D0983785

Anti-Puritan Satire
1572-1642

BY WILLIAM P. HOLDEN

ARCHON BOOKS, 1968

[*Yale Studies in English, Vol.* 126]

LIBRARY OF CONGRESS CATALOG CARD NUMBER: 68-15347
PRINTED IN THE UNITED STATES OF AMERICA

For C. M. H.

PREFACE

THIS BOOK examines the central ideas of English Puritanism and the satire which was directed against the Puritans in England from 1572 to 1642; the chosen limits indicate points of clarification and of eruption. With the publication of the two Admonitions in 1572 a program of ecclesiastical reform had been presented, a program which made possible the drawing of lines of battle both in church and state. With the development of the details of the serious arguments, a tradition of satirical writing grew up, enforcing and enriching the polemical, the philosophical, and the theological. When open fighting broke out in 1642 there came a logical—not to say necessary—break in the development of the discussion. Arguments in favor of either side had become academic: the strength of the respective armies was of more import than pamphlets on the government of the Anglican church or plays on the hypocrisies of the Puritans.

The core of the argument to 1642 is beyond question religious; and religion having been a central concern of the age, political and economic considerations, although they are present, are subservient to the real issue, the correct manner for worshiping God. Throughout the dispute, serious and flippant, there appears, in the discussion of theological niceties, a laborious search for a center of toleration. In this search, the years to 1642 anticipate the outcome; but the outcome was to be achieved only after the Commonwealth and the Restoration. The solution involved the limitation of the crown to an extent which would have been unthinkable to a Caroline royalist, and the preservation of the episcopacy in a way which would have been abhorrent to a Commonwealth Puritan. This search in the direction of a solution appears to an extent in a number of the more enduring of the polemical writers; the solution is also to be found clearly anticipated in the anti-Puritan satire at its best.

I am particularly indebted to Douglas Bush under whose direction large portions of this book were originally written, for official purposes, at Harvard University. I have received helpful criticism on a variety of matters from Charles T. Prouty, Roland H. Bainton, and E. Talbot Donaldson. A research fellowship from Yale University was used in part in the completion of the book.

Contents

List of Illustrations

The illustrations are from the Yale University Library.

I. The Evolving Pattern of Religious Dispute

IT IS A platitude of the historian that literature reflects the age which produces it and that the closest approach to an event is not through the official records but through the books, pamphlets, plays, and poems which came out of the event. However, the historian complicates his platitude when he asks whether the event produced the literature, or the literature the event. The question is imponderable, since cause and effect mingle indistinguishably in the event and the writings: the writer records action, but he also precipitates it. The events and the literature of the English Puritan movement are related in just this ambiguous manner; the precedence of the one over the other cannot be determined in a formula of action and of writing, for the order shifts from one moment to another and, indeed, as with all revolutionary movements, the writing is itself a part of the event.

The evolution of Puritan thought and action from the lenient beginnings to the violence of 1642 cannot be found in a consistent, or even thoroughly conscious, program laid down by a few leaders and pursued by a body of reformers in common agreement. It is rather to be found in a small number of attitudes and intentions which remain more or less unchanged through the years, and a large number of changing beliefs and practices which come to be attached, by accident or by necessity, to the reformers.[1]

The belief that religious reform was necessary was not something new to England in the seventeenth century: the figure of Piers Plowman, John Wyclif, and a mass of writing of religious protest and satire from the fourteenth century on testify to the fact that the need for change was no sudden discovery of the Puritans. In many respects the religious reformers of the age of Elizabeth reflect the intentions of those of the past. The later period had far more specific complaints and more precise remedies for the corruptions of the world; but at the same time the tone of the later writers is frequently similar to that of the earlier. Both groups are concerned with the evil ways of the clergy and the Christian communicant: if Lady Mead is bribery, the Whore of Babylon, sung by

1. M. M. Knappen, *Tudor Puritanism* (Chicago, University of Chicago Press, 1939), 339: "The Puritanism of 1567 differed from that of 1566; the Puritan of 1573 was one thing and the 1574 variety was quite another person. Nor is it possible merely to select one individual as representing the average and describe his fluctuations as typical."
The place of publication of all printed items is London, unless otherwise indicated.

later preachers and poets, is also a symbol for evil. The tradition of protest and the urge to reform are, then, not things which are peculiarly the
product of the Reformation in England: to writers and men of action
in the state and church, protest and reform, with its handmaiden satire,
were neither new nor strange.[2] But a problem of definition arises in the
difference between mere call for reform of abuses and the formulation of
a program politically and religiously Puritan.

The shift from the more general to the more specific occurs as the
reforming groups, with the passing of time, become aware of their particular desires and express in action and in writing the peculiar modes
which come, finally, to mark them out as belonging to one group or another. The reforming Roman Catholic of the fourteenth century in certain respects resembles the Anglican of Henry VIII's time: both operate
within the framework of a Christian morality, and both believe that
there are in the church abuses to be remedied by change. It is a convenient fiction for the commentator in the time of Henry VIII to say that the
Anglican is not a dissenter, and not a schismatic, a fact which is perfectly true in terms of a new and English church. But to the Roman
Catholic, the Anglican of any age is a heretic who would destroy the
church. The earliest significant difference is of degree of protest rather
than kind of protest; much later, a difference in kind does arise, but that
difference is not to be found in the earliest years of English reform. At
the beginning, the forces are ranged in this order: Roman Catholic, reforming Roman Catholic, Anglican, and reforming Anglican.[3] It is to
the last group that the term *Puritan* is properly attached after the passage of some time and the clarification of a program which marks out
the reforming Anglicans as irreconcilably in opposition to the center
group. And, having had their way, the reformers necessarily are trans-
formed from a pattern of revolution to a pattern of conservatism: if the
church has been cured, then it is well, and more purging will only weaken
it. Thus, in the dispute, reformers, some Anglican and some dissenters,
whose experiments with church polity, rite, and doctrine were neither
slight nor mild, were eventually placed in the difficult position of the

2. Attacks, satirical and nonsatirical, on the church, are common in the early sixteenth century. The poetry has the reforming tone of *The Vision of William Concerning
Piers the Plowman;* the prose conforms in general to the writings of complaint which
came from the Lollards. Representative are *Rede Me and Be Not Wrothe* (Strasbourg,
1528), most probably by William Roy and Jerome Barlow, both associates of Tyndale;
and a series by William Turner, *The Hunting and Finding Out of the Romish Fox*
(Basel, 1543), *The Seconde Course of the Hunter at the Romish Fox and His Advocate*
(Zurich? 1545), and *The Hunting of the Romish Wolfe* (1554). Modern reprints of religious complaint are *Political Poems and Songs,* ed. Thomas Wright (2 vols. 1859);
Remains of the Early Popular Poetry of England, ed. William C. Hazlitt (1856); and
Arber Reprint, No. 28 (1871).

3. Knappen in *Tudor Puritanism,* 493, extends the list to "Flat Atheist, Profane . . ."
on the left. But he is using terms more common in later years with the growth of new
groups and fragmentation among the old.

defenders of an established order, while the left wing of their own movement was to lead the people on to a paradise—or a wilderness—of still greater change.

At the basis of the English reform movement, as well as of English Puritanism, is Calvin's account of the universe and of man's place in the universe, an account which, in its theological aspects, is almost as agreeable to the Anglican as to the Puritan. To describe the Puritan as a mere faultfinder is unjust; but it is no more unjust than to see the Anglican as a theological and political reactionary blindly refusing to permit heaven to come to earth via the *Institutes*. English Puritanism did, to an understandable degree, usurp the word *Calvinist*. And if the Anglicans followed Calvin for most of the journey to salvation, the Puritans went all the way.

Calvin's total account of man and God was set forth in increasing detail in the various editions of the *Institutes*. The first account was comparatively short; it appeared in 1536. The definitive edition, that of 1559, was several times as long, but was in important respects unchanged from the first. The central principles are definite and, although they have been variously interpreted on details of meaning, there is little disagreement on the basic issues.

At the heart of Calvin's account is the idea of an all-ruling God who is good; and the purpose of the *Institutes* is to explain the knowledge which man has both of God and of himself. With this knowledge man will be able to accept his place and fulfill his part in God's total plan. The universe at large and the world in particular display the glory of God; man once had a direct and intimate knowledge of God.[4] But this knowledge man subsequently lost by ignorance and wickedness, and so he knew God inadequately. God then gave man the gift of Scripture, a divine communication through which he can achieve the necessary knowledge of God. Among other things revealed in the Bible is the purity of man at his creation: he was then without sin. In addition, man had free will. He could have chosen to resist temptation; instead, he chose to fall, he was utterly corrupted, and there has since been no good in him. But God, having given man the freedom of choice to stand or fall, was in no way at fault. God's foreknowledge enabled him to know that man would fall; but God did not foreordain the fall.[5] Man, fallen in Adam, no longer has

---

4. *Institutes,* Bk. I, chap. I, "The Connection between the Knowledge of God and the Knowledge of Ourselves"; chap. 3, "The Human Mind Naturally Endued with the Knowledge of God." References are to the translation of John Allen (7th Am. ed. 2 vols. Philadelphia, Presbyterian Board, 1936). The influence of Ulrich Zwingli on English Puritanism was more considerable than Calvin, at least in the early years; but Calvin came to be the authoritative voice for the English Puritan.

5. *Ibid.,* Bk. I, chap. 4, "This Knowledge Extinguished . . . by Ignorance . . . Wickedness"; 6, ". . . Scripture Necessary to Lead to the Knowledge of God . . ."; 15, ". . . Man at His Creation . . . Free Will . . . Purity of His Nature"; Bk. II, chap. I, "The Fall and Defection of Adam . . . The Doctrine of Original Sin."

free will. Within man there is only evil, and he is powerless to achieve salvation unless he can be reconciled with God. This forgiveness can come only from outside himself, from God's grace through Christ.[6]

The total purpose of the Bible is now clear. It is not only to reveal God, but in addition to show man the means to find God once more. To the Jews the means was revealed under the law of the Old Testament; to Christians the means has been revealed fully in the New Testament. Therefore, the believing Christian, undeserving, may receive the righteousness of Christ, and through Christ, ultimate regeneration and forgiveness. The process of regeneration is marked by a sense of repentance for evil and by the exercise of prayer; good works, although they may be indicative of God's grace, are useless for salvation, since man's depravity is so complete that any good which he may do is nothing in the sight of God. A portion of mankind has, through all eternity, been determined by God's election or choice, free and undeserved, for salvation; the remainder has been determined for destruction. God has made his election of those who are to be saved without regard to good works; at the same time, his damnation of the remainder is both just and beyond the understanding of man.[7]

All believers, united in the church, must follow God's order of offices and government of the church as described in the Old and New Testaments. In the biblical church there are only two offices, the pastor and the teacher. The proper functions of the pastor are discipline, the administering of the sacraments, presiding over the church, and the interpreting of the Scripture in preaching. The teacher is concerned with the interpretation of the Scripture. The pastor is ordained by the laying on of hands; but in addition, he is legitimately in office only when he has been approved by the lay members of the church.

The government of the church is in the hands of the pastors (who are also called presbyters or bishops), of elders or lay presbyters, and of deacons. There is a chief bishop or presbyter who functions only as a moderator: he presides over a deliberative group; and he has no superior

6. *Ibid.*, Bk. II, chap. 2, "Man, in His Present State, Despoiled of Freedom of Will . . ."; 3, "Every Thing That Proceeds from the Corrupt Nature of Man Worthy of Condemnation"; 6, "Redemption for Lost Man to Be Sought in Christ."

7. *Ibid.*, Bk. II, chap. 9, "Christ, Though Known to the Jews . . . Clearly Revealed only in the Gospel"; Bk. III, chap. 3, "On Repentance"; 15, "Boasting of the Merit of Works, Equally Subversive of God's Glory in the Gift of Righteousness, and of the Certainty of Salvation"; 18, "Justification from Works Not to Be Inferred from the Promise of a Reward"; 21, "Eternal Election, or God's Predestination of Some to Salvation, and of Others to Destruction." Calvin says, p. 181: "In conformity, therefore, to the clear doctrine of the Scripture, we assert, that by an eternal and immutable counsel, God has once for all determined, both whom he would admit to salvation and whom he would condemn to destruction. We affirm that this counsel, as far as concerns the elect, is founded on his gratuitous mercy, totally irrespective of human merit; but that to those whom he devotes to condemnation, the gate of life is closed by a just and irreprehensible, but incomprehensible, judgment."

authority of decision. Like the ordinary pastor, the bishop is subject to the approval of the congregation.[8]

The only sacraments of the church are baptism and communion: other so-called sacraments are later corruptions away from the original church. Baptism in itself does not purify man of sin; rather, the water of baptism is the symbolic representation of the blood of Christ by which alone man is saved. Communion, the other true sacrament, is a continuing reminder to man throughout his life that Christ's body was given for man's salvation. The two sacraments without the meaning behind them, without a consciousness of the biblical doctrines of sin and redemption, are without force and, indeed, are not sacraments.[9]

God's church has a specific relationship to the civil government; and the members of the church have upon them certain obligations which arise from the church and apply to society. The church must find refuge and strength in good government; conversely, the civil government, to be good, must express the deepest moral and social principles of the church. Church and state are consequently separate, but are not opposed to each other in any way.

The civil government may be of various forms; it may be monarchical or aristocratic, for instance, but the best form is that in which power is with the many and not the few. Obedience to the civil magistrate is the duty of the godly man; since the good magistrate expresses the divine order, to oppose him is to oppose God. Like the pastor, the magistrate is the particular representative of God; and the sovereign as magistrate exercises a divine right in ruling. To the instructions on the Christian man's duty of obedience, there is one important exception. If a magistrate goes plainly against God's laws, then the subject must disobey him.[1]

As has been pointed out, the greater part of these, the central proposals of Calvinism, were acceptable to Anglicans of all degrees. In particular, the theological account of the universe, of God's purpose and

8. *Ibid.*, Bk. IV, chap. I, "The True Church, and the Necessity of Our Union with Her, Being the Mother of All the Pious; 3, "The Teachers and Ministers of the Church; Their Election and Office"; 4, "The State of the Ancient Church, and the Mode of Government Practised before the Papacy."

9. *Ibid.*, Bk. IV, chap. 14, "The Sacraments"; 15, "Baptism"; 17, "The Lord's Supper and Its Advantages."

1. *Ibid.*, Bk. IV, chap. 20, "On Civil Government." The instruction on disobedience of the magistrate is explicit (p. 805): "The Lord, therefore, is the King of kings . . . we are subject to those men who preside over us; but no otherwise than in him. If they command anything against him, it ought not to have the least attention; nor, in this case, ought we to pay any regard to all that dignity attached to magistrates . . . On this principle Daniel denied that he had committed any crime against the king in disobeying his impious decree . . ." The theory of resistance to the magistrate, and the justification of war in general, did not originate with Calvin but came from the Christian Roman Empire and the Middle Ages. See Roland H. Bainton's "Congregationalism: from the Just War to the Crusade," *The Andover Newton Theological School Bulletin*, 35 (April 1943), 1–20.

nature, of man's corruption and need for grace, are commonplaces of Anglican thought; they were approved repeatedly both by the government and by the clergy. The inability of man to save himself by his own efforts is, for instance, a point which the Anglican church entered in the official articles of faith.

But Anglican opinion parted sharply from Puritan on a number of important points. For example, the question of right church government was less that of the number and nature of the offices than the source of the authority. By the Anglican view, power flowed in a gently descending stream from the fountainhead of king and bishop to the quiet pool of an obedient people. By the Puritan view, no officer of the church was legitimate if he lacked the approval of the lay members of the church; and, what was to prove more important, church members were enjoined to disobey a civil officer who plainly went against God's plan and order. To the Anglican, not only power but social order came from above. The ultimate source for the power might be the crown, or the bishop (in the sense of a royally appointed official), or some other source removed from the confusion and passion of popular opinion. But the source must be above; it must not be the "mere popularity" of the Puritans. Again, Anglican opinion split from Puritan on the questions of polity, rite, and moral law as observed in the primitive church. Both groups subscribed fiercely to the belief that the right church must be the church in its original form; but the original form, as described in the Bible, was subject to widely varying interpretations; and the varying interpretations gave rise to disputes. In addition, the Calvinistic account was plainly directed toward increased attention to preaching, to the study and interpretation of the Bible, and to the simplification of elaborate rites which had become unbiblical distractions in the worship of God. A specific example of the multitude of divergencies is found in the matter of vows and oaths. The state required oaths under various circumstances, some ecclesiastical and some legal; the "et cetera oath" of 1640, not to alter the government of the church, was one. But Calvin had restricted the use of oaths virtually to the assertion of man's belief in God and in the two sacraments.[2] How, then, could a Christian swear to something which was in part undefined, and which in part required him to uphold an unscriptural polity?

These problems of the later years are anticipated by two groups in the reign of Henry VIII; both the man of action and the man of ideas mark themselves as belonging frequently to the center party of com-

---

2. *Institutes,* Bk. IV, chap. 13, "Vows: The Misery of Rashly Making Them," p. 537: "Yet I would not be thought to carry my recommendation, even of those vows which I maintain to be holy, so far as to wish their daily use . . . if any person would follow my advice, he will make none but such as are sober, and of short duration. For if any one often recur to the making of many vows, all religion will be injured by their frequency, and there will be great danger of falling into superstition."

pleted reform or to the party of the left and of further changes: the archetypes of the Elizabethan Anglican and Puritan are on the stage long before 1558.[3] There are clearly interconnections of opinion from reforming Anglican to Puritan, and the similarities of intention in the early years can be seen in the attitudes and conduct of numbers of religious leaders during the reigns of Henry VIII, Edward VI, and Mary. Specifically, the fact that the terms *Anglican* and *Puritan* are by no means polar appears in the mixed programs of religious leaders throughout the early part of the sixteenth century.

William Tyndale (d. 1536) is typically the Puritan. The influence of continental reform was heavy upon him; but at the same time he was at least vocally submissive to his sovereign. Although he could not accept passive obedience as a principle, he did in his writings accept passive resistance: he intended to sponsor no revolution, even against a Roman Catholic monarch. In exile on the Continent for his heretical opinions, Tyndale translated part of the Bible; his work was to form the basis for the Authorized Version of 1611. From the Bible in English the people would get all that was necessary for salvation; they could order their lives, their church, and their society. The Anglican of the time would not have gone so far; at the top of his hierarchy was a God not notably different from the God of Tyndale, but for the Anglican there were the intermediate links of the monarch and the visible church to interpret and control. On the other hand, the revolutionary implications of Tyndale's beliefs are not difficult to see. If salvation could be had outside the Established Church, then that church and monarchy were not necessary elements for a Christian order. Tyndale and the reforming Anglican clearly met in one area and parted company in another.

John Hooper (d. 1555) has been called the father of English dissent; but Hooper differs not at all in principles from a number of his Anglican contemporaries, and he is of particular interest as an example of the cleric who started in Henry's church, advanced to become a reforming bishop under Edward, and died for his Protestantism under Mary. Early in his career he had advanced opinions; the influence of continental thought was for him, as for Tyndale, of crucial import. Hooper's beliefs sent him into exile under Henry and brought contact with the reformers Bullinger and à Lasco abroad. Returning to England in 1549, Hooper grew famous as a preacher with the force, severity, and simplicity which were later to be the hallmarks of the Puritan divines, and he gained particular note from his objections to the wearing of vestments for his consecration as a bishop. For a time he was jailed, but he finally con-

3. James Gairdner in *The English Church in the Sixteenth Century* (Macmillan, 1902), 283, echoes the common opinion that John Hooper was "the father of nonconformity." Knappen in *Tudor Puritanism*, 3–30, finds in William Tyndale a pattern typical of early English Puritanism. It is perfectly possible to speak of Anglican Puritans in the early years. See Knappen, 339.

sented to put on the orthodox clothing. As bishop of Gloucester, Hooper the Anglican showed the zeal of the Puritan: he preached three or four times a day; he questioned the clergy on their learning; and he attempted to remedy the ignorance which he found so widespread. On Mary's succession he refused, unlike Cox and so many others, to leave the country. In 1555 he was degraded, excommunicated, and burned as a heretic for his teachings on the Eucharist.[4]

William Whittingham (1524?–79) is, like Tyndale, the extreme Protestant, with the literary flair of the Puritan translator, diary writer, and preacher. At Frankfurt during the exile, Whittingham almost certainly wrote *A Brief Discourse* (Zurich? 1574), an account which tells of the disputes of the Anglicans and the extreme reformers at Frankfurt, and of the rightness of Calvinist service and polity. On Mary's death, Whittingham, instead of returning to England, stayed in Geneva and played a most important part in the completion of the Geneva Bible (1560). After his return home, he became an Anglican dean, and then offended the High Church party by his objections to the vestments. He believed deeply in the need of continued reform, in the importance of continental religious thought, and in the possibility of discovering in the Bible God's own instructions for a perfect life and a perfect church.[5]

Richard Cox (1500–81) exemplifies the nice balance of tradition and revolt: he is an Anglican, but he is also a reformer who accepts much change with the eager spirit of the Puritan. Cox sided with Henry VIII on the annulment of his marriage to Anne of Cleves, and played an important role both in the writing of the Prayer Book of 1549 and in the revision of 1552. Again, Cox introduced the Protestant Peter Martyr to the English universities. Finally, as an indication of the way in which the Anglican could sometimes take on the coloring of the hot Puritan of later years, Cox was one of seven royal visitors who engaged in the destruction of books in schools and colleges. His "mad work," as Anthony à Wood called it, was to be repeated in the troubled years after 1642. During the Marian exile Cox was on the Continent and, at Frankfurt, sided with the conservatives who insisted on the Prayer Book and a service with rites which would make it a continuation of Henry's church; there were definite if unpredictable limits to Cox's reforming spirit. But still later in his career, Cox showed more marks of the Puritan beast: after his return to England under Elizabeth's Protestant

---

4. The classical account of Hooper is in John Foxe's *Acts and Monuments*, ed. Josiah Pratt (8 vols. n.d.), *6*, 636–76. John Strype's retelling in *Ecclesiastical Memorials* (3 vols. Oxford, 1822), *3*, Pt. I, 282–8, is based on Foxe. See also Gairdner's *The English Church*, 281–4 and Knappen's *Tudor Puritanism*, 82–9. Hooper's opinions can be had from letters of his reprinted in *Original Letters Relative to the English Reformation*, ed. Hastings Robinson, The Parker Society (2 vols. Cambridge, England, 1846–47).

5. J. Hay Colligan's *William Whittingham* (Simpkin Marshall, 1934) is a short account. Strype in *Eccl. Mem.*, *3*, Pt. I, 404–17, tells of the disputes at Frankfurt.

dispensation, he found the crucifix and lights in the queen's chapel too Romish for his liking.[6]

The intention of reform is, generally, similar in all four men. The degree of difference which marks out a Hooper from a Cox is the significant element which later years developed into a characteristically Puritan pattern. It is simply that the early reformers to the time of Elizabeth are united in a number of complaints against the Roman Catholic church, in a number of beliefs which are at variance with Roman Catholic doctrine, and in a number of intentions of change. Basic to the English Reformation are the objections to the powers of the pope and his church in England and to the corruptions of the clergy. In its simplest terms, the objection to the powers of the pope involved the proposal that he was not religiously and morally supreme in the Christian world, and that he had come to interfere in areas which rightfully belonged to the civil authority. Henry's marital ventures had caused an early clash, but the taxes which Rome collected from England were not less a source of conflict. It was the old problem of the proper area of concern of the church. If it was morals, did that fact mean that an ecclesiastical court took precedence over a civil court? And what was the authority of Rome in respect to taxes in England? Did the right of Rome to her income precede the right of the sovereign to his? With a monarchy gaining in power, it was obvious that one authority must conflict with the other. In the later disputes between Anglican and Puritan, the old problems would survive from the Henrican establishment to plague, in new guises, the moderate reformers themselves.

Much of the corruption of the Roman church likewise remained after the supposed remedy of separation. In the early writings of Anglicans and Puritans, one of the major themes is the dishonesty, indolence, lechery, and ignorance of the clergy both high and low. Among the early writers the loudest complaints also come from the extremists; the Roman Catholic or the Anglican frequently accepts an amount of corruption as the inevitable characteristic of an institution which, if of divine inspiration, is of merely human constitution. But out of the ignorance and indolence of the clergy had grown, supposedly, both the ignorance of the people on their religion and the overembellishment of the rites of the church to the obfuscation of the original teachings of Christ. The reformer frequently asked whether the intervention of a corrupt priest was necessary to the salvation of a layman who, by comparison with the priest, might be both virtuous and learned.[7]

6. Strype, *The Life and Acts of Archbishop Grindal* (Oxford, 1821), 15–18; The *DNB* quotes Anthony à Wood; Knappen, *Tudor Puritanism*, 127–33.

7. See, for example, Tyndale on justifications by faith in *The Work of William Tindale*, ed. S. L. Greenslade (Blackie, 1938), 167–80. Tyndale says, 172: "Hereby see we, that deeds and works are but outward signs of the bounteous and plenteous mercy of God, freely received without all merits of deeds, yea, and before all deeds." He attacks

Thus, a group of positive beliefs, held by Anglicans and Puritans alike in Elizabeth's reign, derived logically from the complaints and objections which had helped originally to cause the separation from Rome. The reformers were, consciously or not, antisacerdotal. If the corrupt priest could be dispensed with, and if learning would bring virtue in place of ignorance and corruption, then the clergy no longer constituted a necessary link in the chain of salvation from God to man. Salvation for Anglican and Puritan would come from faith in the word of God, from the grace of God, and from the observance of the rules of conduct to be found in the Bible. The concern of the reformers with accurate translations made widely available to a literate populace then becomes clear; and the prejudice of some of the extremists against Latin becomes at least intelligible. The interpreting ecclesiast, coming between the Christian and the word of God, perverted the truth and kept the layman in darkness. Indeed, if the Bible had been obscured and perverted by the corrupt professionals of the old church, the teachings of Christ in particular had been overelaborated and distorted until religion had become a series of gaudy rites: a reversion to the unadorned letter of the law was necessary.[8]

Opinion on the validity of personal interpretation of the Bible was not by any means unanimous among the reformers. During part of Henry's reign, while the Roman Catholic church still was supreme, the authorities were necessarily ranged against the extremists who spoke for the Bible in the hands of the lay reader. Under Edward and during the Marian exile, the Roman Catholic ideal of an authoritative hierarchy was taken over to an extent by the Anglicans, while the forces of Puritanism insisted with increasing vehemence on a Calvinist interpretation of the Bible discovered, at least in theory, by the average reader. But it is scarcely accurate to say that the Anglicans had adapted the ideal of the Roman Catholic church to the ideal of a national church which would be at once English and within the community of saints. Anglican bibliolatry would remain, through the sixteenth century, almost as devout as that of the Puritans, and the Anglican church, with the sovereign at the head, would be more English than Catholic. In addition, both the right and the left wings of the reformers, in deposing one authority, would only set up another, whether the king, the bishop, or the presbyter. And finally, as it turned out, the Bible in English would be susceptible to even more varied interpretations than the Bible in Hebrew, Greek, or Latin.

---

the church (123–48) on such points as abuses of the pope, bishops, and lower clergy, the wealth of the church, ceremonies, images and relics, saints, the decay of the mass from that of the primitive church, confession, and purgatory.

8. *Ibid.,* 159–60: "Thou shalt understand, therefore, that the scripture hath but one sense, which is the literal sense . . . No place of the scripture may have a private exposition; that is, it may not be expounded after the will of man, or after the will of the flesh . . ."

For the reforming left, particularly, the benign view of an international church of Christ, under Puritan and biblical auspices, turned out to be most difficult of realization. It is true that the Puritans had a view of a biblical city of God on earth; but they had neglected to decide what *biblical* meant. As with the Anglicans, there was less than universal agreement on the definition of the word. Both Puritans and Anglicans were thus similar in that they had cast off old authority and had found, at least in theory, a new order which would be less corruptible than the old.

The intentions of the various forces of reform encompassed remedies on which all were united; beyond these principles there were troublesome details which, at first of small concern, were later to give rise to enormous difficulties. There was, for instance, the general proposal that the English church, whatever form it might eventually take, would be no part of the Roman Catholic church. A difference in attitude between the extremists and the moderates can be roughly indicated. To the moderate, England was in the process of developing a church which, although it owed no obedience to Rome, was neither heretical nor schismatic. As the moderates developed an apologetic, they would discover that their church was not new but was simply a revival of the original church, the child of the primitive church of Christ without the pope as midwife. Extremists, under the influence more clearly of continental thought, argued that the Roman church had become so corrupt that it was in many important respects unchristian. Their intention was the re-establishment of the pure order and practice of the Bible. All reforming parties agreed that there should be some simplification of rites and practices, that the service should be less for the glorification of the ecclesiast, and more for the edification of the communicant. Thus, for example, a well-constructed sermon in good English would be of more importance than the number of candles on the altar.[9]

The government of the church, separated from Rome, would necessarily be altered: its new head, according to the moderates, would be the sovereign with his bishops in an episcopacy. But, both under Edward and during the exile, there was a second group which found in the teachings of John Calvin and in certain passages of the Bible good reasons to argue for a new order of polity based on the model of the Protestant church at Geneva. The first group was obviously devoted to a national church, similar in basic teachings to the old church before its alleged corruption; the second group was devoted to the same ideal, with the chief difference that it believed reformation incomplete. More changes

9. A typical statement of Puritan intentions is "A Declaration of the Preachers in Prison," in Foxe's *Acts, 6,* 550–3. Emphasis is laid on a simple service in English; the use of the Bible; and the willingness of the reformers to submit to authority. It is dated May 1554 and is signed by John Rogers and Miles Coverdale, among others.

were needed to make the new church consonant with the biblical church; a virtuous Protestant on the throne would see the light and make the alterations. Through the reign of Mary, when Protestantism was heresy, the reformers were in general united in their beliefs and in their intentions for the future. Among them there were few who advocated an ecclesiastical order apart from the government; the most common opinion was that, since the present government was Roman Catholic, they would passively resist until it became Protestant.[1]

On the death of Mary in 1558, a Protestant might have looked back at the events of the past five years and felt that the tribulations of a Romish monarch had truly been sent by God to test the fiber of the English and to show them more surely the way to reform. If the reign had begun with mildness, the trials and executions of the last four years had tested the fiber of the Protestantism which had been born under Henry and had grown under Edward.[2] The charge from the throne against the new order had been heresy, not treason. Actually the Protestants, in defying Roman Catholicism, had opposed both the legally constituted government and its church. But whatever the logic of the charge, the result had been that English Protestantism had been driven either underground or overseas. At home, groups of communicants did meet, worship, and conduct the necessary business of a church. But they were cut off in small groups from the rest of the Protestant community: they could look to no supreme head for guidance, to no general opinion for communal decisions. The result was that those who worshiped outside the law worshiped perforce outside any generally developing tradition of a national church and they took for themselves the decisions which seemed to them in accord with what might have been done had there been the uniformity of a Protestant and a state religion. For these newly isolated groups of communicants, the hierarchy of rule ended with the congregation itself: there could be no Protestant bishop since there was no Protestant king. The habit of independence was acquired; and once acquired, it was not in later years easily lost.[3]

As the Protestant looked abroad in 1558, he would have seen that his

1. *Ibid.*, 553. Statements of pacific intentions and of persecutions suffered are very common among the reformers from the advent of Mary to 1642. The protestations are entirely sincere, but frequently at variance with the facts. Christina H. Garrett in *The Marian Exiles* (Cambridge, University Press, 1938) concludes that the exile was at the beginning voluntary. She says, 15: "Very soon they [the exiles] came, as all others have done, to believe ardently in their own fiction. Only in deference to truth it should at last be recognized that it *was* a fiction and that by their seditious action abroad they very probably induced for others the persecution which in their own case was imaginary."

2. Foxe is the most enduring account. Subjected to much denigration during the nineteenth century, his reputation is now secure. See Knappen, *Tudor Puritanism*, 495.

3. Sir John Cheke, writing from Strasbourg to John Calvin 20 October 1555, speaks of "the universal church, scattered as it is far and wide . . ." (*Original Letters*, I, 142–7). The discussion of the old and new disciplines in *A Brief Discourse* demonstrates the need for, and habit of, independent action in the church in exile.

cause had flourished very well in exile. Unhappily, dissension seemed to plague the English on the Continent; but Henry's church had not died. In it there was a hard core of diligent and learned divines, and a number of crucial questions had at least been posed in the course of the controversies which had gone on at a discreet distance from the stake at Smithfield. English Protestants abroad, like those at home, had frequently been divided by necessity into small, self-sufficient groups. Many of the exiles were poor, having left most of their wealth in England, and geographical distance compelled the congregation to develop by itself. Thus, as at home, self-rule among the English on the Continent had become something of a habit. Without a head, and, indeed, without any polity which transcended the communal group, the exiles had tasted the heady wine of independency. More dangerous still, Calvin had furnished the English with a carefully constructed justification for an order in which power was not centered in a monarch and his appointed bishops. But this new order was no democratic aberration intended to destroy the Protestant monarchy; it was simply a readjustment of ecclesiastical polity to God's ordinance, plainly set forth in the Bible.

There were, then, the reformers who were for the retention of the episcopacy, and there were the reformers who were for a Presbyterian polity. The history of the colony of English at Frankfurt during the exile perfectly illustrates the clash. William Whittingham, John Knox, and William Turner, among others, had arrived at Frankfurt with the determination to set up a church which would conform to a Calvinist rather than to an Anglican pattern. The result differed from the reformed church of Henry and Edward chiefly in respect to its complete (if necessary) independence from any central authority and in the simplification of its rites and services. Neither point was in any way separatist: the communicants remained by their own judgment within the English church, and departed from its practices in ways which, in their estimation, would have been logically necessary had reform not given place to Mary's reaction. But the simplicity of service, anti-Roman to a point of affectation, did not meet with the approval of a later group which joined the congregation. More conservative in their intentions, but not different in their attitude toward Rome, the pope, or the abuses of the old church, the newcomers insisted on the retention of the rites, practices, and liturgy of the Edwardian church. The clash was bitter; the conservatives won, and the radicals moved on to Basel. The Puritan program of reform without tarrying was set against the Anglican intent to preserve the national church under the sovereign with Calvinist elements confined largely to the unpolitical area of doctrine. But if Frankfurt showed the clash of two ideals, the troubles among the extremists themselves at Basel indicated that even had they won at Frankfurt, there would have been less than perfect peace. At Basel they fought over scriptural meanings; the polity of the primitive church was not quite beyond dispute; and there was the old puzzle of the adiaphora and the essentials.[4]

The hypothetical Protestant looking abroad in 1558 might, then, with sufficient perspicacity, have seen the future alignment of Anglican against Puritan and, in addition, the beginnings of the complications which were to arise among the Puritans themselves. He might have seen that the question of the degree of reform within the English church would prove to be even more vexatious than the separation from Rome, and that the new problem of ecclesiastical polity would ultimately involve questions of far more trouble to English society than mere authority in the church. Religion, a major concern of the period, could become politics; and there might be difficulties if in the future a sovereign could not find a pattern and practice satisfying to the diverse opinions of all factions. But faction becomes party as the number of supporters grows and as intentions are expressed in a coherent program. After about 1572 the Puritans took their place as a major force in English life. The old split in degree of reform in the church, apparent in the age of Henry and Edward, had become clarified in the two sections, not perfectly defined, but generally opposed to each other in the court, in the church, and in parliament. Finally, there was the extended controversy which examined in detail the issues at stake in the program of reform.

The appearance of *An Admonition to the Parliament* and *A Second Admonition to the Parliament,* both in 1572, marks an important point of coalition and clarification.[5] That the Admonitions were the first, or even early, expressions of the Puritan program is not true; nor can it be said that the two manifestoes added new complaints on abuses or new arguments for reform. All that is in the Admonitions had been written before as a usual part of the pattern of complaint from one or another shade of reformist opinion. However, the Admonitions are of importance for the clarity and preciseness with which they express the

---

4. Whittingham, *A Brief Discourse* (ed. 1846), 189: "For where as all the reformed churches differ amonge them selves in divers ceremonies, and yet agree in the unitie of doctrine: we se no inconvenience if we use ceremonies divers from them, so that we agree in the chief points of oure religion." See also Knappen, *Tudor Puritanism,* 118–34. Knappen gives a summary of John Bale's account of the troubles at Basel as reported in Strype.

5. See *Puritan Manifestoes,* ed. W. H. Frere and C. E. Douglas (Society for Promoting Christian Knowledge, 1907) for an introduction to, and the texts of, the two Admonitions. Donald J. McGinn's *The Admonition Controversy* (New Brunswick, N. J., Rutgers University Press, 1949) prints extensive sections of the dispute between Whitgift and Cartwright which followed the Admonitions. *The Works of John D. Whitgift,* ed. John Ayre, The Parker Society (3 vols. Cambridge, England, 1851–53), prints all of Whitgift's part in the argument and much of Cartwright's. The best account of Cartwright is A. F. Scott Pearson's *Thomas Cartwright and Elizabethan Puritanism* (Cambridge, University Press, 1925).

growing body of Puritan thought in the reign of Elizabeth, and the degree to which they define an alignment, at this point largely ecclesiastical, throughout England.

For one thing, the immediate situation which called forth the Admonitions directly reflected the events of the past fifty years. A major theme in the Admonitions, for instance, was the question of the propriety of the vestments: should the clergy wear clothing different from that of the laity? Did the Bible order any such clothing? Or was it merely a survival Romish, and hence, evil? The problem had arisen before. During the reign of Edward VI there had been a hot dispute on the subject, and many of the reforming party had favored either simplification or elimination of clerical dress. Again, attacks on the Edwardian Prayer Book had been common from the time of its publication: revision was necessary to cleanse it entirely of elements of the Roman mass book. A large part of the early troubles had hinged on just these two points, vestments and the services of the Prayer Book, and were echoed in the arguments of the Admonitions.[6] In addition, events from the death of Mary to 1572 had made the appearance of the Admonitions entirely understandable. With the re-establishment of the Anglican church in 1558, the Protestant disputes, carried on *sub rosa* in Mary's England, broke out afresh, and when ecclesiastical convocation met in 1563, the country once more had a legal place for the airing of proposals for religious change. The radicals appeared on behalf of a plainly dressed clergy and a prayer book without Romish taint; they were defeated narrowly, even though they were gaining in strength. Anglicanism was strong with the support of Elizabeth who, as pilot of the church, set a course which was adjusted more to the dangers of the voyage than to the comfort of the crew and passengers.[7] The failure of convocation to support the reforms set a pattern for the future; from a merely hostile bloc, the conservative assembly was to become finally a goad in the side of the extreme party. Effort at reform by a different means took place in the 1571 parliament when the Puritans, having failed in convocation, attempted to get through the legislative body measures which by tradition were the concern only of the sovereign and his ecclesiastical advisers. Bills for changes in vestments, for the alteration of the Prayer Book, and for the simplification of rites were offered. More bills for the legalizing of Puritan innovations in

6. *Original Letters*, 2, 466: ". . . master Hooper likewise . . . has committed such havoc with the pontifical ceremonies . . . For he nobly stood forth in the king's council against those bishops who strenuously supported the vestments and such-like triflings . . ." The date is 1550. For further accounts of Hooper on Romish vestments, see 2, 571, 583, 674. *A Brief Discourse*, 34–9, reports Calvin's strictures on the English Prayer Book and Knox's sermon against it at Frankfurt.

7. Knappen, *Tudor Puritanism*, 168–71, 184–5, 192; William Haller, *The Rise of Puritanism* (New York, Columbia University Press, 1938), 7.

worship were introduced, and, finally, on 22 May 1572, the queen decreed that no more bills on religion should be presented unless they were "liked by the clergy." [8]

Probably about a month later, *An Admonition to the Parliament* appeared; [9] it was an appeal by the Puritans from the legally constituted authorities, the crown and the convocation, to the legislative body for ecclesiastical reform of the most radical sort. The pamphlet was immediately popular; if it has become dull reading to subsequent ages, the reason is simply that the government of the church and the conduct of rites have come to be of less than burning interest. But the English of the first Admonition is still direct, clear, and forceful; as a model for controversy it is far superior to the run of pamphlets for years to come. Its arguments are presented in good order and there is a minimum of redundancy. The line of reasoning hews to two points which were of particular appeal at the time: the need for a Presbyterian government, and the corruptions of the Anglican establishment. In general, the text avoids the dull presentation of biblical support; there are references to Holy Writ, but the references by no means carry the weight of proof. In addition, there is an effective appeal for interest by the promise of sensational charges, and indignant threats of disclosures of evil. Throughout the pamphlet there is often a conscious reference to authority of one sort or another, the primitive church, what is "right," and what is in accord with God's command. The reader is compelled either to agree with the Admonition or to align himself with Satan; and it is apparent in terms of the events which followed that large numbers were eager to approve the Puritan arguments even without the persuasive adornments of rhetoric and divine instruction.

The preface "To the Godly Readers" consists of a short, vigorous attack on the whole of the Anglican hierarchy from archbishop to curate. The central charge is that the authority and order which have been established in the English church are contrary to God's order and, necessarily, wrong. It is not that the authors object to authority; it is simply that the authority must not be patterned by man, but in accord with divine instructions. The first section of the Admonition develops in more detail the reforms which are necessary for the establishment of the new and proper order. Three points are crucial, and these three points remain, with minor changes, unaltered to the revolution of 1642. First is the religious instruction of the people. The Roman Catholic church had failed; and the English church from the time of Henry VIII had done little to instruct the common man in the moral principles and practices of Christianity. Through a learned clergy, able to preach, and restricted

8. Frere, *Puritan Manifestoes,* i–xiii.
9. Strype, *Life of Aylmer* (Oxford, 1821), 37; *Life of Archbishop Parker* (Oxford, 1821), *2,* 109–10; Frere, *Puritan Manifestoes,* xiii.

in their cures so that they could preach regularly, the evil of religious ignorance could be remedied.

The second point, that of the manner of administering the sacraments, is largely an expression of the anti-Romanism of the reformers. The pamphlet complains that the Communion and baptism have been elaborated and corrupted with nonscriptural irrelevancies, vestiges from Rome. Plainness and simplicity both in the conduct of rites and the dress of the clergy will remedy the evil. The communicant should sit, for instance, rather than kneel during Communion, for kneeling implies the real presence, a popish superstition. The third point, the most important in respect to the future of Puritanism, is the question of the government of the church. By the Puritan reading of the Bible, the rule of the church should be by the Calvinist orders of members: ministers, elders, and deacons. The function of the minister should be to preach and govern; of the elder, to govern with the minister; the office of the deacon should be to gather and distribute alms. Authority rests with these three orders, and other officers are an irrelevancy. The section ends with a reassertion of the need for a return to the primitive church under biblical rule. The heart of the argument has been delivered; and the section bears properly the title of the volume.

The next section, "A View of Popishe Abuses," goes over the same arguments to a certain extent, repeats the exhortations of the first and second parts, but centers more particularly on the corruptions of the Prayer Book, an outworn relic of Rome. The Prayer Book is full of unscriptural elements and it sets up an order of church government which is contrary to God's command. The Articles of Religion are for the most part sound doctrinally, but it is not possible to separate doctrine from polity, and the Prayer Book attempts that separation. The conclusion, "To the Christian Reader," expresses the willingness of the reformers to put themselves in danger for the cause of godly reformation; there is in addition a statement of devotion to the queen and the inevitability of her concurrence in the program of change. The two letters appended to the first Admonition are simply an appeal to the prestige of continental Protestantism for the need of reform in England.

A Second Admonition to the Parliament is of considerably less interest simply because it adds little which is new; the style of the second is repetitious, while its length suggests the dullness of controversial writings of the future. The value of the second Admonition lies chiefly in the fact that some details are given for the proposed reform in ecclesiastical government. One of the first points in the pamphlet is the specific praise of the Geneva Bible with its marginalia, even then a major prop to Puritan arguments.[1] The pamphlet continues that the reformers do not

---

1. Knappen's chapter "The Puritan Doctrine of Authority," *Tudor Puritanism,* 354–66, is an account of Puritan bibliolatry and the attendant difficulties.

despise authority, and do not question the supremacy of the queen. On
the contrary, the sovereign rules rightfully over the whole of the state
and the church. The seeming contradiction with the argument of the first
Admonition on the same subject disappears when it is pointed out that
her majesty, necessarily the agent of God's order, must act in accordance
with his instructions. The instructions are to be found in the Bible and
the queen will presently carry them out.

In the purified church the basic unit of decision and appointment is
the congregation; on its request a minister is chosen by the conference
(which is later defined), and sent to the congregation for approval. The
congregation is led by pastors and teachers; the order is generally the
same as that prescribed in the first Admonition, which is to say, radically
opposed to that of the establishment. Above the congregation, but consisting of ". . . ministers and other brethren . . ." is the conference
representing a loosely defined but small geographic area. Above the conference is the provincial synod, and at the top of the administrative pile
is the national synod. Divine justification for the whole order is found,
of course, in the Geneva Bible; the technique for arriving at the order
is an extreme eclecticism which quotes supporting passages in the
peculiarly Calvinistic translation and disregards divine instructions
which might disarrange the symmetry of the perfect church.[2] Inter-
mingled with the plan for the ordering of the church is the usual attack
on Romish practices and abuses of omission and commission. Almost at
the end of the pamphlet there is once more an appeal to the queen as the
"supreme governour in all causes," and the assurance of the loyalty
and submission of the reformers; but also, there is the plain statement
that the queen's way must be God's way, which is to say, the Puritan's
way.[3]

The immediate result of the two Admonitions was a flood of controversial writing from both sides: infinite repetition of arguments
yielded some slight clarification of positions. The chief contestants were
John Whitgift, supporter of the Elizabethan establishment and later
archbishop, against Thomas Cartwright, most vocal of the Puritan reformers of the moment. The Anglican fought the difficult fight of

2. In, for example, the Geneva Bible of 1560, 1 Cor. 11:28, reads: ". . . And God hath
ordeined some in the Church: as first, Apostles, secondly Prophetes, thirdly teachers,
then them that do miracles: after that, the giftes of healing, helpers, governours, diversi-
tie of tongues." The gloss reads: "As Deacons, As Elders." 1 Tim. 5:17, speaks of the
honors due to "elders" of the church. The Calvinist tone is obvious. M. M. Knappen in
Tudor Puritanism, 144, says: "But the most important contribution . . . to the intellectual armory of the Puritan faction was the Geneva translation of the Bible . . . as
in the earlier translations, the marginal comments were not the least important part of
the volume. When it was stated that the locusts of the Apocalyse were not only heretics
and monks but 'Archbishops, and Bishops, Doctors, Bachelors, and Masters which for-
sake Christ to maintain false doctrine,' a handle was provided for future attacks on the
episcopacy."
3. The most important sections on polity are in *Puritan Manifestoes*, 96–130.

defense; his opposite attacked to destroy.[4] Perhaps the most important development in the course of this dreary and extended bickering is the setting forth of the multitude of ambiguities involved in the Anglican and Puritan concepts of civil authority. Throughout the two Admonitions the Puritan party line had piously maintained that remedy would come from a godly sovereign. In addition, the reformers had pledged more than once their obedience to the civil arm, and nowhere in the Admonitions was there the suggestion that the government should be changed, or that the church should be in any ordinary sense above the state.

But Cartwright moves a distance from the Erastianism of early Puritanism, and Whitgift sees the move. The Puritan theory of the total order has allowed for dangerous speculations and the Anglican defender, far more than his opponent, is aware of the political implications in the new statement of the old theory. The two accused authors of the first Admonition, when jailed, had to an extent recanted, and had insisted that they really desired only a mild reform of abuses, rites, and polity.[5] It was the common difficulty of a Puritanism more revolutionary than it knew. Cartwright continued the line of argument as best he could: on the one hand he attempts to be more conciliatory than the Admonitions, but on the other hand he makes proposals which are, in their implications, at least as radical as those of his predecessors. The Church of England is certainly Christian; in addition, it is possible for there to be variations in rite and practice from one church to another and from one time to another. It is true that elaborate vestments are evil, and that Romanism is evil, but those faults are not enough to vitiate all good in a church. On the other hand, the English church is wrong in that it centers ecclesiastical power in a civil head. The principle of a canon law promulgated by a convocation to reform and regulate is right. Many heads are better than one; church law should be made by the clergy as a body, and the proper function of the crown should be to administer, not to legislate, in matters of religion. However, the elected legislative bodies may occasionally pass laws which are "unlawful"; then the crown may interpose its supreme authority and alter the law.[6] The nature of a wrong law, and the wisdom to recognize its wrongness, are unfortunately not described.

4. The following are the items in the controversy: John Whitgift, *An Answere to a Certen Libel* (1572); Thomas Cartwright, *A Replie to an Answere* (1573?); Whitgift, *The Defense of the Aunswere* (1574); Cartwright, *The Second Replie* (1575) and *The Rest of the Second Replie* (1577).

5. *The Seconde Parte of a Register,* ed. Albert Peel (2 vols. Cambridge, University Press, 1915), 1, 83–7; Knappen, *Tudor Puritanism,* 237. But the recantation insists on a Presbyterian polity and simple ceremonies, and is thus scarcely an act of perfect contrition.

6. Whitgift, *Works* (1851), *1*, 195, Cartwright says: ". . . we deny not but that certain things are left to the order of the church, because they are of that nature which are

In the controversy between Whitgift and Cartwright, the question of
the superiority of argument is of less interest than the points of agreement and of difference, with, particularly, the anticipations of the future
Puritan program. The Anglican and the Puritan, deriving as they do
from a single party of reform, have still much in common. They are both
bitterly, if not quite equally, anti-Roman : the prospect of the Tractarian
movement at Oxford in the nineteenth century would have been almost
as horrid to Whitgift as to Cartwright. At the moment of dispute, they
both subscribe to a biblical order in the church, and they both find in the
Bible precise, if widely divergent, instructions. What Gibbon calls the
great law of impartiality compels the conclusion that each has found
what he believes in, to wit, divine approval of an episcopacy or of a
presbytery.

The differences between the two are, thus, both of degree and kind.
Quite aside from the reform of abuses in the English church, a matter
which was at least officially the concern also of Anglicans, the Puritans
want a simplicity which the Anglicans do not approve, and Cartwright
wants a relocation of power to alter radically the constitution of the
English state. If Cartwright is not precisely for the separation of civil
and ecclesiastical government, he at least believes that power should
be moved from the sovereign and the convocation of a royally appointed
clergy to the parliament and a popularly elected body of clergy. Rule
would then shift from the few to the many. But the many who ruled
would not rule popularly; they would rule in a godly manner.[7] For the
Elizabethan Puritan is not the exponent of religious liberty. The
reasons, conscious and unconscious, for his leveling tendencies are fairly
easy to see : considerable numbers both in the Commons and among the
people were shifting to the Puritan side. The Commons showed sympathies which were with the passing of each year more ardently Puritan.
Among the people both in and out of London the cause of reform was
growing : Puritan preachers met with increasing acclaim. If power
moved down in the hierarchy, God's cause would win. The change from
an episcopacy would, without doubt, be a revolution. A presbytery in
control of the church would leave little room for a sovereign as supreme
governor, and none for royal bishops. Whitgift, like other moderates of

---

varied by times, places, persons . . ." For Cartwright on the vestments and Romanism
see *2*, 1, 3, 6, 7. On the supremacy of the crown, he says, *3* (1853), 311: ". . . if when
there is a lawful ministry it shall agree of any unlawful or unmeet order . . . the prince
ought to stay that order, and not to suffer it . . ." Throughout the argument, both Whitgift and Cartwright refer interminably to the Bible and Calvin.

7. See A. F. Scott Pearson's *Church and State* (Cambridge, University Press, 1928),
9–64, for an exposition of the Puritan theory of authority. Pearson says, 41: "Certain
aspects of his two-kingdom theory make it obvious that Cartwright did not believe in
the absolute sovereignty of the earthly monarch. The Christian magistrate is a member
of the Church . . ."

his time, might well ask whether the Puritan program would stop with the government of the church, and whether the Puritans aimed at the overthrow of the government of the nation. The answer from the Puritans was resolute, unvarying, and altogether honest, if not at all times convincing: they were in every way loyal to the crown.[8]

Richard Hooker's *Of Ecclesiastical Polity,* the classical justification of the Anglican position, did not appear for some years after the controversy between Whitgift and Cartwright, but Hooker was intimately concerned with the same problems and with the same conflict of beliefs and groupings of ambitions in the church and state.[9] In the years which immediately followed the publication of the Admonitions, the popularity of both Calvinist theology and polity grew. So widespread, indeed, was the esteem with which England held the teachings of Calvin that English Anglicanism was, normally, at one with Geneva on doctrine, and at serious odds with Geneva only in respect to the rites and government of the church.[1] Thus, when Hooker wrote against the Puritans in the 90's, the nature of his argument was specifically indicated in his title, *Of Ecclesiastical Polity.* Although the work is ultimately a philosophical refutation of several of the basic tenets of Calvinism, it is immediately an attack on Calvin's theory of church government.

The book found its beginnings both in the need of the Anglican party for a large apologetic and in the particular event of a clash between Hooker, the new master of the Temple in 1585, and the Puritan Walter Travers, his

8. Cartwright tells of the mild intentions of the Puritans (in Whitgift, *Works, 1,* 79): "It is all true you here allege of the anabaptists: God be praised there is nothing of it true in us. If through these questions moved the church be disquieted, the disquietness riseth in that the truth and sincerity which is offered is not received. We seek it in no tumultuous manner, but by humble suit unto them to whom the redress of things pertain . . ." But Whitgift was suspicious of the Puritans, ". . . contentious persons and disturbers of the peace of the church . . ." (*ibid.,* 80).

9. The standard edition of Hooker was edited by John Keble (3 vols. Oxford, 1845). Some recent studies of Hooker are Alexander Passerin d'Entrèves' *The Medieval Contribution to Political Thought* (Oxford, Oxford University Press, 1939), 88–142; Ebenezer T. Davies' *The Political Ideas of Richard Hooker* (Society for Promoting Christian Knowledge, 1946); and F. J. Shirley's *Richard Hooker and Contemporary Political Ideas* (Society for Promoting Christian Knowledge, 1949). A clear warning of the revolutionary intentions of the Puritans appeared in Richard Bancroft's *Daungerous Positions* (1593) and *A Survey of the Pretended Holy Discipline* (1593). Bancroft, a chaplain of Richard Cox as bishop of Ely, was instrumental in the apprehension of the printers of the Marprelate tracts (1588–89). He showed extreme hostility to the Puritans at the Hampton Court conference of 1604 and in the same year succeeded his close friend Whitgift as archbishop of Canterbury.

1. Perry Miller, *Orthodoxy in Massachusetts* (Cambridge, Harvard University Press, 1933), 18: "The Thirty-Nine Articles as framed in 1563 were, as Fuller says, 'purposely couched . . . in general terms . . . to include all such dissenters within the comprehensiveness of the expressions.' They declared that Scripture contained everything necessary for salvation, and advisedly avoided more explicit description of the outward means . . . Indeed, if the Establishment had at first any theological tone, it was predominantly Calvinistic, as Whitgift demonstrated in the Lambeth Articles of 1595."

preacher.[2] Travers had already published his *Ecclesiasticae Disciplinae* at Geneva in 1580; the work had been translated into English by Cartwright and published in 1584 at Cambridge, a heaven, or perhaps, a wasps' nest, of nonconformity. In 1587 John Bridges—later to be consecrated bishop of Oxford by Whitgift—had published his *Defence of the Government Established in the Church of England,* 1,401 pages of confused polemics, precisely the kind of justification which the Church of England did not need. In 1588, the year which marked the end of the greatest danger of Roman Catholic invasion, the Marprelate tracts, aimed at the ponderosity of Bridges, the ineptness of the Anglican officials, and the corruptions of the clergy, showed clearly that Geneva was the major threat.[3] Hooker thus directed his arguments against the Puritans rather than against the Roman Catholics and, controversy and polemics having produced little of enduring value as an apologetic for the establishment, he pitched his arguments on a general rather than a particular level. Although Puritanism was the nonconformity which he was to discredit, he was at the same time to demonstrate the validity of the middle position of the English church; and he was to be less concerned with the particulars of church government and of rites than with the general basis for social and ecclesiastical order.

Central to Hooker's justification of Anglicanism is his concept of human society: every man is at once a member of his society and of the

---

2. Hardin Craig, "Of the Laws of Ecclesiastical Polity—First Form," *Journal of the History of Ideas, 5* (1944), 91–104, summarizes opinions and concludes that 1593 is the year of publication. C. J. Sisson in *The Judicious Marriage of Mr. Hooker and the Birth of the Laws of Ecclesiastical Polity* (Cambridge, University Press, 1940), 64, says: "The fact is, therefore, that . . . the manuscript had gone straight to press after the contract was signed and the copy registered, and that printing was finished before 13 March 1593, in the space of one and a half months." Craig says, 94–6, of Hooker's intentions: "We have two sermons which embody doctrines to which Travers took exception and we have both Travers' *Supplication* and Hooker's *Answer.* These documents make it plain that Hooker's sermons on *The Certainty and Perpetuity of Faith in the Elect* and *A Learned Discourse of Justification, Works, and How the Foundation of Faith is Overthrown* contain the gist of what Travers objected to in Hooker's doctrine and what Hooker sought to substantiate by his profound study and thought . . . Travers reproves Hooker for an utterance at slight variance with Calvin . . . The point is that Hooker had presumed to appeal to his own reason against an authorized interpretation of Scripture . . . In other words, Hooker came finally squarely out with the thesis (against Calvin and all comers) that Scripture is not the only rule of all things ecclesiastical . . . *Of the Laws of Ecclesiastical Polity* as originally conceived was a work directed against Walter Travers and what he had so ably advocated." Wilbur K. Jordan in *The Development of Religious Toleration* (4 vols., Cambridge, Harvard University Press, 1932–40), *1,* 226, says of Hooker's heterodoxy: "In his earliest sermons Hooker committed himself to a view concerning the divine Will which comprehended the salvation of all men, seeking, however, to couch this heterodox view in terms that should not clash with the current predestinarian theology."

3. Sisson, *The Judicious Marriage, 7:* "For Hooker too the Roman field was won . . . Indeed, in some measure Rome and Canterbury had now the same ground to defend . . . by 1588 the main danger was over with the signal defeat of the Armada." Hooker was regarded by some as dangerously lenient with Rome.

church of that society. Specifically, in a Christian society, each person is necessarily both a citizen and a member of the church which is supported by the state and upon which, conversely, the state is based. Hooker thus presents a Calvinistic view of the parallelism of church and state, but he rejects the Roman Catholic concept of the pope as the unique head of a single, universal church. If Hooker's proposal seems on the face of it to deny the catholicity of a national church, one of the central principles of Anglicanism, and to put in its place a number of merely state churches, the answer to this objection of religious fragmentation and particularization is to be found in his account of law. It is perfectly true that within the Anglican pattern, as explained by Hooker, each national society will have, or at least may have, a national church which differs in many respects from other national churches. The ruler in each state, identical both by his civil function and by his adherence to Christian morality with the head of the church, would exact conformity to the state church, and would oppose toleration of serious deviation from the religious practices of the state.

But the imposition of general ecclesiastical conformity would arise from a series of laws in the universe, all designed to make it possible for man to live in society, and all reflecting the nature of God as revealed to man or as found in man himself. A law is not, Hooker explains, something imposed by a superior authority; it is, rather, a principle of procedure for carrying out actions; it is that which is pragmatically necessary for the achievement of an end.[4] Human society being a desirable convenience, good or right law must produce a workable order. For all true law is good law, and is by definition productive of desirable ends in human life. All true law indeed proceeds from God and expresses His perfect nature: the pragmatic test again applies, for the goodness can be determined by the fact that in the opinion of most humans the law produces a desirable result. Now man, being a creature of God, is by nature inclined to good; if, in addition, he will choose to follow the law which God has given him, man will express his godly nature by the goodness of his life and the goodness of his society.

Hooker's specific list of laws reflects the hierarchical view of the universe, inherited from the past and usual to his time: first is the law

4. Hooker, *Works, 1,* 200: "For unto every end every operation will not serve. That which doth assign unto each thing the kind, that which doth moderate the force and power, that which doth appoint the form and measure, of working, the same we term a Law." Sisson, *The Judicious Marriage,* 9: "For Rome, the Pope is the Vicar of Christ, therefore the Sovereign cannot be head of the Church. With Geneva, the Church ought to rule the State as God's kingdom upon earth. With Canterbury and Hooker, the sovereign is head of the Commonwealth and therefore of the Church which is coextensive with it. Heresy was not only heresy: it was sedition, a more serious matter in Tudor eyes." For an analysis of Hooker's law, and of consent as the justification of power, see Passerin d'Entrèves' *The Medieval Contribution to Political Thought,* 117–42. Passerin d'Entrèves finds that Thomas Aquinas furnishes at least the outlines of Hooker's theory.

of nature by which heaven and earth move in a divine order; then there
is celestial law for spiritual beings; finally, there is human law. In human
law there is the law of reason, the faculty of decision which has to do
with moral conduct; human positive laws, related to the law of reason,
but concerned with the particular regulations of human conduct in
society; and divine law, communicated to man through the Bible. The
most important of the divisions of human law is the law of reason: upon
this Hooker hinges the largest part of his argument for the concept of a
church which is both national and catholic. Reason is the peculiarly
divine element in man: it moves him most immediately to goodness; it
enables him to decide freely and thus in a godly manner, and it inclines
him toward order rather than chaos. Man's reason enables him to
achieve, to arrange, and to understand his place in the plan of things.
Again, out of the law of reason arises human society. A contract of a
sort exists among men: by obedience to rules of order, consented to by
humans, society becomes possible. Good law, then, in addition to being
in accord with God, is measured by the consent of large numbers of a
society for a long time; and the function of the state is fulfilled if the
good laws, the laws of reason, are consistently imposed for the preservation of society.[5]

Two points of particular importance are immediately apparent for
the discrediting of religious and political theory both to the right and to
the left of Anglicanism. For one thing, the law of Scripture is not
antecedent to the law of reason in respect to the Christian church; and
for another, the law of reason is not a specific code, unaltered and
unalterable in time and space, but rather the generalized concept of free
action which is productive of the good (in particular, of order) and which
abolishes evil (in particular, disorder). Calvin's divinely ordained polity,
then, disappears in a cloud of particular trivialities: presbyters or bishops
is an irrelevant question. Reason may find presbyters right in one time
and place, while in another bishops may be right. That government is
good which expresses the divine law of reason and which conforms to
custom in each particular society. There can be, in this view of political
and ecclesiastical order, no uniquely right church; but at the same time,
Christian societies can be connected to the extent that, despite variations
in particulars, they have in common a heavenly order.

Divine law is confused and perverted by the Puritans. It is contained
in the Bible, it concerns salvation, but it delivers no specific commands
for the government of the church or the state. Properly understood,
divine law instructs man chiefly in the nature of faith, hope, and charity
as the means for his redemption, and it offers general moral principles
for his conduct. But the Bible can be understood only by the use of

5. The whole of Bk. 1 (*Works, 1,* 197–285) is concerned with the examination of law,
human and divine.

reason so that, ultimately, even divine law depends on man's reasonable faculty. On this very point the Puritans have erred: they have acted as though reason were not necessary for the understanding of divine law; they have treated divine law as though it were concerned with particulars of human government instead of moral and spiritual principles; and they have, finally, substituted the anarchy of private whim for collective tradition. If they would preserve the differences among the laws of various sorts, they would not look to the Bible for things which it cannot possibly contain, and they would not abolish order by denying reason.[6]

It might be said that for Hooker, collective human reason is the ultimate measure of right and wrong. But his key phrase is scarcely different from the "popularity" with which the Puritans had been charged, and which constituted in the eyes of the Anglicans' a most serious fault. In actual practice there was little to choose between Hooker's collective reason and the regard for the opinion of the educated leaders of the community as advocated by the Puritans, except that one group of educated leaders, unhappily, was Anglican, and the other was Puritan. Both Puritan and Anglican apologetics accept the force of social consent, the dual obligation of the subject to obey, and of the government to exact obedience in respect to the area within which the subject approves obedience. Again, it is useless to pretend that Hooker looks to a medieval tradition of order and hierarchical gradations in power, and at the same time to pretend that the Puritans were unaware of Christian thought on the state and the church before 1500. Both look into the past for an orderly society; each finds an order which is different from that of the other. Hooker, however, is more clearly the conservative, acutely aware of the value of established patterns, and deeply suspicious of change for its own sake. The Puritan, on the other hand, finds both in the government and the morals of the English church serious discrepancies with the apostolic church; and by his position, the Puritan is amorous of change. Hooker turns from the revealed instructions of the Bible to the collective reason of society: he discards Calvinist bibliolatry, a failing of Anglican and Puritan alike, and demands at least an outward conformity to established practice in religious matters. His system allows certainly for evolution in worship, just as it allows for differences of time and place. The conformity which he demands is rather a catholic acceptance of central principles upon which men would generally agree, and his concept of society is different from that of the Elizabethan Puritan: Hooker cannot admit of a society divided as to church and state. In a proper society, the state is itself a Christian personality with the obligations of the Christian, but with the unique powers of the state

6. The section on the light of reason (*ibid., 1*, 225–37) is central to Hooker's account. In his "Preface" (*1*, 125–96) he has already delivered a measured attack on the confusion and unreason of the Puritans.

over each individual. Since the state receives sanction from the whole
social body, its power transcends that of any member, and its will transcends that of any member. As a Christian authority, the state is indeed
a church, and must perforce conform to precisely the ideals which the
Christian church, itself a part of the community, sets up. The two are
one: the church is a part of the Christian state; but the state, being
Christian, is a part of the church. There can be no division of allegiance,
as the Puritans or the Roman Catholics would insist; and there can properly be no division of aim and end. Such a view, however well it may
justify conformity in the central doctrines of a national church, at the
same time offers no argument for the unique rightness of a polity of king
and bishop: Hooker's strength in the long view is also his weakness in
an age which is looking for assurances and supports of official policy.[7]
Could the godlike opinions of reasonable men support the rule of king
and bishop if those men received instructions from a heaven quite different from Hooker's, but not less dependable?

Midway between the reforming zeal of the Admonitions on the left
and the traditionalism of Hooker on the right, are the religious opinions
of Francis Bacon. Bacon's position, however, is not precisely that of the
devout moderate who favors reform: his oblique skepticism, coupled with
his political caution, expresses an attitude which is markedly different
from that of the supernaturalist of any camp.[8] In addition, Bacon is
of particular interest because he speaks intermittently on the subject of
religious dispute from about 1589, a few years before the appearance of
Hooker's justification of Anglicanism, to around 1625 and the death of
James I. Perhaps through lack of interest, or perhaps through an understandable timidity in pronouncing on questions which were not safely
and singly philosophical but were dangerously political, Bacon generally
avoided in his discussions the examination of a basis for faith and practice; what he says becomes at times like the cry of the skeptic smothered
in the seas of doctrinal disputes. There is no chronological development
in Bacon's point of view; toward the end of his life his harshness against

7. See Sisson, *The Judicious Marriage*, 107–8. Hooker's lenient treatment of Roman
Catholicism made his nineteenth-century editor, the Anglican Keble, somewhat uneasy.

8. Jordan in *Religious Toleration, 2* (1936), 457–72, discusses Bacon's treatment of religion and of Puritanism with particular stress on his Erastianism. Jordan argues
cogently that Bacon's rejection of reason in the comprehension of ultimate religious
mysteries was a first step toward a detached and tolerant view of theological differences.
It should be pointed out, however, that skepticism, comparatively rare in the period, was
only one of a number of forces tending to produce religious toleration. The principle of
subjectivism or private judgment, so common among the sects, was much more important. Jordan says of Bacon, *2*, 460: "It can scarcely be argued that this attitude did
not cloak a real scepticism, and the powerful influence which Bacon's philosophy and
method were to exercise contributed importantly towards the development of the scepti-
cal temper of mind. For when religious truth is held to be unsusceptible of rational proof,
when it has been reduced to faith subjectively apprehended . . . the basis of religious
infallibility and, it follows, of religious intolerance has been swept away."

the sects is perhaps more marked than at the beginning; but he is also constantly aware of corruption in the establishment and an overconcern with externals of worship: for Bacon, religious strife is murder for a penny. Bacon illustrates the position of the secularist, unattached to a theological system, and supporting Anglicanism not because it is expressive of Hooker's divine reason, but because it is convenient.

An early expression of Bacon's opinion of the troubles is *An Advertisement Touching the Controversies of the Church of England* (1640). The pamphlet was probably written in 1589.[9] Bacon's sympathies are obviously divided: he is a conforming Anglican, but he is at the same time sympathetic to variations in worship, and he recognizes the need for the reform of abuses within the establishment. His refrain is neither the divine perfection of the Anglican church nor the necessity of a Calvinist polity, but the desirability of peace. In a survey of the complaints of the Puritans and the answers of the Anglicans, Bacon points out faults on both sides and suggests that each could give way to the other. The corruptions of the church, for example, are known beyond dispute: the authorities should attend and seek a remedy. The theory that a good service is one which has no elements from Rome is patently absurd: the abolition of all the old rites and the strict imitation of the reformed churches of the Continent would be futile innovation with the danger of irreparable damage to Christianity in England. The Anglicans have been too eager to deprive clergymen who would not conform in all respects. At the end of the pamphlet, Bacon warns of the peril in stirring up the common people with religious controversy. The average man is no fit judge of such matters, and there are both the wild preachings of untrained zealots and the immoderate charges of the orthodox clergy to cause public turmoil.

Bacon speaks plainly, if cautiously, for a degree of toleration in *Certain Considerations Touching the Better Pacification and Edification of the Church of England* (1604).[1] The tone of the pamphlet is generally consonant with the first. Writing in a studiously oblique manner, he says that innovation is desirable in the church and that reform must allow for differences of opinion which will be expressed in differences of worship. He argues, like Hooker, that the form of church government is a nonessential and insufficient ground for schism; a belief in "one faith, one baptism," is important, and on that the nation can agree. The fact that the nation could not agree on precisely that point must have been apparent by 1604, but Bacon's impatience does not arise from his inability to understand what is going on around him; it stems rather from his

9. *The Works of Francis Bacon*, ed. James Spedding *et al.* (14 vols. 1858–68), *8* (1862), 74–95. Spedding, 72–3, dates the pamphlet as about the summer of 1589 and connects it with the Marprelate controversy.

1. Bacon, *Works, 10* (1868), 103–27. Spedding, 102, discusses the circumstances surrounding the writing and publication. There was a reprint in 1641.

belief that the points at issue are beyond human resolution and can best be determined on the side of peace, order, and custom, and without unceasing concern for the inscrutable will of God in the church government of England. The rest of *Certain Considerations* goes over a number of the most important abuses of the Anglicans: the argument is scarcely balanced, as it was in *An Advertisement*. Bacon clearly supports a program of moderate reform at least in respect to the ignorance of the clergy, the lack of preaching, nonresidency, and pluralities.

It is notable that Bacon's program fits approximately the demands of the moderate Presbyterians at the time of the Millenary Petition in 1603.[2] However, he differs from the petitioners in a most important respect: like Hooker, he regards a particular polity as of minor importance. Although he agrees with the Presbyterians on the abuses which they had found, he then differs in allowing for a nonconformity and toleration which was no part of Elizabethan Puritanism. Bacon's attitude is thus much different from that of the devout and devoted Anglican or Puritan. Bacon does not say that nonconformity is right, nor that the Presbyterian order of government is right; he does say that elements like polity are less important than central doctrines of faith. On the other hand, he does not say that the Anglican order is right, but rather that it is an established and therefore convenient form for England. To this extent he echoes Hooker. Yet in allowing for a considerable degree of deviation in what he regarded as adiaphora, he denied the positivist positions of both the right and the left, and, indeed, the nationalistic basis of Hooker's church and society.

Both in advice which Bacon seems to have given, about 1616, to George Villiers, first duke of Buckingham, and in the 1625 version of the essay "Of Unity in Religion," there is the same complaint against those whose arguments are more subtle than substantial.[3] Religious change for slight reason is dangerous, and the chief of those who imperil the state are "Roman Catholiques . . . Anabaptists and Separatists and Sectaries . . ." Bacon still supports ecclesiastical order under the sovereign.[4] But Bacon's Erastianism is again quite different from that of

2. Strype in *The Life and Acts of Archbishop Whitgift* (4 vols. Oxford, 1822), *2*, 478–502, sums up the chief points of the petition, a document of moderate Puritanism in 1603. The signers declared for a simplification of rites, more preaching, less church music, stricter observance of the Sabbath, the elimination of plural livings, and a "church disciple . . . according to Christ's own institutions . . ."

3. Bacon, *Works*, 6 (1858), 381–4. James Spedding's *An Account of the Life and Times of Francis Bacon* (2 vols. Boston, Mass., 1878), *2*, 151–66, contains "A Letter of Advice, Written by Sir Francis Bacon to the Duke of Buckingham, When He Became Favorite to King James." A second version which differs from the first in wording but not in sense appears in Spedding's *The Letters and Life of Francis Bacon*, ed. James Spedding (7 vols. 1861–74), 6 (1872), 27–56, and is titled: "A Copy of a Letter Conceived to Be Written to the Late Duke of Buckingham When He First Became a Favorite to King James . . ."

4. Bacon in Spedding's *An Account*, *2*, 156–7: "If any question be moved concerning

Hooker; indeed, Hooker does not think of a civil governor supreme over the church, but rather of a Christian governor expressing the moral identity of state and church. Bacon's road is paved with skepticism expressed through a religious circumspection which substitutes, almost convincingly, the word *faith* for *doubt*. For Bacon rejects Hooker's function of reason in the comprehension of final religious truths; and if man's reason cannot discover the nature of God or the government of God's church, there can then be little justification, on the basis of reason, for Hooker's Anglicanism. Bacon equally shrouds the mysteries of Holy Writ in darkness; and if the Geneva Bible is a mystery, it is difficult to be certain that presbyters are better or worse than bishops. In short, if man's reasonable faculty cannot discover religious truth, that truth must be regarded as undiscoverable, or it must be accepted on faith. If there is no religious certainty, then the believer can look for no true church beyond the dictates of his faith, his desire to believe. The concept of a "right" church becomes meaningless both in the rational sense of a Hooker and in the biblical and illative sense of a Cartwright; and there remains only the rightness of the established order, the rightness of a social convenience. An Englishman should be, in general, an Anglican, since in general, his Anglicanism will tend to preserve society.

It is no cynical aspersion to fail to find in Bacon a shining city of God. To Bacon several points at issue, of crucial import to the Puritan and the Anglican polemicists, are trivial irrelevancies; and the strenuous efforts of the assorted partisans to discover for their churches a justification which will be not merely social but also ethical and indeed divine strike Bacon as presumptuous displays of human vanity. Bacon by 1625 had anticipated the temper of the much later times of hydra-headed nonconformities when Anglicans and Puritans alike were compelled to accept the distasteful fact that "Christ's coat indeed had no seam, but the church's vesture was of diverse colours . . ." [5]

With the opening of the Long Parliament in 1640 a violent attack on the bishops began; anti-Anglican pamphlets came from the presses and, more notably, a London petition which called for the abolition of episcopacy "root and branch" was introduced.[6] On the other side, in

---

the doctrine of the Church of England expressed in the 39 Articles, give not the least ear to the movers thereof. That is so soundly and so orthodoxly settled as cannot be questioned without extreme danger to the honor and stability of our Religion . . . But to settle your judgment, mark but the admonition of the wisest of men, King Solomon, Prov. xxvii.21. My son, fear God and the King, and meddle not with those who are given to change."

5. Bacon, "Of Unity in Religion," *Works*, 6, 382.
6. See Godfrey Davies, *The Early Stuarts* (Oxford, Oxford University Press, 1937), 188 ff., for an account of parliament and the Root and Branch Bill. The commons were by no means united on the desirability of abolishing episcopacy. Of the anti-Anglican pamphlets, the *DNB*, "Joseph Hall," observes: "No less than 140 of these passed the press before the session was very far advanced."

defense of the established order, Joseph Hall's *Episcopacie by Divine
Right* (1640) appeared as a major statement in opposition both to the
propaganda of the Puritans and the threat of reform by law. James
Ussher stood side by side with Hall. The most celebrated of the Puritan
opposition were John Milton and the group of Presbyterian divines who
signed themselves Smectymnuus.[7] The arguments of the writers on each
side have a great deal in common with those of their opponents: both
sides, for example, are much concerned with the government and the
officials of the church, and with the manner of conducting rites and services. Indeed the disputants, writing as they do near the moment of
open fighting, sum up the chief points, indicate the attitudes of each
side at the moment of conflict, and serve to furnish a comparison with
the tone of the dispute in earlier years.

The basis of the Anglican argument is not notably different in 1640
from that in 1572. Hooker's account of the nature of human reason has
counted for little to many of the apologists for the establishment; and the
Episcopal church, at least to Hall, remains ". . . not only an holy and
lawful, but a divine institution . . ." Conversely, Presbyterianism is
without "true footing" in the past or present.[8] His arguments, biblical
and traditional, make Anglican liturgy and polity things to be derived
from God's written instructions and, consequently, beyond violation and
above improvement. James Ussher supports Hall with a clever but conventional account of the origin of bishops: they were the leaders chosen
by elders of the apostolic church.[9] Neither Hall nor Ussher has the least
doubt about the sufficiency of unevolving tradition and biblical authority
as seen through Anglican eyes. Unlike Hooker, they do not recognize
the danger of resting on Scripture when the enemy has already said that

7. The name is a compound of the initials of Stephen Marshall, Edmund Calamy,
Thomas Young, Matthew Newcomen, and William Spurstowe. Of their and Milton's
intentions at the time, Arthur Barker in *Milton and the Puritan Dilemma, 1641–60*
(Toronto, University of Toronto Press, 1942), 127, says: "The general political ideas
incidentally expressed in the early pamphlets are those of moderate Puritanism. Civil
no less than ecclesiastical liberty according to God's will finds its place in Milton's
thinking at this time; but he is at one with Smectymnuuans in placing the emphasis on
reformation rather than on freedom." Haller's chapter "Root and Branch" in *The
Rise of Puritanism,* 324–63, connects the literary events to the political. The standard
edition is *The Works of the Right Reverend Joseph Hall, D.D.,* ed. Philip Wynter (10
vols. Oxford, 1863). The divine origin of episcopacy and the fallacies of Presbyterianism, together with an account of the dangers of admitting "lay elders" (i.e., Puritans) to
any authority in the church are illustrated in *Episcopacie by Divine Right* (1640),
Works, 9, 142–281. The essentials of the argument are in the two "Propositions," 141.
Jordan in *Religious Toleration, 2,* 146, points out that Hall was a moderate Anglican and
that Laud actually disliked him.

8. Hall, *An Humble Remonstrance to the High Court of Parliament* (1641), *Works,
9,* 282–96.

9. In his *The Judgement of Doctor Rainoldes* (1641), reprinted in *The Whole Works
of the Most Rev. James Ussher, D.D.,* ed. Charles R. Elrington *et al.* (17 vols. Dublin,
1864), 7, 75–85. The quotation on which the pamphlet is based is from *The Summe of
the Conference betweene John Rainolds and John Hart* (1584).

the Anglicans are blind and that only a Puritan can read the Scripture. Smectymnuus and Milton answer with consistency and detail the proposals of Hall and Ussher. The refutation is delivered over some period of time, and in a number of writings, but the sum is fairly simple and generally coherent. The government of the church is the chief question at issue: on this point they agree with their opponents. But the Anglicans are in serious error in their biblical and historical claims for episcopacy. Episcopacy is not the form of government which was used in the apostolic church; in addition, it is not now and never has been universal to the church. Episcopacy is the result of time and decay, it is simply a human institution arbitrarily imposed on the original order which was quite different from that which now exists in England. Actually, the present order opposes the Gospel, it promotes schism, and it tends to destroy the monarchy.[1] "The diseased tumor of Prelacie" should be cut out and England should turn to a truly biblical order, which is to say a presbytery. But if the presence of bishops is evil, their manner of election and their conduct in office are further offenses against God: they are appointed, rather than chosen by popular election; and having been appointed, they corrupt the church, the universities, and the civil government with their neglect and their dishonesty.[2]

A third major item of dispute, the service, is commingled with the arguments over polity and the authority of bishops. On the subject of the service, the attack is much what it was in the days of the two Admonitions: the Puritans still would simplify, since much of the service is wrong in that it is Romish and unhistorical. It has reached a point in the Anglican church where elaborate ceremony is an excuse for escaping

1. Haller says in *The Rise of Puritanism*, 350: "Milton in 1641, putting aside all authority but scripture and all guidance but reason, thought that the type of church government plainly delineated in holy writ was Presbyterianism." Milton stated the Presbyterian position in the following pamphlets: *Of Reformation Touching Church-Discipline in England* (1641), *Of Prelaticall Episcopacy* (1641), *Animadversions upon the Remonstrants Defence, against Smectymnuus* (1641), *The Reason of Church-government Urg'd against Prelaty* (1642) and *An Apology against a Pamphlet Call'd a Modest Confutation* (1642). They are reprinted in *The Works of John Milton*, ed. Frank A. Patterson *et al.* (18 vols., New York, Columbia University Press, 1931–38), *3* (1931). The Smectymnuuans spoke in *An Answer to a Booke Entituled, an Humble Remonstrance* (1641) and *A Vindication of the Answer to the Humble Remonstrance* (1641). With Milton, the merely indignant frequently blends into the witty and satirical: ". . . besides errors, tautologies, impertinences, as those thanks in the womans Churching for her delivery from Sunburning and Moonblasting, as if she had bin travailing not in her bed, but in the deserts of Arabia. So that while some men cease not to admire the incomparable frame of our Liturgy, I cannot but admire as fast what they think is become of judgement, and tast in other men, that they can hope to be heard without laughter." (*An Apology against a Pamphlet, Works, 3,* 352.)

2. Don M. Wolfe summarizes the opposition in *Milton in the Puritan Revolution* (New York, Nelson, 1941), 51: "Milton opposed the prelates, then, for their worldliness, their aristocratic church structure, their oblique detraction from the dignity and worth of the Christian layman and preaching minister, and their insistence on ceremonial conformity."

the trouble of preaching, and the liturgy is of more importance than the instruction of the people: "We stand for a Popish Liturgy as for the ark of our Cov'nant. And so little does it appear our prayers are from the heart, that multitudes of us declare, they know not how to pray but by rote." [3] Out of the Romish practices, worse corruptions have been perpetuated: the inequitable distribution of church income, the non-resident clergy, pluralities, and the perverting of justice for ecclesiastical fees.

However, the accounts, both Puritan and Anglican, of the correct order of the state have come to be much more in agreement than during the years of Elizabeth. Both sides now subscribe, at least officially, to an extreme Erastianism; it is, certainly, a Christian Erastianism of the sort that both Whitgift and Cartwright could have approved, though for different reasons. Both sides now eagerly place the crown above the miter, one side perhaps because it sees in the crown the best protection for the miter, and the other side because it does not like the miter. [4] But then each side accuses the other of the intention to subvert civil discipline and to destroy the rule of the sovereign. The old charge of civil disorder, common enough in Anglican pamphlets against the Puritans, and fairly easy to sustain on the basis of Puritan recommendations for the alter-ation of the government of the church, is now turned against the Anglicans on a number of counts. The ecclesiasts have invaded courts in which they have no right; they have failed to confront the accused with the witnesses against him; they have required no more than one witness for a conviction. And there is the old, but still lively, issue of the bishops in the House of Lords. Their presence means usually more power for the Anglicans; their absence, if only by default, a gain for the Puritans. So, each side calls on God and proves that the bishops should, or should not, have seats in the Lords. [5] Finally, the Puritans charge the Anglicans with ruin of the crown and the nation: ". . . the Prelats, as they are to the subjects a calamity, so are they the greatest underminers and be-trayers of the Monarch . . . hinder or break the happy assembling of Parlaments . . . crosse . . . and traduce all Parlamentary proceed-ings." [6]

In point of fact, the arguments of Hall and Ussher, and of Smec-tymnuus and Milton are not markedly different in content from those of Whitgift and Cartwright. The central issues are the same in 1642 as

3. *An Apology against a Pamphlet, Works, 3,* 356.
4. Smectymnuus, *A Vindication of the Answer, 7;* Hall, *A Short Answer to the Tedious Vindication of Smectymnuus* (1641), *Works, 9,* 385–443, is an appeal to "The Most High Court of Parliament."
5. Hall, *A Short Answer . . . against the Bishops Sitting in Parliament, Works, 8,* 273–6, proves that the bishops should sit in the lords; Smectymnuus in *An Answer to a Booke,* 45, proves that they should not.
6. Milton, *The Reason of Church Government, Works, 3,* 276–7.

they were in 1572, although the positions of the two disputing parties are changed. Each side supports, or pretends to support, a monarchy which rules an orderly and Christian state; one side insists on the need for the preservation of accustomed patterns of rule and worship; the other side insists that change is essential. But if the content is generally the same, the tone of the argument is much different from that of earlier years. Even Bacon the moderate conformist is generally foreign to Hall and Ussher; although Hall was no hot Anglican, he was at least very warm when he faced the reforming zeal of a John Milton. And, equally, Milton could curse an opponent who would not see the need for a purge of the most radical sort within the church.[7] Each side is deeply sure that it is right, that it represents God's revealed order in the world, and that the opposition is corruption and ruin. Hooker has small part in the Anglican apologetic at this moment; and he has planted no doubts in the mind of the keenest of the Puritan polemicists.

Hall and Ussher no longer speak, like Whitgift, with a mildness that concedes elements of agreement with the other side, or with a tone that implies that the arguments of the establishment are delivered, at least to some extent, in the hope of converting error. The latter-day Anglicans are plainly denouncing, and have accepted the depravity of the reforming party. Milton and Smectymnuus likewise talk openly of the threat of destruction of the monarchy—not that they wish to see the monarchy destroyed—but the destruction will come if the institution is not extracted from the evil machinations of Satan's cohorts. The tunes are the same as those sung by Whitgift and Cartwright and, indeed, not so different from those of Cox and Tyndale. Some new variations have been devised; but the music is very much louder. The increasing bitterness of the argument indicates the approach of violence and the profound change which has taken place in the tone of the debate on ecclesiastical reform since Elizabeth's time.

From the varying expressions of each side, from the shifts in tone and nature of the arguments, it is possible to understand both the revolutionary aspects of Puritanism and the evolution toward violence in civil war. One of the most obvious changes is, for instance, the enlargement of the area involved in some of the central problems dealt with in the

7. Milton's *Of Reformation* ends with a prayer to God (*Works, 3,* 76–9) and a curse (79) on the Anglicans; the curse is notable for the fury of invective or, through Anglican eyes, its immoderation: "But they contrary that by the impairing and diminution of the true Faith, the distresses and servitude of their Countrey aspire to high Dignity, Rule and Promotion here, after a shamefull end in this Life (which God grant them) shall be thrown downe eternally into the darkest and deepest Gulfe of Hell, where under the despightfull controule, the trample and spurne of all the other Damned, that in the anguish of their Torture shall have no other ease then to exercise a Raving and Bestiall Tyranny over them as their Slaves and Negro's, they shall remaine in that plight for ever, the basest, the lowermost, the most dejected, most underfoot and downe-trodden Vassals of Perdition."

dispute. Polity, rites, and abuses in the church are primarily questions of reform into the age of Elizabeth. In the earlier years the reformers rarely intended a political revolution and would have been shocked at the suggestion that the sovereign might be deposed. Later, ecclesiastical reform became a question of government in the largest sense, not merely of party but of the structure of the state. The Puritan program takes on unmistakable political overtones by 1572, and, by the Long Parliament of 1640 is as much political as religious. It is also true that to the end of the peaceful negotiations, the Puritans usually believe that they are concerned with a reform of the church, and they cannot accept the fact that they are in the process of fomenting social and political revolt. To indicate the process of evolution in one item only, the Puritans continue to insist on the need for a simplification of rites; but what had been in the past chiefly anti-Romanism, as manifested by Hooper, for example, did come to be, under Elizabeth, James, and Charles, a particular defiance of the express orders of Protestant monarchs. A clergyman's refusal to follow instructions on vestments or the manner of administering Communion began in qualms of conscience; a persistent refusal to obey instructions from his superiors simply applied the pre-Calvinist principle that the crown, when it persisted in violating God's instructions, ought to be defied.[8] Elizabeth's technique of attrition kept the Puritans politically in hand without at the same time alienating them from the crown. James I in the Hampton Court conference of 1604 showed that he was aware of the dangers of allowing defiance of authority; but James was more forthright than Elizabeth.

But by 1640, the Puritans, who had been mainly the party of religious reform, had become the political left; they were on the point of destroying the old order and setting up a new order of their own. As innovators, they could promise to reform abuses which had existed for years in the old church; on this they could claim support from virtuous moderates,

---

8. Knappen is generally right in arguing in *Tudor Puritanism* that a principle of Elizabethan Puritanism was passive resistance. See, for instance, his chapter on separatism, 303–16. But it must also be remembered that since the Puritans steadily believed that the government was defying God's order of the church, active resistance could easily become a Christian necessity. Cartwright's tone is not openly rebellious as is John Milton's, but Cartwright's proposed reforms could certainly not have been achieved by passive reforms unless the government had quietly abdicated to the Puritan party. Perry Miller in *Orthodoxy in Massachusetts* (Cambridge, Harvard University Press, 1933), 50, describes the course of the later years: "They believed in the Supremacy; they had to believe in it, because it was the assumption of their age and because it was essential to their discipline. And so they swore fervent allegiance to a King who ingeniously tortured them, denied their basic conviction, assumed functions that belonged only to Christ, commanded their adherence to a Popish ceremonial, and deliberately enjoined the desecration of the Sabbath . . . Their whole cause would have been lost had they once broken the national uniformity; they could no more envisage themselves existing as a separate church alongside the Establishment than the prelates could have permitted it . . . So Puritan reasoning went round in hopeless circles, and Winthrop in 1629 had good cause to be worried about the future of England."

and enjoy the prestige of the diligent reformer. But at the same time it was obvious that as extremists they would be compelled to destroy, and it was not at all certain that all of England, or even the greater part of England, was ready for wholesale reform in church and state. With good reason, the Anglicans thus seized upon the undeniable fact that the Puritans were revolutionaries.

The Anglicans could, by comparison, take on the contrasting virtues of preservers of the nation as well as the preservers of an ecclesiastical establishment: they would guard faithfully and loyally the social and political system, tried, tested, and agreeable to large sections of English society. There had been, in the past, revolutionary aspects of Anglicanism; the English church had separated from Rome, and, through the rebellious Henry, the enlargement of the powers of the crown in English society had hastened the development of a more unified state. But the religious and political innovations so intimately connected with Anglicanism were necessarily forgotten when Anglicanism and the crown were faced with a new force for change; the church with the crown developed a position of comparative immobility.

It was theologically desirable to strengthen the feeling that the church was both English and catholic and that it was in the main stream of western Christianity; in addition, it became less dangerous to admit the debt to Rome.[9] The new apologetic could offer a church with the ancient roots of Roman Catholicism, but with the decayed branches of innovation and corruption pruned away. The point is of particular interest since it underscores the fact that Anglicanism remained, in respect to its ideal of an improved church, very close to English Puritanism. However far apart the two groups had moved since the Marian exile, they were still connected by the strong bond of the English Reformation which had given birth to both parties. So the Anglican argument was understandably designed to make the reformers less attractive: the Puritans had no monopoly on reform. Another point of attraction in Anglican doctrine was that the old claims to biblical exactness of worship and polity, often as extreme as those of the hottest Presbyterians, were at least to some extent disappearing. By the time of the canons of 1604, many in the church admitted that Scripture could not be the sole and sufficient guide for determining all questions. This increasing acceptance of human reason guaranteed Anglicanism a much wider appeal than it had had before; but as human reason came in, much of the strength of the old positivist and supernaturalist position went out. Under the old

9. Douglas Bush's *English Literature in the Earlier Seventeenth Century* (Oxford, Oxford University Press, 1945), 318 ff., contains a summary of the changes in both the Anglican and Puritan positions after 1600: ". . . Earlier generations of Anglicans had naturally stressed their Protestant remoteness from Rome; now that the time of active revolt was past, a larger view was possible. The Church of England was defended as a true Catholic Church, purified from the accumulated inventions and abuses of Rome . . ."

dispensation, the sovereign and his bishops had interpreted the truth as contained in the Bible: then there was a right answer to a question. A good part of the strength of Jewel in his early attacks on the chief adversary, Rome, had come not only from his Protestant God, but also from his Protestant sovereign. The later church of Andrewes went far in the direction of the ideal of a truly catholic church, but at the same time it lost much of its old strength.

And just as the statements on polity and authority became less apodictic, so the doctrine of the church became less harsh as well as less certain. The doctrinal Calvinism of Elizabeth's establishment had offered difficulties if the preacher was to persuade the congregation to follow the paths of virtue: man's fate having been decided already, could he choose between good and evil? But an unofficial semitolerance could let the beliefs of the average man alone; and the English church had never been overly concerned with doctrine. The Anglican shift in the course of the controversy then, had been, after the accession of Elizabeth and to the advent of Charles and Laud, in the direction of less certain authority from crown and bishop. Hooker's reason had given a generous and noble account of Christian practice, but the same reason had to an extent weakened the Anglican cause. For survival in the face of the advancing forces of revolution, Hall with his episcopacy divinely appointed promised at least something certain to fight for.

The Puritans had, like the Anglicans, changed, but in many respects the Puritans had strengthened themselves in the process. They had particularly identified themselves with Geneva, and the strongest single bond between them and the Anglicans was the central doctrine of Calvin, that of predestination and its logical postulate, election. Within the scheme, no man could do a deed pleasing to God, and each man had been through all eternity assigned to heaven or to hell.[1] Now, the themes of predestination, election, the vileness of man, and the grace of God were preached unceasingly by Puritan and Anglican, and there can, on the basis of the number of sermons printed, be no question of the attraction of the subjects to the sixteenth- and seventeenth-century mind. But just as the Anglicans came, after the turn of the seventeenth century, to alter the harshness of the doctrine, so the Puritans discovered more positive worth in good works, and a clearer hope for salvation in the hereafter.

The shifts in emphasis did not destroy the tablets from Mount Geneva;

---

1. Haller, *The Rise of Puritanism*, 83–5: ". . . we must endeavor to grasp the meaning of the central dogma of Puritanism as it applied to the life of men . . . This was a conception of an all-embracing determinism, theologically formulated as the doctrine of predestination. It is a conception which, especially in its postulates of an absolute human depravity and a purely arbitrary human redemption, has often seemed absurd to the common sense and abhorrent to the humanitarian sentiment of later generations . . . The history of Puritan thought in England is primarily the history of the setting forth of the basic doctrine of predestination in terms calculated to appeal to the English populace."

Of predestynacion.

That man that lokyth for to haue a rewarde
Whiche he hath nat deseruyd to obtayne
And lenyth his body vpon a rede forwarde
Whiche for waykenes may hym nat well sustayne
Forsoth this fole may longe so loke in vayne
And on the Crauys he styll shall bacwarde ryde
Cryenge with the doue, whose flyght shall hym ay gyde.

An early attack in English on the doctrine of predestination. From Alexander Barclay's *The Ship of Fools*
(1509), ed. 1874. Barclay is translating and adapting
Sebastian Brant's *Das Narrenschiff* (Basel, 1494).

37

it was simply that there were oblique concessions to free will. If man had no choice about the state of his soul, it was true that the elect might show their predetermined state of grace by their good works on earth. The principle was in accord with Calvin; the stressing of the principle made Puritanism more attractive. Man could believe in predestination and still believe that his good life revealed his heavenly destination. It may also be true that covenant theology of the seventeenth century made salvation available to all who would accept God's grace, although the contractual element in the theory has probably been exaggerated.[2]

Puritanism becomes then, through the years, more diffuse, and the later propaganda by its variety is more appealing in the controversy with Anglicanism.[3] But at the same time, Puritanism suffers from the identical difficulty of the new Anglican ideal of a more rationalistic faith: a multifaceted nonconformity is able to rise, and the sects at last flourish with more power than the old Presbyterianism. In a sense, the acceptance of human reason and a degree of choice meant for the Puritans a weakening of their position by diversity of opinion and the dispersal of a comparatively united front in the face of opposition. After 1642 the process of fragmentation is completed. Politically and religiously to the left of the Presbyterians were the Independents or Congregationalists. Although they were numerically too weak to control the Puritan forces, it was possible to effect a coalition with the sects, which were even farther to the left than the Congregationalists. Within the coalition, diversity of opinion was so great that the principle of religious toleration was necessary for survival.[4] From this changing pattern of Puritanism

2. Perry Miller's account in *The New England Mind* (New York, Macmillan, 1939), 365–97, perhaps stresses too much the contractual element. He says, 377: "Sibbes therefore defined the Covenant of Grace in terms common to all writers: 'It hath pleased the great God to enter into a treaty and covenant of agreement with us his poor creatures, the articles of which agreement are here comprised. God, for his part, undertakes to convey all that concerns our happiness, upon our receiving of them, by believing on him. Every one in particular that recites these articles from a spirit of faith makes good this condition.'" Miller observes, 396: "Here then was a revision of Calvinism which by skillful dialectic preserved the essential tenets of piety—the absolute God, the depraved man, the redeeming and unmerited grace—and yet contrived at the same time that justification by faith should not produce a moral laxity. It aimed throughout to prove that faith without performance was impossible, a contradiction in terms, that the performance required is stated in the moral law, in the Ten Commandments . . ."

3. An example of the shift from harshness to mildness is the difference between Calvin and Milton on works. In the sixteenth century, Calvin says in the *Institutes*, Bk. III, chap. 16 (ed. Allen, *2*, 40): "They pretend that God is appeased by their frivolous satisfactions [good works], which are no better than dung; we assert . . . that the displeasure of God is too great to be appeased by these worthless satisfactions . . ." After the Restoration, Milton's Adam, and all mankind, are told in *Paradise Lost* (XII, 424 ff.):

> Thy ransom paid, which Man from death redeems,
> His death for Man, as many as offer'd Life
> Neglect not, and the benefit embrace
> By faith not void of works . . .

4. See A. S. P. Woodhouse's introduction to his *Puritanism and Liberty Being the Army Debates (1647–49) from the Clarke Manuscripts* (Dent, 1938) for an account of

is to be had the explanation for the great variety of the writing: the propaganda is often confused and contradictory because the movement is a composite of disparate forces. It changes from the beginning, and it is not uniform even at one moment. However, for the right, middle, and left religion is always a moving force, and there is the ideal, not different from that of the Anglican or the Roman Catholic, of an orderly world under Christian rule. The movement is reforming, it is always dynamic, and it is more experimental than traditional. Finally, usually by accident, there is the end product of religious liberty and greater intellectual freedom. It can well be argued that Anglicanism would have been more tolerant in less time had it won, but the fact remains that Anglicanism did not win; and that out of the Puritan struggle came a more generous concept of man's right to his own opinions.

The fact that the reforming Puritan so gradually through the years became the revolutionary is the result of necessity: sweet reason had to become violence. It is true beyond dispute that the Puritan was honest in his protestations of loyalty to the crown; it is also true that the Anglican saw clearly the political implications of the program when the Puritan missed them completely. The Puritan, even after the advent of James, customarily salts his appeals for church reforms with hymns to the sovereign as the source for true belief and practice; but it must be remembered that the Puritan is always speaking of a sovereign who will see the Christian rightness of the reforming party and the evil of the establishment. In the later years of James, and for a time under Charles, the Puritan found no answer to the impossible position of supporting a king who supported a corrupt church. Finally, the Puritan became an open revolutionary because he had to; there was only one possible choice when he was faced with the order of Christ as opposed to a king who would not follow the order of Christ.[5]

On the journey from ardent reformer to revolutionary and regicide, the Puritan was watched and commented on by the Anglican; the Puritan in turn watched the Anglican and aimed at him the barbed arrows of decay, neglect, and positive wrongdoing in the church. But the observations of the Anglican were usually more complex, more varied, and more pointed, if only because the sins of saints are more

---

the principal groupings of forces and the shift of power which took place in the course of the fighting. He says, 17-18: "The Parties of the Left, the Sectaries, religious and political, were a heterogeneous company among whom the winds of doctrine assumed the proportions of a tempest. They were descended from the Separatists and Anabaptists, as the Independents were from the more sedate Congregationalists, and were, so to speak, the Independents' poor relations." Woodhouse finds that after 1646 there is a new concern among the Puritans for free discussion. His summary of Puritanism, 86 ff., is rather too idealized to be a reflection of what the Puritans most commonly wrote and preached.

5. Perry Miller, *Orthodoxy in Massachusetts*, 41: "By 1630 the rift between the King and his Puritan subjects was a yawning chasm, and the Puritans were not colossal enough to straddle it; they could not preach limitation of the King . . . and still be accounted loyal citizens."

notable than the sins of ordinary humans: throughout the years there accumulated a list of anti-Puritan charges from the conformists. Some of the charges were abundantly supported by evidence; others were based on a plainly distorted picture; and still others had no perceptible basis in fact.

There was, for one thing, the ample charge that the Puritans were extremists intent on religious, social, and political revolution. The charge was not difficult to sustain, either on the basis of the content of the Puritan proposals, or the course of events in the Puritan parliaments. The best serious expression of this charge is found in the writings of men like Whitgift and Hooker; lesser Anglicans are often more extreme, and, although it transpires that they are right, the rightness is the product of the accident of immoderation rather than of wisdom before the event.[6] But the complaint, pitched at its most general level, is persuasive, both as a positive recommendation for orthodoxy and as a restraint from hasty action. The argument was the strongest one in the arsenal of the right—and in the right must be included the moderates as well as the conservatives—which held that reform could fail if it proceeded without a due regard for filling with something better the vacuum left after the destruction of the old. The argument, when it came from the moderate who supported the reform of obvious faults, did give a warning of what would happen in the triumph of Puritanism when England would search for a religious uniformity better than the old and a new form of civil government also better than the old.

A second charge, and one that struck at the very basis of the Puritan's frame of justification for his proposed reforms, was his esteem for the literal word of the Bible. And there again, within certain obvious limits, the Anglican could justify his attack. It was perfectly true that the Puritan frequently found in the Bible the answer to all possible questions; and it was also true that the particular translation to which he turned was rendered by his own kind in a vocabulary heavily weighted to prove the rightness of any particular argument which he wished to support. The Anglican might, in the earlier years, say that the Bible could be translated in more than one way to give more than one sense, and in the later years he might say that the Bible was not the only rule for conduct and the ordering of society. So that again, within the limits of the facts, it was true that the Puritan was often over literal and naïve in his attempts to prove his propositions with his own peculiar version of God's word.[7]

6. As, for instance, in the writings of Richard Bancroft.

7. Hooker points out the Puritans' peculiar use of words and their discovery of things in the Bible which other readers cannot discover. He says, *Works, I,* 149–50: ". . . their conceits perverted beforehand, by being taught, that an 'elder' doth signify a layman admitted only to the office or rule of government in the Church; a 'doctor,' one which may only teach, and neither preach nor administer the Sacraments; a 'deacon,' one

Still another observation which the Anglican commonly made was that the Puritan was precise. The Puritan was precise when he scrupled over details of the service or when he found it a sin to bow at the name of Jesus; the Puritan was precise when he saw sin in the wedding ring, and the word *Christmas* as a Romish abomination; most of all, the Puritan was precise in his infinite willingness to debate infinitely any smallest detail of doctrine or rite. True, the Anglican entered into the fray with a delight at least as great as that of his opponent. But the Anglican could always argue with some truth that the Puritan had first offered the objections, and that without them the church, triumphant and united, could have given spiritual peace to England.

Finally, one of the most persistent and damaging of the Anglican's indictments of the Puritan was that of hypocrisy. At the heart of the charge was certainly the fact that he so frequently protested his loyalty to the crown and his devotion to the established patterns of English society when he was moving to abolish the crown and change English society; he could even, finally, talk seriously of preserving the king from evil by overthrowing both his church and his rule. The contradiction is plain to the Anglican, but it is more complex than mere political and religious hypocrisy. In a large number of areas the Puritan seemed to say one thing and promptly do the opposite, and the cumulative result was that he appeared as a shifty and unreliable scoundrel who could be depended to head in the opposite direction from that in which he looked.

In the Puritan's view, the difficulty was not impossible to explain, and the charge could be disposed of, provided always that one was willing to accept certain premises. The Anglican order was destructive of Christian rule; and the Puritan could honestly pledge allegiance to his king, provided that he had a godly king. But if the king finally rejected God's order, then the Puritan was quite honest and not at all hypocritical in rebelling against the government while he talked of preserving right government. In the earlier years of Elizabeth, it was also true that the Puritan in his earnest desire for reform was only slightly conscious of the implications of his demands. Cartwright sincerely believed that what he wanted was not a revolution, even though it plainly was. Whitgift recognized that it was a revolution; Hooker recognized that it was; Bacon recognized that it was; and John Milton did say for the Puritan side that it was.

Attached to the charge of political and religious hypocrisy was an assortment of other evils. Many of the charges cannot be supported in fact; they increase in bitterness, and often are, particularly after the

---

which hath charge of the almsbox, and of nothing else . . . as if purposely the Holy Ghost had therein meant to foresignify, what the authors of Admonitions to the Parliament . . . should either do or suffer in behalf of this their cause . . . they discern those things in the word, which others reading yet discern them not."

execution of Charles I, merely rhetoric of indignation. There is the picture of John Milton, the evil Polyphemus, punished with blindness for his wicked life: ". . . monstrum horrendum, informe, ingens, cui lumen ademptum . . ." [8] The Puritans, again, were greedy for money despite their pretended unworldliness. But, it might have been pointed out, the Puritans were not an extremely ascetic group, they made fewer pretensions to unworldliness than to moderation, and they did not regard wealth as in itself evil. Miserliness and cheating again came to be attached to the Puritans. The chief reasons can be guessed at: they were often to be found among the rising merchants in the cities, and since the Puritan movement had grown in strength in almost all classes, the fact that Puritans appeared with increasing frequency among land-owners did not necessarily prove that they prospered by evil means. The Puritans were accused of ignorance underneath their pretensions to learning. The basis of the story is not hard to find: attached to the Puritan movement were large numbers of semiliterate and illiterate people, as well as numbers of learned. The Puritans at Cambridge in Cartwright's time were not notable for their lack of learning; but the hypocrisy of ignorance with a pretense to learning could more convincingly be displayed with the nonconformist preachers as examples. The Puritans made much of the sermon; common people with no learning "revealed" and taught with more regard to the spirit than the word; the result was that the "lecture," delivered from the top of an overturned tub, could be offered as a sample of the vaunted wisdom of the reformers.

It must be remembered that one of the well-springs of inspiration for disreputable stories of the Puritans was the habit of the right to fail to make differences in the left. The most careful commentators do not make the confusion, either before or after the fighting, but the lesser ones do. *Anabaptist,* a rather vague and terrifying word, describes all varieties of dissenters; *Brownist* has similar emotive force; and *Familist* serves as a substitute for "sexually promiscuous," although sexual promiscuity was no part of the teachings of the group. Limited to eccentricities of worship in the sects, the charge of extremism could have been supported very well. But there was no good reason for confining the propaganda within the limits of accuracy; indeed, propaganda serves better if it disregards to an extent the facts. It is true that English Puritanism was not, at least before the revolution was well under way, an agglomeration of eccentric sects in coalition. It was largely Presbyterian and Congregational, with a general uniformity and a hierarchy as strict as that of the

8. The attack appeared in the younger Peter du Moulin's *Regii Sanguinis Clamor Ad Coelum Adversus Parricidas Anglicanos* (The Hague, 1652). The Virgilian phrase is in the "Epistola Dedicatoria," 5 verso. In the same volume there is, 140–8, an extensive verse attack, "In Impurissimum Nebulonem Johannem Miltonum Parricidarum & Parricidii Advocatum." Milton's answer is in *Pro Populo Anglicano Defensio Secunda* (1654), *Works, 8* (1933). The specific passage on his blindness is 67–71.

Anglicans; its service and rites were different from those of the Anglicans, but certainly not less sober.

The Puritan picture of the Anglican is, by comparison, very simple: the Anglican is a corrupt and decadent conservative intent on preserving an evil order in the church and devoted to fleshly pleasures forbidden to a Christian. The picture changes little through the years, but the colors do become brighter and the shading heavier as the Puritan comments go from the court of Elizabeth to James, and finally to Charles I. The view of the Anglican as a conservative unwilling to exchange the old and false for the new and true originates simply in his resistance to change in polity and practice. The opinion that the Anglican clergy is corrupt is based on a generalization frequently, but not always, valid: it was too easy for the Puritan to regard all virtuous bishops as Puritans and all corrupt ones as Anglicans. At the same time, bishops did die rich; livings by the fours and fives went to single incumbents chosen for their connections rather than for their learning, piety, or virtue; and large areas of the country were for months or years without sermons and religious instruction.

The charges went back and forth; each side lavished threat, indignation, and the horror of outraged decency upon the opposition. The great mass of the writing was on the most serious level. Most of it was of the moment, and has perished, save as it has preserved for the historian or the antiquary, the average spirit of the moment. But the serious writers who have been examined, although they represent only a small part of the mass of opinion, do indicate a general pattern of enduring belief, both in the Anglican camp and in God's army across the river. These major writers have come to be in later times symbols of the programs which they supported: Hooker is as much the philosophic saint of Anglicanism as Milton is the poet of Puritanism. Another body of writers, numerically much smaller than the polemicists, the philosophers, and the epic poets, enlisted the artillery of wit, and complemented the earnest writers with satire. In the satirists there is often revealed a correspondence of opinion with the serious writers. If Hooker is concerned with the Puritans' facile neglect of the law of reason in the interpretation of Scripture, so is John Taylor the water poet when he writes a parody of a Puritan's exposition of a biblical text. If one of the most serious of Puritan charges against the Anglicans is that of ignorance and neglect, Martin Marprelate uses the same charge as almost the central point in his clownish attack. Thus the relationship from the serious to the satirical is generally close and, more important, in the satirists at their best, as in the serious writers at their best, there is the anticipation of the ultimate solutions which came out of the conflict.

2. Prose and Verse Satire

Martin Marprelate: Satire versus Polemic

ALTHOUGH, in the early years of the satiric exchange, the Anglicans did win for the most part on the counts of quantity and quality, there is one notable exception: in the Marprelate controversy the Puritans not only triumphed argumentatively, but they also succeeded in producing a group of tracts of historical interest in the development of English satire. In 1588 and 1589 seven pamphlets which epitomize the dispute over the government of the church came from an unknown writer or writers, Martin Marprelate.[1] The importance of the pamphlets as early satire has long been recognized: the complaints which they register against Anglican polity include the sorest points in dispute; and the responses which they called forth are fair examples of anti-Puritan attacks for the discrediting of the reformers.

There was, as so often happened, a background of polemical writing. In 1584 there had appeared an anonymous volume with the paralyzing title, *A Briefe and Plaine Declaration, Concerning the Desires of All Those Faithfull Ministers, That Have and Do Seeke for the Discipline and Reformation of the Church of Englande.* Its success was immediate, and it came to be known by the running head of the first edition, *A*

---

1. Two chief sources for the facts of the controversy are William Pierce's *An Historical Introduction to the Marprelate Tracts* (Constable, 1908) and Walter Kirkland Greene's "The Martin Marprelate Controversy" (unpublished dissertation, Harvard University, 1922). All references to the tracts themselves are from William Pierce, ed., *The Marprelate Tracts 1588, 1589* (Clarke, 1911). The author of the Marprelate tracts remains unknown despite all efforts to identify him. William Maskell, *A History of the Martin Marprelate Controversy* (1845), 213, argues for joint authorship, and believes that John Penry, who was executed for his connection with the pamphlets, was undoubtedly involved in the writing. Edward Arber in *An Introductory Sketch to the Martin Marprelate Controversy* (1879), 196, believes that John Penry and Job Throckmorton, who denied complicity at the trial of Penry, were the authors. William Pierce's *An Historical Introduction,* 308, holds that the balance of the questionable evidence points to Throckmorton or to a completely unknown person. J. Dover Wilson's "The Marprelate Controversy," *CHEL, 3,* 425–52, argues for Throckmorton as the chief author. G. Bonnard, *La Controverse de Martin Marprelate* (Jullien, Geneva, 1916), 214, is inclined to believe that Throckmorton wrote the pamphlets. Walter Kirkland Greene in "The Martin Marprelate Controversy," 855 ff., rejects all candidates for the authorship and constructs an unknown writer who was a Puritan, a lawyer, a bachelor, and a Londoner. Donald J. McGinn, "The Real Martin Marprelate," *PMLA, 58* (1943), 84–107, reviews the opinions, considers Job Throckmorton as a possible candidate, but decides in favor of Penry.

Learned Discourse of Ecclesiasticall Government.[2] An important part of the argument is, not unpredictably, the corruption of the Anglican clergy and the need for extensive reform.

John Bridges, dean of Salisbury, answered *A Learned Discourse* in a sermon at Paul's Cross, and later published his objections in *A Defence of the Government Established in the Church of Englande* (1587), a weighty vindication which damned the Roman Catholics, and said that ". . . the controversies betwixt us and our Brethren are matters, or rather (as they call them) but manners, and formes of the Churches regiment . . ."[3] One section of the Puritan party, however, did not feel that the questions at issue were simple matters or manners and forms, and Bridges' work furnished the immediate stimulus for the Marprelate series.

There are in all seven titles. Two, printed in 1588, have title pages which are almost identical in the first lines. The earlier of them begins: *Oh read over D. John Bridges for it is a worthy worke: Or an epitome.* This is known as *The Epistle.* The second is known as *The Epitome.* The others, printed in 1589, are *Certaine Minerall and Metaphisicall Schoolpoints; Hay Any Worke for Cooper; Theses Martinianae; The Just Censure and Reproofe;* and *The Protestation.* Several threads which run through all the pamphlets reveal a common pattern of subject and attitude. There is some discussion of doctrine, but the largest issues are the nature of church government and the powers and duties of the clergy; in general, the Martinist position is simply a reflection of extreme Presbyterian proposals for reform. Although the logical argument of serious polemic is replaced by casual banter and witty denunciation, at the same time it is possible to extract from the series a coherent program. The first pamphlet, *The Epistle,* charges that the bishops are "petty popes and petty antichrists" holding civil titles in an unscriptural ministry.[4] *The Epitome* presents the argument on behalf of a "scriptural" polity, unalterable, in accord with Christ's instructions and, of course, without bishops.[5] The question of the survival of the crown and its authority is disposed of, perhaps too easily, in *Certain Minerall and Metaphisicall Schoolpoints:* the bishops in their opposition to God's order weaken the crown; hence, opposition to the bishops will strengthen the crown.[6]

Hay Any Worke for Cooper and *Theses Martinianae* complete the

2. See the *CBEL, 1,* 690. The author is traditionally William Fulke of Cambridge.

3. *A Defence of the Government,* 43. Dudley Fenner answered Bridges in *A Defence of the Godlie Ministers, against the Slaunders of D. Bridges* (1587). Walter Travers' *A Defence of the Ecclesiasticall Discipline Ordained of God to be Used in His Church* (1588) attacks Bridges.

4. Pierce, *The Marprelate Tracts, The Epistle,* 23–5.

5. *Ibid., The Epitome,* 126–8, 143–4.

6. *Ibid., Certaine Minerall and Metaphysicall Schoolpoints,* 194–6. The original was a broadside.

anti-Episcopal argument. The first maintains that the civil authority can perfectly well abolish a merely human order in the church and replace that order with the divine offices of pastor, doctor, elder, and deacon. The change will abolish the bishops, ". . . the greatest enemies that now our state hath . . ." *Theses Martinianae* even contends that loyalty to the crown demands opposition to the episcopacy.[7]

The point of importance next to the government of the church is the corruption of the clergy, and the argument repeats the reformers' old list of abuses.[8] The last two pamphlets, *The Just Censure and Reproofe* and *The Protestation of Martin Marprelate* add nothing beyond some striking invective.

From 1588 until about 1595 there was an amount of writing produced with the intention of discrediting Martin Marprelate, and it is probable that a countercampaign was organized by Richard Bancroft, afterward archbishop of Canterbury.[9] The answers fail generally to refute Martin's charges of corruption in the church and, still more seriously, they fall far short of Martin in force, wit, and variety of expression. Unlike Martin, the defense seems to have little heart for the Lord's work, and with few exceptions they depend on abuse, obscenity, quips, and puns, many of which have become meaningless with the passing of time. The anti-Martinist press was for the most part anonymous, but a sufficient number of the answers were signed so that it is possible to attach some names to the group: the most notable are Greene, Lyly, Nashe, Richard Harvey, and Thomas Cooper. The general line of attack from these authors, not all notable for their devotion to order and morality, was to charge Martin with blasphemy and treason. Treason was not difficult to argue since the bishops were the chosen servants of the crown; and an attack on the bishops was, if one wished to press the point, an attack on her majesty. Nor was blasphemy too hard to demonstrate, since the order of bishops was of divine appointment.

If John Bridges' *Defence* (1587) had furnished fuel for Martin's first bonfire, Thomas Cooper's *An Admonition to the People of England* (1589) was just as usable. Both documents suffer from the handicaps

7. *Ibid., Hay Any Worke for Cooper,* 229–36, 239, 242; *Theses Martinianae,* 306–16. Marprelate in *Theses,* 315, quotes in part Tyndale's *The Practice of Prelates* (Antwerp? 1530): ". . . by the doctrine of the Church of England it is not possible that, naturally, there can be any good lord bishop . . . a bishopric is a superfluous honour, and a lewd libertie . . . servants of the Beast . . . ministers of antichrist . . ."

8. *Ibid., The Epistle,* 79–80; *The Epitome,* 149; *Minerall and Metaphisicall School-points,* 188–94; *Theses Martinianae,* 319. *The Epistle,* 28 ff., numbers over the sins of the clergy: ". . . All our Lord Bishops, I say, are petty popes, and petty usurping anti-christs . . . they will breed young popes and anti-christs."

9. According to the *DNB* he is ". . . said to have originated the idea of replying to the tracts in a like satirical vein . . ." Detailed accounts of the anti-Martinist writings occur in Pierce, *An Historical Introduction,* 219–54; and Greene, "The Martin Marprelate Controversy," 168–629.

of sobriety and weight. Cooper's arguments are sound enough; and even in respect to eloquence they are far above the general level of anti-Martinist writing. But soundness is not sufficient to answer the easy wit of *The Epistle* and *The Epitome*. Cooper's chief point is that no church can be perfect and that Martin is unfair in demanding perfection from the establishment; the specific attack on the reformers is slight.[1] Cooper's reward was Martin's answer *Hay Any Worke for Cooper*, the title being a London street cry. *Mar-Martine* (n.d.), seven pages of doggerel, and *Anti-Martinus* (1589),[2] a warning in Latin, attack the morals and the integrity of Martin Marprelate, and accuse him of sedition; the first finds him ". . . in hart a friend to the Papa." *A Whip for an Ape* (n.d.), later republished as *Rythmes against Martin Marre-Prelate*, is 26 stanzas of invective which compare Martin to Tarleton the clown. In *Martins Months Mind* (1589) there is at least a sustained satirical pattern, although it wears thin: the pamphlet purports to be the account of the death, the funeral, the will, and the epitaph of Martin Marprelate. He repents his many sins and confesses that he has been guilty of blasphemy and sedition. At the same time there is scarcely a word on the charges which Martin had made against the establishment. T. T.'s *A Mirrour for Martinists* (1589) speaks in pious tones of the shattered unity of the English church, but the pamphlet lacks wit and force, mutters against the Brownists, and ends with a plea for uniformity.

Pappe with an Hatchet (1589), commonly ascribed to Lyly, is full of obscure witticisms and reiterates the charges of contention, hypocrisy, and sedition. One good story is that of the Martinist who borrowed some money and then refused to repay it so that he would not be guilty of the sin of usury.[3] An anti-Martinist effort of Nashe is *A Countercuffe Given to Martin Junior* (1589): the pamphlet is short and carefully skirts the edge of theological controversy, in the intricacies of which the author was, perhaps, not perfectly equipped to mix. In *The Returne of the Renowned Cavaliero Pasquill of England* (1589), Nashe continues with a description of the Puritans in a passage which rises to some eloquence.[4] *The First Parte of Pasquils Apologie* (1590) follows

---

1. See *An Admonition to the People of England*, 122-3 for the most particular of Cooper's denunciations of the Puritans.
2. *Anti-Martinus* is signed "A.L."
3. *Pappe with an Hatchet* (ed. 1844).
4. *The Works of Thomas Nashe*, ed. Ronald B. McKerrow (5 vols. Bullen, 1904-10), *I* (1904), 51-68; 69-103. In *A Countercuffe* (*1, 62*) there is some eloquent denunciation: "By these meanes shall you see Religion haled with violence into her grave, the goodly frame of this Commonweale shall fall, and Banck-roupes and Atheists pocket uppe the peeces . . ." In *The Returne of the Renouwned Cavaliero* (*1, 73*) Nashe says: "They have an itch in their eares, that would be clawed with new points of doctrine never dreamed of; and an itch in their fingers, that woulde be nointed with the golden *Aenulatum* of the Church. I knowe they are commonly called Puritans, and not amisse, that

Pasquill, but centers its attention on John Penry, possible author of the Marprelate tracts. Nashe finds, a bit prematurely, that the church has ". . . cast out the foul spirit of the Faction . . ." and that the trouble is finally over. If necessary, the queen should drive the Puritans out of England.[5] Nashe is patently incapable of talking about church government as something aside from civil government. It may be perfectly true that he is writing from a point of view in which he has been instructed by the church; but it is also true that for him and for most of his sympathizers there is no difference between an attack on the archbishop of Canterbury and an attack on Queen Elizabeth. Certain Puritans, among them Martin Marprelate, had attempted a false dichotomy of king and bishop. In common with the other writers who attempt an answer to Martin, Nashe does not go beyond the cry of treason. It was perhaps too soon to say with James i: "No bishop, no king," but it was not too soon to explain that civil government and ecclesiastical government were the same and that one could not be altered by itself. *An Almond for a Parrat* (1590?), doubtfully ascribed to Nashe, is much concerned with Penry; unfortunately, the account is a plain mixture of fact and wishful thinking, and the two cannot be sorted. Penry, according to the author, arrived at Cambridge a papist, and then was successively a Brownist and an Anabaptist; finally he wrote the Marprelate tracts. The story is too convenient to be credible. All in all, the pamphlet is rambling, confused, and pointless. There is much name calling; one passage at least is interesting for its emphasis on the identity of ecclesiastical and civil rule.[6] But the passage is exceptional, for Nashe ordinarily does not grapple, in serious or even in satiric terms, with Martin's central charges, and fluent invective generally does duty for wit and a knowledge of the issues.

---

title is one of the marks they beare about them. They have a marke in the heade, they are selfe conceited, They take themselves to be pure, when they are filthy in Gods sight; They have a mark in the eye, their lookes are haughtie; They have a marke in the mouth, a verie blacke tooth, they are A generation that cursse their father."

5. *Ibid., 1*, 109–36. Nashe calls on the queen to defend the bishops (*1*, 133): "This is the conclusion of Penries prayer in his Epistle to the *Treatise,* that the Bishoppes may be thrust as one man out of the Church. . . . Nowe is the broode of hell broken loose. . . . The spirite of the Lord shall come upon her Majestie, and kindle her sacred hart with a newe courage to strike home, that there may not one couple of the Faction be left together in the Realme of Englande . . ."

6. *Ibid., 3* (1905), 339–76. McKerrow doubts that Nashe is the author. The best account of Penry is William Pierce's *John Penry* (Hodder, 1923). In *An Almond for a Parrat* one passage which emphasizes the identity of ecclesiastical and civil rule is the following (Nashe, ed. McKerrow, *3*, 353): "Hast not thou in thy firste booke . . . excluded her Highnesse from all Ecclesiasticall governement, saying shee hath neither skill nor commission, as shee is a Magistrate, to substitute anie member or minister in the Church? And in an other place, that there is neither use nor place in the Church for members, ministers, or officers of the magistrates making? If this will not come in compasse of treason, then farewell the title of Supremacie, and welcome againe unto Poperie."

Several items are of interest for the fact that they occupy a position more or less between Martin and his attackers, and indicate the existence of a center group opposed to extremists both in the Puritan and the Anglican camps. A sermon of Richard Harvey, a pamphlet of Leonard Wright, and two anonymous tracts either deplore the dispute and blame both sides for immoderation, or rebuke Martin Marprelate in fairly moderate terms. The Harvey sermon, *A Theologicall Discourse of the Lamb of God* (1590), condemns the Martinists for having confused simple people and for having failed in loyalty to church and state. Leonard Wright's *A Friendly Admonition to Martine Marprelate and His Mates* (1590), a six-page tract, tells Martin that he has done wrong to pit the parliament against the sovereign; the Church of England is Christian and scriptural. The anonymous *Plaine Percevall the Peace-Maker of England* (n.d.) pretends to attempt a reconciliation between Martin and the opposition. All Englishmen should be reconciled since they belong to the same church of Christ. *Marre Mar-Martin* (n.d.) is as clumsy as its title. Its chief point is that the country is in a religious turmoil over the argument between Marprelate and the church. All these writers, mild in their strictures, or even at the midpoint of disgust with both parties, fail as the Anglicans fail. In the neutral pamphlets there is a lack of spirit, wit, and knowledge of the issues necessary to match the learned impudence of Martin Marprelate.[7]

In consideration of the religious satire which was to follow in the years after 1588, the Marprelate tracts occupy an exceptional position. The pamphlets center on two of the most serious points at issue, polity and the reform of abuses; at the same time, the arguments are presented by means of a bantering, humorous style which bridges the gap between serious polemic and clowning. What Martin Marprelate did had been done before in satiric attacks on the Roman Catholic church, and it is not possible to talk with accuracy of the Marprelate tracts as having given birth to English satire. But it is true that the Marprelate tracts brought to the Puritan controversy a breath of life and lightness which had been lacking, and demonstrated that all discussion of God and His order on earth need not necessarily be dull.

7. There should be mention of a number of items which speak passingly of the Marprelate controversy, or which are in some way connected with it. *M. Some Laid Open in His Coulers* (1589), possibly by Penry or Throckmorton, attacks the moderate Robert Some for his plural livings, and urges freedom of religious discussion. Its attitudes are very close to those of the Marprelate pamphlets. Some denounced pluralities, but attacked the extremists in *A Godly Treatise* (1588). Passing references to the Martinists are fairly common in the polemic writings of the 1590's. In 1593 Richard Bancroft made two sorry attacks on the Martinists. They are in *Daungerous Positions and Proceedings* and *A Survey of the Pretended Holy Discipline*. Job Throckmorton in *The Defence of Job Throkmorton* (1594) denies that he is Martin Marprelate. However, Matthew Sutcliffe accuses Throckmorton of being chiefly responsible for the tracts in *An Answere unto a Certaine Calumnious Letter* (1595).

In satiric technique, Martin shows an imaginativeness and an ability to comprehend serious issues in comic terms; his opponents here are always his inferiors. Perhaps the greatest single quality of the Marprelate pamphlets is this mixture of the serious and the comic to produce the thoughtful laugh, one of the commonest elements of satire. On the other hand, the pages of the pamphlets are full of boisterous chatter; and Martin sounds frequently like a clown on the stage.[8] But mixed with his talk there are almost always the themes of corruption and error; these charges return again and again until, at the end of the series, the reader has a far clearer picture of the essentials of Puritan reform than he can get from most of the solemn volumes of logically marshaled argument. The mixture of serious and comic, however, extends to more than the main points in the argument. Throughout the tracts there are numberless accounts of the idiosyncrasies of church personages. Bridges, for instance, is attacked, as are Aylmer, bishop of London, and Cooper, bishop of Winchester; and even the rhetorical eccentricities of one churchman are specifically burlesqued.[9] These attacks are more than personal spite; the clerics' failings are of a sort which reflect directly on their competence to guide the people, or bring into question their honesty in handling church affairs. If the bishop of Gloucester's preaching sounds silly when Martin mocks it with an imitation of the bishop's unhappy trick of repeating single words *ad nauseam,* the account is more than spiteful. It says, in effect: "Good preaching is a part of good worship. Get preachers who are cultivated men, who know the Bible, and who can speak English." [1]

The extremely mixed style of the pamphlets gives informality, pertness, and a popular tone which sober dialectic could not have; there are the rich invective, the slang, the meaningless sounds like street cries of the time, the puns, each a device supporting in its way the serious observations on the evils of the church. One trick, irony, is used with particular effect. In *Certaine Minerall and Metaphysicall Schoolpoints* Martin demolishes both the Anglican position and the dullness of theological controversy by means of a list of impossible proposals framed in the wordy solemnities of the theologians.[2] The list from the hand of an earlier Puritan writer would have been the central tenets of Presby-

---

8. See George P. Krapp's *The Rise of English Literary Prose* (New York, Oxford University Press, 1915), 118–30. Krapp says, 118: "Martin indeed was a dramatically conceived character, unified and consistent, like the Piers Plowman and Jack Upland of earlier periods of English religious controversy, and he sums up the spirit and tone of one large section of the Puritan party of the last quarter of the sixteenth century."

9. Pierce, *The Marprelate Tracts,* 90 ff.

1. *Ibid.,* 100: ". . . you shame yourselves when you use any continued speech; because your style is so rude and barbarous."

2. *Ibid.,* 173–96. Number seven, for instance, 187: "That the public fasts and the prayers of the Puritans were the cause of the invasion of the Spaniards, and of all other troubles and turmoils within the land . . ."

terianism or the errors of the opposition, but Martin makes the list a parody of what his opponents believe. Refutation would be otiose; the ironic perversities admit the reader at once to the secret that the Anglicans are fools, and the list persuades more than a dozen solemn analyses.

By comparison, the anti-Martinists are thin; when they are not serious, they coin words, make obscene puns, and are frequently coarse without being funny; personal invective is stretched to destroy the heretic and traitor who threatens church and state. And so they fail where Martin succeeds. Usually, they do not manage to connect the libels with any particular weakness in the reformer's position. They make fun of Martin, but they do not make fun of what he stands for.[3] They curse Martin for his impudence, but they do not rise to his challenge and, with a humorous account of the failings of the Puritans, prove that Anglicanism is, for all its corruptions, much the best form of worship for England. Again, they are unable to point up their personal attacks on Martin so that they will be generalized satire of the religious reformer, or the zealot, or even the Puritan hypocrite of a growing myth. It must, certainly, be admitted that the anti-Martinists could not see the fox they were chasing, but at the same time they knew the nature of the beast, and they could have hunted better than they did. Their ranting invective is dull for its repetition; there is no parody of the Puritan proposals; Martin to the end remains undemolished.

Serious polemicists like Cooper and Bridges could not see what had happened: the Martin Marprelate tracts had most seriously complicated the discussion of the religious issues. Theological dialectic in a 400-page book, with arguments ordered and supporting references to Holy Writ in the margins, would no longer be necessarily the surest way of converting the English people to an ecclesiastical position. In the future the force of logic would be only one persuasion beside the force of satire: the ponderosities of the anti-Martinists had failed to answer Martin the comic actor, the clown, and the monologist. In short, Martin Marprelate was the witty commentator on the religious scene. His pose would be used increasingly; and satire would take its place by controversy in the dispute over religion.[4] However, with the greatest strength of the tracts in the manner and style, the greatest weakness is in the argument. The series is concerned with the reform of abuses in the church and the government of the church. The first is the more promising as a point for

3. Krapp, *The Rise of English Literary Prose*, 126–7: "The tract (*Pappe with an Hatchet*) is much more noisy and scurrilous than Martin, lacking of course Martin's underlying seriousness of purpose. . . ."

4. *Ibid.*, 129–30: "The model employed by the inventor of the character of Martin may have been, as was frequently charged against him, some popular actor of the day, like Tarleton or Kemp. Martin always monologizes. He appears alone upon the stage, figuratively speaking, and pours forth his torrent of invective in the ranting, huff-snuff style which had been made familiar to the public not only by comic actors but by many a dithyrambic popular preacher. . . ."

satire of enduring interest; but the second occupies enough space so that, in general, the pamphlets are of interest chiefly to the historian of the church, or the historian of literary forms. In the centering of the argument to a large part on church government, Martin Marprelate only shows his closeness to the serious polemicists of his age: he echoes one of the chief points of the two Admonitions, and of Cartwright in his controversy with Whitgift.

The Common Opinion, Serious and Satiric

OF THE various kinds of writing against the Puritans, the prose pamphlets and the nondramatic verse are the most obvious connecting links between theological controversy and literary satire. On the level of casual prose, and verse which is hortatory or occasional, the difference between the merely indignant and the satirical is slight: Martin Marprelate can be for a moment as sober as the most earnest Puritan preacher, or John Milton can be bitterly satiric in a discussion of church government. A blend of the polemical and the satiric occurs in a number of prose pamphlets and an amount of verse printed from about 1580 through 1630; after 1630 the satiric note is common. Writers of indifferent skill treat the Puritans in the simplest terms, and the result is no more than gross libel. In the same years other literary forms, more complex, more exacting, come into use, and from the more complex forms come developed satire.

However, on the simplest level, the tone and pattern of the whole attack is set: in many respects, what the crude ballads say is echoed, in a more elaborate and more elegant, but not a different, manner by the epigrammatists, the character writers, and the dramatists; and similarly, the prose pamphlet, setting out from the point of polemic, reaches hot denunciation, then becomes dominantly satirical, and finally arrives at the parody of the Puritan tract. The bawds and lechers of the anti-puritan ballads are first cousins to the smooth, hypocritical sectaries of the Jacobean and Caroline drama, while the rantings in prose against the Anabaptists in Elizabeth's reign take on wit and form both in the drama and in the burlesques of Puritan pulpit oratory after 1600.

The connection between the dispute and the satire appears in many areas; it appears, for instance, in the attention, at first official and ecclesiastical, and later literary, paid to the Family of Love. The Family, a small, and by sixteenth-century standards, an eccentric, religious group, had damnation from the government at an early point, and for years was the target of assorted attacks. Elizabeth in 1580 described the books of the Family as "lewd, heretical," and officially, at least, abolished it. The attack from the pamphleteers had begun some years before; popular opinion held that the group clandestinely practiced sexual rites of an outrageous sort. There is comparative mildness in the account of John Rogers' *The Displaying of an Horrible Secte of Grosse and Wicked Heretiques* (1578), for the writer admits that the Family is not guilty of much that it is charged with, and in his detailed account of doctrine the *maximae culpae* are the holding of communal property, the granting of divorce, and the belief that each member is as perfect as Christ. The last would be the most offensive, since it denied the utter depravity of man. Rogers is, by comparison with his contemporaries, extremely fair. He does not lose his temper over the heresies of the sect, and he condemns it for reasons which were to his time valid.[1] A more typical attack comes from the Anglican pulpit; the speaker is Edwin Sandys, an archbishop with strongly Puritan sympathies. He complains of the Familists' secrecy, their lies and hypocrisy, and their separation from the body of the Christian church. Hooker's reasoned examination in the preface of *Of Ecclesiastical Polity* is in contrast to Sandys.[2] The common opinion is that Henry Nicholas (usually referred to as *H.N.*) introduced the group to England; his writings were published about 1575 in English. The denunciation of the sect continued on a serious level after the turn of the century in *A Supplication of the Family of Love . . . Examined* (Cambridge, 1606); the result of an appeal from the Family for toleration, the tract condemns the sect on all the old charges of sedition, schism, and immorality. But in the meantime the attack spread to satire: one pamphlet, indignant and humorous, reads on the title page: "Love one another: A Tub Lecture, Preached at Watford in Hartfordshire at a Conventicle on the 25th of December last, being Christmas day, by John Alexander, a Joyner. His text was taken out of the Epistle of Saint John, and himselfe was taken by Captain Bird, Lieutenant Rock, and other officers, from whom he received such usage as his doctrine did deserve . . ." About 1602 Thomas Middleton's *The Family of Love* presented a satirical picture of the Family in all their hypocrisy and clandestine immorality. In point of fact, the

---

1. *By the Queen. A Proclamation against the Sectaries of the Family of Love* (1580). The proclamation provides punishment for members; *The Displaying of an Horrible Sect,* J4 verso ff.

2. See the preface to *Of Ecclesiastical Polity, Works,* ed. Keble, *1,* 148 ff. In *The Sermons of Edwin Sandys,* ed. John Ayre (Cambridge, England, 1842), 130, 191, there are the following passages:

> Which practice the Family of Love hath lately drawn to a precept, and hath newly broached it as saleable doctrine, that men need not openly be of any religion whereby they may endanger themselves; that it is good christendom to lie, swear, and forswear, to say and unsay to any . . .

> It is the property of froward sectaries, whose inventions cannot abide the light, to make obscure conventicles, when the doctrine of truth is set at liberty. The Donatists, the Arians, the Anabaptists, the Family of Love, with all others of the like sort, fostered up their errors in secret and dark corners. But such as be of the flock of the great shepherd Christ ought to assemble themselves in one sheepfold.

Family of Love, from the evidence available, appears to have been a mild and harmless group; indeed, by comparison with the Presbyterians, they were innocent of political overtones.[3]

Before 1600 the denunciations of the Puritans in prose and verse become common. Greene, Nashe, Marston, and Dekker all speak of the immorality, the hypocrisy, and the preciseness of the dissenters, and usually they make no attempt to distinguish between the reforming party of the moderate right and the more eccentric groups of the extreme left. Robert Greene shows plainly a mixture of dislike and admiration when he is in his mood of confession and revulsion against his misdeeds. On the one hand, a vicar in *A Quip for an Upstart Courtier* (1592), when asked if he is a Puritan, indignantly denies that he is, and complains that the reformers are immoderate and violent and that they have "preached good workes out of our Parish . . ." The specfiic objection is centered on a doctrinal point common to Anglican and Puritan alike: in theory, at least, good works could save an Anglican no more than a Puritan. On the other hand, in *The Repentance of R. Greene* (1592), the writer deplores the wickedness of his life and plainly states that evil companions have seduced him from a better morality, taught by the Puritan preachers.[4] Thomas Nashe, more extreme than Greene, has nothing good to say of the Puritans. Cheating deceit and hypocrisy are their marks, and their pretenses to reform in the church are only tricks to overthrow order and abolish good works. One venomous passage looks back to the indignant objections of the polemicists and at the same time anticipates the hypocrisy of the conventional stage Puritan of later

3. *A Supplication of the Family of Love,* 18, 32 ff. A good account of the beliefs of the sect appears in *Mirabilia Opera Dei which Happened to H.N. Published by Tobias a Fellow Elder* (n.d.) The actual writings of Henry Nicholas were published in English about 1575. Rufus M. Jones describes the literature, beliefs, and practices of the Family in *Studies in Mystical Religion* (MacMillan, 1909), 428–48. He concludes that they were guilty of no sexual irregularities in their worship, that their most unorthodox belief was in the goodness of man as contrasted with the Calvinist doctrine of utter depravity, and that they were generally misrepresented. Jones says of Nicholas' teachings, 434: "He maintains that the only righteousness that amounts to anything is one which appears in the person himself . . . this righteousness, this new life, comes from a spiritual incorporation of the person into God's life, so that the person, once a mere man, becomes 'godded,' or made conformable to Christ . . ." He concludes of the Familists, 447: "They had, for more than a hundred years, maintained in England a steady testimony to the spiritual nature of religion, to the fact of a Divine Light and Life in the soul . . . They had insisted on spiritualizing this life rather than on dogmatizing about the next life, and they had been practising, as far as they could, in the society in which they lived, the Sermon on the Mount."

4. *The Life and Complete Works of Robert Greene,* ed. Alexander B. Grosart (15 vols. 1881–86): *11* (1881–83), 280–1; *12* (1881–83), 176: ". . . I sorrowed for my wickednesse of life . . . the Preachers wordes had taken a deepe impression on my conscience . . . they fell upon me in jeasting manner, calling me Puritane and Precizian, and wished I might have a Pulpit, with such other scoffing tearmes, that by their foolish persuasion the good and wholesome lesson I had learned went quite out of my remembrance . . ."

years: "It is not the writhing of the face, the heaving uppe of the eyes
to heaven, that shall keepe these men, from having their portion in hell.
Might they be saved by their booke, they have the Bible alwaies in their
bosome, and so had the Pharisies the Lawe embroidered in their gar-
ments." [5] They are immoderate in their denunciations of men's sins, and
they have confused religion. But two of their worst sins are their dull
sermons with their opposition to learning and literature. If they have
their way, poetry will disappear and wit will be a crime.[6] The charge of
opposition by the Puritans to learning is not easily supported; it can,
however, be said that they opposed various aspects of education in the
universities, controlled by the church, and that the Puritans complained
of lacks in the education of the clergy. In addition, the Puritans undoubtedly opposed the theater, as the propaganda on both sides was beginning to demonstrate as early as the 1570's. Nashe is unlike Greene
in the total rejection of the Puritan program and the denial of any
possibility of good from the reforming program. Puritanism is a pious
fraud being imposed on the English people.

John Marston likewise damns the Puritans: they are mealy-mouthed
frauds; but his verse satire has life, wit, point, and it does not labor the
obvious. The precisian

> . . . cries "Good brother," "Kind sister," makes a duck
> After the antique grace, can always pluck
> A sacred book out of his civil hose,
> And at th' o'p'ning and at our stomach's close,
> Says with a turn'd-up eye a solemn grace
> Of half an hour; then with silken face
> Smiles on the holy crew, and then doth cry,
> "O manners. O times of impurity!" [7]

If his descriptions of the "lewd precisians" and their irreverence toward
Christian rites are not just, they are lively. Thomas Dekker agrees with
Marston, but Dekker centers his attack on the deceit and dishonesty of
the Puritans: they lie and cheat their way about England. Two of
Dekker's stage players talk to each other and reveal that the stock

5. *The Works of Thomas Nashe,* ed. McKerrow, *1* (1904), *Pierce Penilesse* (1592),
220: ". . . under villanie I comprehend murder, treason, theft . . . under hypocrisie, all
Machiavilisme, puritanisme, and outward gloasing with a mans enemie . . ."; *2,
Christs Teares* (1593), 118; *1, The Anatomie of Absurditie* (1589), 22.

6. *Ibid., 1, The Anatomie of Absurditie, 27*: The precisians ". . . overshoote themselves . . . in senceless stoicall austeritie, accounting Poetrie impietie, and witte follie."
3 (1905), *To the Gentlemen Students* (n.d.), 321–3, charges that the "reformatorie
Churchmen" would crush literature. *1, The Anatomie of Absurditie,* 20, says that the
Puritans talk ". . . of whoredome, as though they had beene Eunuches from their
cradle . . ."

7. *The Works of John Marston,* ed. A. H. Bullen (3 vols. 1887), *3,* "Satire II," 271;
"The Scourge of Villainy" (1598), 315.

Puritan of the drama is a scoundrel.[8] A fairly extended description of the Puritan in Thomas Heywood's *Troia Britanica* (1609) sums up the opinions of Greene, Nashe, Marston, and Dekker. The Puritan is precise, hypocritical, sour, ignorant, and overbearing. He hates all learning, all beauty in the church service, and all pastimes which may give pleasure, such as "Hunting, Hawking, Cockes, and plaies." [9]

The intensely religious manner, the devout talk, and the pious behavior of the Puritan must certainly have been an irritation; the charge of hypocrisy could arise in the course of a diligent search for faults, since the Puritan could scarcely be in all respects perfect, and the demands of satire could enlarge minor lapses to crimes. At any rate, the precisian as a hypocrite comes to be almost central to the satire. The supposed hairsplitting and dishonest carping gave rise to a conventional picture, as in George Wither's *Abuses Stript and Whipt* (1613); in a series of anonymous satires, *The Times' Whistle* (c. 1614), by R. C.; and in *Exchange Ware at the Second Hand* (2d ed. 1615). The attack in *The Times' Whistle* is in undistinguished couplets and covers the usual charges of heresy and sedition; there is the old charge that the Anglican church stands between the two immoralities of Rome and Puritanism. The author tells the story of Mistress Simula, the Puritan wife ". . . Ready to faint if she an oth but hear . . ." but not so pure but that she was

> . . . tane in bed
> With a young, tender, smoothfacd Ganimed,
> Her husbands prentice. Out, lascivious whore! [1]

The poet asks rhetorically if her adultery is the only product of the Puritan sermons. Finally, in the course of a vision, the poet speaks with True Religion. She tells how Elizabeth and James preserved her; then

---

8. *The Non-Dramatic Works of Thomas Dekker,* ed. Alexander B. Grosart (4 vols. 1884–86), 2 (1885), *The Seven Deadly Sinnes of London* (1606), 21: "Sometimes hee's a Puritane, he sweares by nothing but Indeede . . . wrapping his crafty Serpents body in the cloake of religion, he does those acts that would become none but a Divell." 2, *Jests to Make You Merie* (1607), 282: ". . . I have so naturally playd the Puritane, that many took me to be one . . . True . . . thou playdst the Puritane so naturally, that thou couldst never play the honest man afterwards . . ." 3 (1885), *The Belman of London* (1608), 95: "A Rogue is knowne to all men by his name, but not to all men by his conditions; no puritane can dissemble more than he . . ."

9. *Troia Britanica,* 89–90. Heywood is describing the "Self-opinion'd Puritan." He says:

> In our reformed Church too, a new man
> Is in few yeares crept up, in strange disguise
> And cald the Selfe-opinion'd Puritan,
> A fellow that can beare himselfe precise . . .

1. *The Times' Whistle,* ed. J. M. Cowper (1871), 26. *Exchange Ware at the Second Hand* (2d ed. 1615), C verso: ". . . You were a horrible Puritane the other day, and very precise, Ruffe." See Wither's *Abuses Stript and Whipt* (1613), R8 ff. on "the counterfeit Elect." Wither later fought for parliament.

she denounces the Puritans and warns that unless they are suppressed, Religion will be destroyed.[2] *The Times' Whistle* is poor stuff, crudely constructed, declamatory and humorless, but it sums up the stock sins and sets a formula for attack which is altered and improved upon, but not discarded, by more nimble-witted writers.

In the last years before the fighting, the charge of sexual immorality was developed and repeated by the pamphleteers and versifiers infinitely. That it was one of the least plausible is of no consequence; the writer could not miss a fine opportunity for humor, for a sensational story, and for the burlesque of Puritan piety and the extremes of seriousness, so frequently apparent in the movement; the stern devotion to a lofty moral ideal did lay the reformers open to attack. The mere rumor of defection could furnish occasion for the pricking of the bubble of perfection.

The stories, sometimes serious, but more often a mixture of the serious and the comic, follow the standard patterns of portraying virtue, seduced and betrayed by hypocrisy, and then redeemed by sturdy Anglican honesty. There is, for instance, the narrative of Mistress Sarah Miller of Banbury who went all unaware to a Brownist meeting. The preacher was "a most Reverend Barber" who picked his nose and prayed in the inflated manner of the sectary: a good part of his prayer was against learning in general and the study of Latin in particular. After the service the preacher seduced Mistress Miller. She became pregnant; her only salvation was that she confessed her sin and returned to the bosom of the Anglican church.[3] The experience of Susanna Snow was less disastrous, but as harrowing. Mistress Snow was led into the Family of Love. There she heard a sermon in which the preacher (seemingly not opposed to all learning), talked of Ovid and Priapus instead of Holy Writ. After the sermon a member of the family seduced her: ". . . she played a maid's part indeed; she said Nay, and yet took it." By a miracle she was saved to return to decent society to tell her story.[4]

The two accounts have in common the picture of Puritan corruption;

2. The poem is in Cooper's edition of *The Times' Whistle* and is entitled "Somnium." True Religion says, 141:

> There is a sort of purest seeming men,
> That aide this monster in her wrongfull cause,
> Those the world nameth—Puritanes I meane—
> Sent to supplant me from the very jawes
> Of hell, I think; by whose apparent shew
> Of sanctity doe greatest evils grow.

3. *The Brownist Haeresies Confuted Their Knavery Anatomised in a True History of One Mistres Sarah Miller of Banbury* (1641). The preacher's prayer reads in part: ". . . May we set our selves with might & main against those Scholars, as Bishops, Deanes, yea and Deacons which strive to construe the Scriptures according to the Translation of the Hebrew, Greek, and Latin, which last Language stinks like a piece of beefe a twelve moneth old, yet never salted."

4. *A Description of the Sect Called the Family of Love* (1641).

but at the same time it might be noted that the ignorant seducer of the first story, the reverend barber, becomes in the second a preacher who uses learning for evil. It is true that in the satiric attacks, the Puritan is frequently the uneducated tradesman, and there is the implication that a good deal of the religious trouble is the result of improper ambitions of the lower classes; but the Puritan can also be the perverse scholar. It is quite useless to seek, in the attacks, for a Puritan typical as to class or occupation: he is, rather, what the writer wants him to be. Although the Puritan of satire comes more commonly from the lower classes than from the upper, he is by no means confined to one social or economic group.

Other sects in addition to the Familists were denounced for sexual irregularities; the term Brownist was commonly used without any intention of singling out those of a particular belief, and the charges of fornication and adultery were pitched only in the general direction of all dissenters. One account with a striking title is *A Nest of Serpents Discovered* (1641); the slight narrative is on the reported habits of the sect of Adamites: they deny the divinity of Christ; they will not marry; they are lascivious nudists who leave their clothes at the door of the meetinghouse. They have arrived from Amsterdam with their beliefs, and they must be suppressed. Other reports of the same year tell of a congregation in Wales and their approval of bastardy and adultery. The members have no ceremonies for marriage or for burial, and their sexual promiscuity is part of their religious doctrine. Again, a total of twenty-nine sects have been discovered in London, ". . . Puritans, Papists, Brownists, Calvinists . . ." Sexual irregularities are common among them. But the worst of all is, as usual, the Family of Love.[5]

The mixed tone of the pamphlets, satiric to a degree, but with, generally, an undertone of serious indignation, becomes obscene humor in the popular poetry and ballads. Freed from the necessity of considering doctrine or biblical authority, the ballad writer can concentrate his attention on his story and, simply by dubbing his sinners Brownists, turn the bawdy incident into a satirical comment on Puritan practices. "Off a Puritane" follows the pattern set by a number of the prose pamphlets, but in this example of popular poetry there is no indignation, no protest. The characters have scriptural names; they are from Amsterdam; they have the false piety of the sects; and in the midst of their sins they talk of God's word.[6] The incident is profane to the point of incredibility, but

5. *A Nest of Serpents Discovered* (1641); Edward Harris, *A True Relation of a Company of Brownists* (1641); *A Discovery of 29 Sects Here in London* (1641).

6. *National Ballad and Song*, ed. John S. Farmer (5 vols. 1897), *1*, 73, "Off a Puritane":

> It was a puritanicall ladd
> that was called Mathias
> and he wold goe to Amsterdam

the situation is at least cleverly sustained with details which do credit to
the invention of the writer. The same story is told over many times by the
versifiers in the early 40's. Sometimes there are lascivious bouts during
the Puritan service; sometimes there is a pious conjugation in a haymow; sometimes the conventiclers pair off after the sermon.[7] The
anonymous poems are vigorous, but scarcely subtle:

> What's he that met a holy Sister
> And in an Hay-cock gently kist her,
> Oh! then his zeal abounded,
> Close underneath a shady willow,
> Her Bible serv'd her for her pillow,
> And there they got a Roundhead.[8]

> to speake with Ananias.
> he had not gone past halfe a mile,
> but he mett his holy sister;
> hee laid his bible under her breeche,
> and merilie hee kist her.

> "Alas! what wold they wicked say?"
> quoth shee, "if they had seene itt!
> my Buttocckes they lie to lowe: I wisht
> appocrypha were in itt!"

The lady has some worries in the course of the performance:

> If wee professors shold bee knowne
> to the English congregation
> either att Leyden or Amsterdam,
> itt wold disgrace our nation . . .

7. *Rump: or an Exact Collection* (1662), "A Curtain Lecture," 28:

> At the last when they must part,
> Male and Female go together
> Join'd in hand, and join'd in heart
> And join'd a little for their pleasure.

> First for a Kisse they will agree,
> And what comes next you may conjecture
> So that the wicked do not see
> And so break up the Roundheads Lecture.

This anthology, together with *A Collection of Loyal Songs Written against the Rump
Parliament* (2 vols. 1731); *Political Ballads of the Seventeenth and Eighteenth Centuries*, ed. W. Walker Wilkins (2 vols. 1860); and *Cavalier and Puritan. Ballads and
Broadsides Illustrating the Period of the Great Rebellion 1640–1660*, ed. Hyder E. Rollins
(New York University Press, New York, 1923), adequately cover the field of political
verse directed against the Puritans. It is of generally poor quality. Most of it was
printed after 1642. The largest single mass of ephemeral writing on the Puritans from
1640 on is in the Thomason Collection of the British Museum. The printed catalogue
usually indicates the general nature of each item. See *Catalogue of the Pamphlets, Books,
Newspapers and Manuscripts Relating to the Civil War, the Commonwealth, and Restoration, Collected by George Thomason, 1640–1661* (The British Museum, 2 vols. 1908).
  8. *Rump*, "The Character of a Roundhead," 42.

Richard Corbett, speaking perhaps as a good Anglican in behalf of his church, treats the same situation with more wit, but in a manner which does not differ materially from that of the unknown poetasters. Corbett's Puritans walk in the fields and discuss the stories

> Of David, and Uriahs lovely wife,
> Of Thamar, and her lustfull brothers strife;
> Then, underneath the hedge that woos them next,
> They may sitt downe, and there act out the text.[9]

John Taylor, one of the most prolific of the anti-Puritan writers, repeats the charge of pious fornication when he describes the act by the use of ridiculously inflated imagery of the sort that the Puritans sometimes employed in their accounts of their religious experiences: the figures of spirit and fire, common in the Puritan confessionals, are turned to unholy use.[1]

It is not possible to argue that the Puritans were depraved libertines intent on destroying Christian morality in England; and in default of statistics on bastardy among dissenters, it is possible to point out only that they represented a fairly complete cross section of English life and, very probably, conducted themselves with average morality. But rumor starts easily concerning a strange religious group by the common suspicion directed against those who do not conform in all respects. And the opportunities for the satirists were too good to be neglected: the reports and rumors of sexual orgies were rich material for the pamphleteer writing in indignation, while a lascivious text plucked from the Bible and acted out in a haymow was even more effective.

In the late 30's and early 40's, with the increasing tension between the parliament and the king and with the strengthening of Puritan forces, much of the writing, both in prose and verse, is increasingly political. It is often more bitter than in the earlier years, and it does center to a greater extent on the question of the intentions of the Puritans toward the king and his government. John Taylor had his usual opinions when he wrote of the disturbances of the state: in many of his pamphlets he

9. *The Poems of Richard Corbet* (ed. 1807), "An Exhortation to Mr. John Hammon," 105. According to the *DNB*, Corbett's poems were first collected in 1647; he died in 1635.

1. John Taylor, *An Apology for Private Preaching* (1642?), A4:

> He . . . may with much ease administer Reformation on a Bed-side, where inspired with the Spirit of Unity, we constantly conclude, and join in a copulative love without the unnecessary assistance of any light, but the flame of our own Zeal . . . the pretious Coals of Devotion; and inflamed by the provoking Administry of the last Doctrine.

John Taylor's prose and poetry have been reprinted in the following: *Works, Comprised in the Folio Edition of 1630.* The Spenser Society (1868–69) and *Works of John Taylor the Water Poet Not Included in the Folio Volume of 1630.* The Spenser Society (5 vols. 1870–78).

specifically discusses the Puritans and the sovereign. His *Englands Comfort, and Londons Joy* (1641) predicts that the monarch will be able

> To cure all wrenches, fractures, spraines and rents,
> Where Church, and Common Wealth is dislocated . . .

The lines were written on the occasion of Charles' return from Scotland in November 1641. If they are inadequate as predictions of future events, they do echo the king-worship of the royalists and curse the roundheads as hypocritical traitors who "shape a strange Religion." [2] A particular strength of Taylor as a propagandist is his ability to find all virtues in the Anglican and all vices in the Puritan. One attack places the sins of rebellion on the lower classes led by their preachers and the Puritan commons. There is bitterness enough, but little effort to create a satirical tone. In *The Hellish Parliament* (1641), Taylor sustains a single image successfully throughout: a meeting of sectaries and Roman Catholics has been called by the devil. The Roman Catholics are led inevitably by Guy Fawkes; the sectaries, by an inspired cobbler-preacher, Sam How. The common target of a lower-class troublemaker is apparent in the cobbler. The convention makes a number of resolutions, the most important of which are for a firm union of Brownists and Roman Catholics, the invasion of England by foreign forces, and the destruction of all learning. That the sects, the Puritans, and the papists were in league was a common charge from the Anglicans just as, through the years, the cry of popery had been hurled at Anglicans by dissenters. A rather thin effort of Taylor, but one which strikes again at the part played by the Commons in the religious troubles, is a plea, entirely serious, which urges the parliament to purge the Christian body of the Brownist plague.[3] However, one of Taylor's wittiest attacks on the Commons is *A Most Learned and Eloquent Speech* (n.d.). The writer pretends to record an address he has heard in the lower house, a Puritan speech full of protestations of loyalty to his majesty. The dissenters have helped the king ". . . by shooting bullets of all sizes at his person, for His Majesties preservation, on purpose to make him a glorious King in another world . . ." It is apparent that Taylor has improved with the years; at his best he avoids the direct, the hotly denunciatory, the purely indignant; he is no master of wit and Puritanism from his pen never becomes the vehicle for a major expression of irony, but he does have his

---

2. See Taylor's *Heads of all Fashions* (1642); and *The noble Cavalier Caracterised, and a rebellious Caviller Cauterised* (n.d.). The title of *Heads of all Fashions* is a slur on the roundheads.

3. Taylor's *The Generall Complaint* (n.d.), A2: ". . . a pestiferous swarme of Preachers, a Mechanick kennell of illiterate Knaves, with the threats and Tyranny that you have used to us, and the execrable Covenants which you have forc'd us to take . . ." The same theme is repeated satirically in his *The Hellish Parliament* (1641). He commonly blames the preachers as the chief instrument for infecting the people.

Heads of all Fashions,

Being,

A Plaine Defection or Definition *of* diverse,

and fundry forts of heads, Butting, Jetting,or pointing
at vulgar opinion.

And Allegorically fhewing the Diverfities of Religion in
thefe diftempered times.

Now very lately written, fince Calves-Heads came in Seafon.

London Printed for *Iohn Morgan,* to be fold in the Old-baily. 1 6 4 2:

say on the dissenters in a clever and an indirect manner which pleases the reader, which points out the failings of the extremists, and which has the therapeutic quality of satire. His central point in the pamphlet is perfectly well taken : the Puritans very frequently protested their loyalty, but their performance did not square with their protestations.

Thomas Jordan's *Rules to Know a Royall King, from A Disloyall Subject* (1642) is generally too earnest to give off any sparks; in the course of the pamphlet Jordan quotes 1 Chron. 16 :22, a favorite with both sides : "Touch not mine anointed, and doe my Prophets no harm." The anointed is, of course, the king; and, Hooker notwithstanding, those who look outside the Bible for instruction will come to no good end. Jordan is scarcely in agreement with the marginal gloss to "mine anointed" in the Geneva Bible of 1560 : "Mine own elect people & them whom I have sanctified." The old issues, so earnestly discussed by the polemicists of Elizabeth's day, endure. Among the crown jewels of the king is the square stone of justice. "I would not have a Brownist look on it, for feare of spoiling his eyes," Jordan says.

The difficulty of definition of "mine anointed," the question of whether the phrase applies to Charles 1 as the particular instrument of God's will or to English Presbyterians, involves the old question of rule, the "mere popularity" of the serious controversy; [4] in addition, there is the view of Puritanism as an uprising of the lower classes, an opinion which comes not only from Taylor, but from other satirical writers on the movement. The central contention is that the revolutionary ideas on government of church and state, along with support for the reform, come from base mechanicals dissatisfied with the condition to which God had ordained them. The question of the support of the Puritan movement is, like the movement itself, both political and religious. But in the turmoil of the later years, the religious aspects may seem to be of less importance than they were, and the unwary reader is sometimes deceived into thinking that Puritanism has become a proletarian movement, supported by the downtrodden and opposed by the privileged who attack the revolutionaries on the single objection that they are poor and humble : "A Phanatique League and Covenant . . . We ignoble men, Barbers, Cobblers, Colliers, Draymen, Grocers, Hucksters . . . Submitting to onely the Government of one Prince, Belzebub Emperor of the Infernal Region . . . resolve . . ." The resolutions which follow include the destruction of all "Decency, Order and Form" in England. The church and the government are to go, and the royal family is to be attacked.[5] The irony of the pamphlet is obviously directed against one class; there

---

4. As both Sandys and Parker charged the Puritans. See Knappen, 238.

5. See also John Harris, *The Puritanes Impuritie* (1641), 5. John Taylor's *Mad Fashions, Od Fashions* (1642) describes the low social and occupational status of the sectaries.

is the proposal that the lower classes are in revolution and that there is
a struggle going on between the educated and the uneducated, the rich
and the poor, for power. Other pamphlets of the period tell of the en-
croachments of the masses in areas formerly restricted to the privileged
and educated. Ignorant tradesmen are supplanting university graduates
in the pulpit; untrained persons are aspiring to become attorneys and
solicitors; the gentry have been frightened so that they want to sell land
and not to buy it; in London even the moneylenders are loth to carry
on their trade.[6] But just as the Marian exiles were drawn from various
classes in England, so, later, the Puritans represented not one group
but many. Poverty was not the necessary mark of the Puritan, as the

6. *The Distractions of Our Times* (1642), "The Roundheads Race," 3-7:

> What ere the Popish hands have built
> Our Hammers shall undoe,
> Wee'l breake the Pipes, and burne the Coapes
>   and pull downe Churches too.
> Wee'l exercise within a Grove,
>   and teach beneath a Tree,
> And make a Pulpit of a Cart,
> And Hey then up goe we.
>
> Wee'l downe with Universities,
>   where Learning is profest
> Because they prattle and maintaine
>   the Language of the Beast.
> Wee'l Drive the Doctors out of doores,
>   and all what ere they be;
> Wee'l cry all Arts and Learning downe,
>   and Hey then up goe we . . .
>
> . . . Wee'l teach the Nobles how to crouch,
>   and keepe the Gentry downe.
> Good manners hath an ill report,
>   and turnes to pride we see;
> Wee'l therefore cry all manners downe
>   and Hey then up goe we.
>
> The name of Lord, shall be abhord
>   for each man is a brother,
> No reason why in Church, or State,
>   one man should rule another.
> But when the change of Government
>   shall set our fingers free,
> Wee'l lay the wanton Sisters downe,
>   and Hey then, up goe we.

Sir Thomas Aston's *A Remonstrance, against Presbytery* (1641?), although not a satire,
is of interest for its account in specific details of the economic ambitions of the Puritans.
Aston complains that the dissenters refuse to pay their tithes, refuse to obey the courts,
will not swear in court, and will not pay the heriot. He says, E2: "Nay, they yet goe
higher, even to the deniall of the right of proprietie in our estates. They would pay no
Fines, do no Boons, nor Duties to their Land-lords . . ."

Puritans in the House of Lords proved. Just as Anglicanism found support in, and drew its strength from, various classes, so Puritanism had in its following artisans and merchants, commoners and lords, city and country. And similarly, to a degree, Puritanism was resisted by all classes. It is also not possible to say that the Anglican apology, serious or satirical, was the product of a cultivated and leisured class: there were anti-Puritan groups of strength not only in the Lords but also in the Commons, in the city and, as King Charles discovered, among all classes in the country.

In the turmoil of controversy, the small voice of moderation is, on occasion, heard, and both sides are damned for their sins. The title of one single sheet reflects the counsel of Bacon: *The Lofty Bishop, the Lazy Brownist, and the Loyall Author* (n.d.). The text reads in part:

> The Brownists noses, want a Ring
> (to draw them with a Rope;)
> The Prelates wings doe cutting neede,
> (least they fly to the Pope.)

But a voice which speaks in behalf of the middle position is rare; feelings were not generally moderate in the controversy, and with the passing of the years moderation did not become more general.

One pointed fable on the errors of Puritanism comes from Henry Peacham the younger. His *Square-Caps Turned into Round-Heads; or, The Bishops Vindication* (1642) is a sprightly dialogue between Time and Opinion. Opinion is fresh from Holland where he has caused the roundheads to triumph. Time speaks for the square-caps, or orthodoxy. He says that the four corners of the square-caps represent the four corners of the world where they have preached and founded universities, churches, and hospitals. Opinion is fairly well convinced by the argument, but he says: ". . . in the mean time I am carried with violence in the throng. I can do no other than I do." Although the pamphlet is only eight pages long, it expresses very well in the oblique terms of its slight allegory both the dislike which a conservative section of English opinion had for Puritanism and the feeling which many must have had of the impossibility of resisting its more immoderate demands. Opinion clearly recognizes that the desire of the throng is not always right, but she at the same time speaks in such a manner that it is apparent that the wishes of the throng, right or not, will probably prevail. What she says is both a repetition of the old objections—generally valid—to a rule which is merely popular without being informed, and an acceptance of what seems to be inevitable, the triumph of popular rule. Aside from the figure of Opinion, however, the pamphlet does not succeed very well. On the title page is a woodcut of the bishops with their heads down and the Puritans with their heads up; the text has little in the way of a definition, serious or satirical, of Puritanism, nor is there any very comprehensive examination of the sins of Puritanism.[7]

Like a number of the Anglican polemicists, Peacham and his fellow satirists frequently look to an idealized past for what they like to think was a time of no dissension: the future is dark; the past was bright. John Taylor, too, believes that the troubles of 1642 are caused by departures from old ways: "The Creede is left out," and the congregation no longer prays: "Give peace in our time O Lord . . ."[8] The dominant note, despite the accompanying invective, is less satiric than elegiac.

Just as Bacon complained of the follies of immoderation among the sects, so the prose satirists commonly use the zealous eccentricities of the Puritans for painting ridiculous pictures of the movement. The religious intensity of the Puritan congregations, their earnest care with small details of rite and practice, the fervent devotion of uneducated speakers, all contributed to an effect of febrility which could easily be burlesqued. With not much exaggeration, the malicious commentator could turn Puritan habits of conduct into extremisms and hysterias which could serve to make the whole movement ridiculous. There were, for instance, the many places in which the dissidents saw, with terror, Romish crosses. *The Resolution of the Round-Heads, to Pull Down Cheapside Crosse* (1641) makes fun of their zeal: "Whereas we are through our great Ignorance and obstinacy growne to a most seditious and malignant head . . ." A felt-maker and a cobbler are to be heads of the church; learning is damned; at the end, a ballad repeats the old charge of treason. The resolution, like the many others of similar sense, ridicules the papers put before the Commons for the reform of the church. Another pamphlet puts the blame for the attack on Cheapside Cross on the preaching by silly women, and still a third offers cures for various diseases of Puritanism: "How to cure one that is troubled with crosses." The patient must "carry no coin," since money has images and even

7. But lack of a sense of proportion is not a failing peculiar to Anglican writers. *A Sad Warning to All Profane, Malignant Spirits* (1642) gives ". . . five sad examples of Gods fearfull and just Judgements . . ." When sinners call one of the elect a roundhead, their legs break and their tongues turn black. The account is as solemn as a tombstone.

8. *An Humble Desired Union* (1642), A3. *A Defensive Vindication of the Publicke Liturgy* (1641) argues similarly for the old forms of worship and against innovation. However, in John Hales' *A Tract Concerning Schisme* (1642) there is a lively and pointed defense of doctrinal change and variation in rites. The author points out that the bishops have not always shown perfect agreement on all matters. Taylor offers arguments for a morality which will arise from conformity in *Religions Enemies* (1641) and *A Cluster of Coxcombes* (1642). The former has some superlative invective. The Anglicans did not, of course, go unanswered. A good attack from the Puritans on the evils of uniformity is *A Dialogue wherein Is Plainly Laid Open the Tyranicall Dealings of Lord Bishops against Gods Children* (1640). The poem beginning on D2 tells over the virtues of the Puritans.

crosses on it. Again, "a man that is possessed with a factious spirit" should avoid excitement and contention in religion. "A cure for him that is troubled with an ovall-pate, (in English) a Round-head . . ." is to cut the head off. The section entitled "The Briefe definition of a Disease cal'd Obstinacie . . ." tells of the destruction of Cheapside Cross and turns upon the Puritans the old charge that they had made for years against the Anglicans, namely, an overconcern with externals of rite and service. In still another pamphlet the Puritan hero, a cobbler, looks about him and has fears over the Romish landscape: "Do you not see how the walks are laid out, and made in the forme of a crosse, which is execrable, abhominable, and intollerable?" The pamphlet ends with a pointless ballad, "Zeal Over-heated." [9] Direct attacks on the Puritans for the destruction of crosses and Communion rails are common enough: the chief argument, and one which has no basis in fact, is that the zealots are interested in destruction for its own sake.

Another sore point for the Puritan was the taking of an oath; and he had particularly violent objections to the *et cetera* oath in the sixth of the canons of 1640.[1] Among others, all clergymen were required to swear to the oath; uniformity in church doctrine, service, and government were to be the happy result. Puritans of varying shades of opinion objected that an oath exacted under duress was no oath, that a man's conscience was his own, and that universal approval of the Church of England could scarcely be had by forcing men to swear that approval. In addition, a turmoil rose over the particular phrase, *et cetera*.[2] Puritan objections do seem somewhat strained: they had enough to complain of in the plain terms of the oath and it is hard to imagine what secret danger could have been hidden in *et cetera*. But at any rate, the complaint which came to be best known was their objection to the undefined phrase, and, understandably, the satire of the Anglicans frequently centered on that objection. John Cleveland in "A Dialogue between Two zealots upon the &c. in the Oath," and "Smectymnuus, or the Club-divines" combines the Puritans' suspicion of Latin, the language of the beast, with their dislike of the oath:

9. *A Threefold Discourse betweene Three Neighbors* (1642). See also *Certain Affirmations in Defense of the Pulling down of Communion Rails Answered by a Gentleman of Worth* (1641). The pamphlet concludes with "Honour thy father . . ." which is calculated to prove that the Puritans in their rebellion against the king are opposing biblical instruction.

1. William H. Hutton, *The English Church from the Accession of Charles I to the Death of Anne* (Macmillan, 1903), 82: "I, A B, do swear that I approve the doctrine and discipline, or government, established in the Church of England, as containing all things necessary to salvation . . . nor will I ever give my consent to alter the government of this Church by arch-bishops, bishops, deans, and archdeacons, *etc.,* as it stands now established . . ."

2. A short statement of the Puritans' objections is *Queries of Some Tender Conscienced Christians* (1642).

> . . . who will not say
> Tongues are confounded in Et Caetera?

And Cleveland proposes a marriage:

> The bans are asked, would but the times give way,
> Betwixt Smectymnuus and Et Caetera.[3]

Despite the refusals to subscribe and the inclination to tear down crosses, Puritan voices continue to protest innocent intentions: "The Puritan intends no mischief to any, you may assure yourselves he does not . . ." And then the author explains that the destruction of windows, altars, organs, railings, and treasure is the work of the lord's anointed.[4] One of many answers to this overheated piety is that of Richard Brathwaite in his *Mercurius Britanicus* (1641), a "tragic comedy." Master Prinner speaks for utter chaos: "First that there be no order . . ." All rites are to be abolished, all set prayers forbidden, and the button-makers of England are to fill the pulpits.

Another source for material in the pamphlets was the Sabbatarian movement with the extreme compunctions of the Puritans against any unseemly activity or, it was sometimes argued, any activity, on Sunday. A nonsatiric account which sets the pattern for the argument is *The Lamentable Complaints of Nick Froth the Tapster* (1641). It tells of Puritan hysteria: people must stay indoors on Sunday to keep out of trouble; trade has been killed through no Sunday amusements. A cook and a bartender talk together. They say "Sunday" and not "the Sabbath" and thus mark themselves clearly as conformists. They complain that now there is no more drinking, no more selling of meat, no more piping and singing on what used to be the best day of the week. The "Church-Wardens, Side-men, and Constables" are ruining honest English trade. The trick of presenting a Puritan attitude as unpopular, that is, as disapproved of by people of humble occupations who are symbols of the common man, is entirely legitimate. But the trick must be recognized for what it is: the tract proves nothing about the popularity or unpopularity of the Sabbatarian movement and only demonstrates the willingness of the Anglicans to appeal to the scorned "mere popularity" when the appeal may reward them with an argument against the Puritans.

An amusing, if fairly crude, sketch of the Puritan is contained in Richard Carter's *The Schismatick Stigmatized* (1641). The author states plainly that he is writing against all ". . . quarrell pickers . . . enemies to Old Englands peace," and goes on with some paragraphs of sprightly

3. *The Poems of John Cleveland*, ed. John M. Berdan (New Haven, Yale University Press, 1911), 120, 125. Both poems were written about 1640. Two of Cleveland's most eloquent efforts are "The Rebel Scot" and "Hue and Cry after Sir John Presbyter." Both are dated about 1644.

4. *Some Careful Considerations* (1642), 6.

THE
LAMENTABLE
COMPLAINTS
OF
Nick Froth the Tapster, and
Rvlerost the Cooke.

*Concerning the restraint lately set forth,
against drinking, potting, and piping on the Sabbath day, and against selling meate.*

Printed in the yeare, 1641.

denunciation of the Puritans: "When we stand up reverently, they unmannerly sit on their Bums." Then Carter introduces a conversation between two Puritans, Nick-all-asse Non-sense and Tomasse Pragmaticus, and the two precisians discuss the general state of the church as well as an approaching service: "Mr. Faction doth teach today, and he came lately from Amsterdam or Rotterdam or some other new Plantation." There will be no service, but only pure "teaching." Among the communicants will be Alice the Adamite,

> As bare as ones naile:
> She shames not her taile.

The two Puritans' hot denunciation of order and learning in the church is perhaps the most successful part of the production.[5]

The essence of the Anglican complaint of a lack of a sense of proportion and decorum is summed up in a thin but interesting allegory of 1641, the anonymous *Dialogue Betwixt Three Travelers, as Accidentally They Did Meet on the Highway*. The homily is delivered in the form of a conversation among "Crucy Cringe, a Papist, Accepted Weighall, a Professour of the Church of England, and Factious Wrestwrit, a Brownist." By the end of the discussion, the two extremes are inevitably converted to the golden mean of the Anglican church; a good part of the discussion consists of a justification of Anglican rites and practices. The central charge against the Puritan (he is no more particularly a Brownist than a Presbyterian) is immoderation. The invective of his first attack is reminiscent of the heated phraseology of the sectarian sermons;[6] although the parody of language lacks almost all of the vivid touches of the dramatists at their best, it does at the same time remind the reader immediately of the Billingsgate in the anti-Roman philippics of the more violent reformers. A good deal of the argument is over the kind of service proper for a Christian church and the nature of the Communion. The first had been a moot point in the serious controversy; the second had been of little consequence in the troubles between Anglican and Puritan. At any rate, the Puritan makes a fool of himself by his ignorance; the Roman Catholic does somewhat better, but is too much the victim of ignorance and superstition to have an understanding

---

5. *The Schismatik Stigmatized*, 13: ". . . away with this dependant government . . . root and branch. Downe with all Universities, Colledges, and Schooles, they doe but maintaine Learning, an enemy to us. Down with Churches, Hospitalls, and Almeshouses . . . Down with all these Crosses . . . Away with all Orthodox Divines . . ."

6. *A Dialogue*, pp. 1–2: ". . . commit thy deeds of darknesse with the Whore of Babilon with more securenesse. . . . Down Dagon, down, I hate thee Cringe; I hate thee and thy late disputed doctrine of the reall presence in the Sacrament, worse than the lawne sleeves of the Prelates, which are but meer rags of Rome, and fit onely for tinder for the Tinder-box of Tophet . . ." An account of excessive zeal occurs in the anonymous *Bartholomew Faire* (1641), 2. A Puritan who sees some pictures for sale buys a wooden backsword and attacks the pictures. Like Factious, he shouts much about rags of Rome.

both true and clear—which is to say Anglican—of the nature of the sacrament. Weighall gives a moderate, logical, and informing account of the Eucharist; and the result is that the extremes of the right and the left are converted to the happy center.[7] The pamphlet is not over-burdened with humor, and is less than convincing, particularly at the moment of instantaneous conversion of one Roman Catholic and one Puritan to the Anglican church. But the pamphlet is not meant to per-suade; it is meant only to assure and please those already persuaded. Its function is much like, for instance, the polemical writings of Bishop Hall. And in certain other respects the pamphlet resembles some of the Anglican apologetic of the reigns of Elizabeth and James. Weighall, for instance, recommends Hooker's reason and the necessity of accepting those things which are in accord with nature—by which he plainly means the ordinary course of the universe—as opposed to superstition. His argument leaves behind a good part of the bibliolatry of the Puritans and the authority of the Roman Catholics, and he allows much more to the subjective judgment of the individual than would be pleasing to the Roman Catholic. Again, Weighall is insistent on presenting the

---

7. *A Dialogue,* 2–6:

Crucy. . . . The doctrine then of the reall presence in the Eucharist.

Factious. The Eucharist! I can forebeare the argument no longer; there is no such word to be read in all the scripture.

Crucy. Very frequently, Sir, in the Greek originall.

Factious. Talk not to me of Greek, I will beleeve no Greek, it is a language that shall carry no authority with me; I hope to see Greek and Latine too, ere it be long, in lesse reputation than they are.

Crucy. I doe not like this fury, E'en God be with you, and grant your zeale more knowledge, and your knowledge more humility . . .

Weighall. . . . I beleeve we ought not to make our approaches to the blessed Sacra-ment, with that overweening familiarity, as the sawcy Brownists; nor yet with such a devout superstition as the abused Papists. That the Bread and wine in the Sacrament should be transubstantiated into the Body of Christ, cannot be admitted into the faith of any sober man, without admitting with it many grosse and grievous errours . . . it is diametrically opposite to reason and nature . . . The elevation of the Host by the Papists, savours of rank idolatry; and the unmannerly sitting of the Brownists at the Communions, of irreverence. A decent and humble posture is most requisite, especially where God is pleased to communicate himselfe to be really, and more peculiarly present . . . Er-rours in the Church result out of too unruly an heat, or too thick and too grave a Superstition; either while we violently are lead by our own ungoverned humours, or while blinded with pompe, or with the shadowes of Antiquitie with a willing reverence we are drawne unto Idolatry. Too much Ceremony and an affected pompe hath begot much Superstition in the Sacrament amongst the Papists. Too carelesse a presumption hath begot much irreverence in the Sacra-ment amongst the Anabaptists. The mean betwixt both is the safe and happy way attended with a persevering care, not to decline, either to the one, or to the other, either to the right hand, or to the left.

John Taylor in *Differing Worships* (1640) pictures the Anglican church as torn by the sects and the Roman Catholics. The title page refers to "Tom Nash . . . the old Martin queller."

Anglican position as central in relation to those of his two opponents.
That argument is his strongest and, presumably, it is the persuasion
which produces the conversions. It is also clear that Weighall is more
anti-Puritan than anti-Roman: like the serious polemicists after 1588,
he feels that the danger is now not from Rome, and that he can safely
point out the affinities of Anglicanism with Rome without loss of face.
It is also probable that the very opposition of the Puritan to Roman
Catholicism has made the Anglican gentler than he would have been: the
Puritan's fears of crosses looks even more silly if the Anglican can
demonstrate by his own actions that, accepting crosses, a man still
stands in no danger of seduction by idolatry.

Excessive Puritan zeal was perhaps most strikingly displayed for the
delight of the Anglican public in the parodies of sermons, tracts, controversies, and confessions. The old and sober charge of *An Admonition
to the Parliament* that the clergy were ignorant and could not write
a sermon was repeated time after time by Puritan writers; in the later
years there are from the Puritans satirical repetitions of the demand for
reform. James is asked not to make the Anglican preachers preach; the
work is too hard.[8] However, the weight of the attack comes from the
Anglicans and is against the Puritan sermons. John Donne asks the
question: "Why Puritans make Long Sermons?" The answer is that
they must keep talking until the congregation wakes up.[9] The argument
on the Puritan sermon as tedious nonsense is amusingly sustained with
accounts of the bizarre posturings of the preachers, the strange subjects
of the discourses, and the hysterical reactions of the congregations. As
with most satire, the picture is not intended to be fair; it is, rather,
sufficiently close to the original to be recognizable and thus apt, and it
depends for its comic effects on the exaggeration and distortion of the
truth. Halfway between the serious and the comic is the story of John
Sherman: Sherman spent two years as a "revealer" before he repented
and returned to the Church of England. An alleged sample of his preaching consists of a series of elaborate puns on clothing, cloth, and terms
from the tailoring trade, all designed as a travesty of the rhetoric of the
sectary, and, by implication, suggesting the superiority of the cultivated

8. *The Humble Petition of the Unpreachable Ministers of England* (n.d.)
9. John Donne, *Juvenilia: or, Certaine Paradoxes, and Problemes* (1633), F2 verso:
"I have thought sometimes that out of Conscience, they allow long measure to course
Ware. And Sometimes that usurping in that place a liberty to speake freely of Kings,
they would raigne as long as they could. But now I thinke they doe it out of a zealous
Imagination, that, It is their duty to preach on till their Auditery wake." See also A. C.
Generosus, *A Satire against Seperatists* (1642), 7. An account of sermonizing females
is the pamphlet *A Discovery of Six Women-Preachers* (1641). One of them declaims:
". . . the Divell was the father of all those which did not love Puritans." In *The Resolution of the Round-heads to Pull Down Cheapside Crosse* (1641), A2, and *The Diseases
of the Times* (1641), A3 ff., there are "she-lecturers" who supervise sexual orgies in
the woods, "feminine divinity," and "Amsterdamian zealots" who plot against the life of
the king.

preacher speaking in behalf of the Established Church.[1] Again, there is the story, perhaps by John Taylor, of a Brownist sermon five hours long, a revelation sent by God specifically to Mr. Hunt. The revelation ended with a brawl in the congregation and their arrest: the anticlimax points the moral. "Townes and cities are filled with a company of *Yeas* and *Verilies* . . . there had everyone a Religion by himself, and everyone a nigher way to Heaven than the other. . . ." [2]

The most successful of the attacks on the Puritan pulpit are the outright burlesques. Taylor again leads the field in prose: in a series of tracts published around 1642 he makes skillful fun of the revelations and prophesyings; and he even goes to the length of carrying on a controversy with himself over just such matters of doctrine and practice as would stir the argumentative lusts of a Presbyterian. Taylor has the happy knack of giving the impression of interminable length and infinite nonsense all within six pages. The following is the thunderous title and the opening of one of his "sermons":

> *A Tale in a Tub or, A Tub Lecture. As it was delivered by My-heele Mendsoale, an Inspired Brownist, and a most upright Translator. In a meeting house neere Bedlam, the one and twentieth of Dembler, Last 1641. Written by J.T.*
> A Tub Lecture,
> Beloved Sisters, and my well infected Brethren, attend this Text, as you shall find it written in the first Chapter of Bell and the Dragon, the third verse, as it followeth,
> *Now the Babylonians had an Idoll they called Bell, and there were spent upon him every day, 12 great measures of fine flower, and 40 sheepe, and six vessels of wine.*
> I will first of all make a Division in the former part of my Text, I will leave the latter to the Last, and expound that as I shall Wax to an End.
> *Now the Babylonians had an Idoll they called Bell.*
> This sentence I shall divide into 4 parts, because your

---

1. *A True Relation of the Lewd Life and Repentant Death of One John Sherman* (1641).

2. *The Discovery of a Swarme of Seperatists; or, a Leathersellers Sermon* (1641). An amusing controversy takes place between Taylor and one Henry Walker, an ironmonger and a sectary. Taylor begins with *A Swarme of Sectaries* (1641). Walker denounces Taylor in *An Answer to a Foolish Pamphlet Entitled A Swarme of Sectaries* (1641); and Taylor answers in *A Reply as True as Steele* (1641). The last word goes to Taylor in *The Whole Life and Progress of Henry Walker the Iron-monger* (1642). See also Taylor's *Lucifers Lacky, or, the Devils New Creature* (1641). Taylor's *The Devil Turn'd Round-head* (1642?) tells how Satan became a Puritan, and agreed to hate ". . . all good manners, all orders, rule, Orthodoxe Divinitie, rule and government . . . all good works, Academian Learning, Charitie, and the publike Liturgie of the Church of England . . ."

> understandings my Beloved Brethren, consisteth chiefly in the
> Knowledge of Divisions, the particles are these.
>   1. The Time. 2. The Nation. 3. The Crime. 4. The Denomi-
> nation.
>   The Time, *Now*. The Nation, *The Babylonians,* The Crime,
> *had an Idoll*. The Denomination, *called Bell,*
>   *Now the Babylonians had an Idoll called Bell.*
>   First I will begin with the time, you must not conceive
> that it was 1. 10. 100. 1000 yeares agoe, but *Now,* at this
> present, *Now the Babylonians,* &c. Beloved there is much evill
> and abomination to be picked out of these three letters
> *Now* . . .

and Taylor picks evil and abomination out of *now*. The sermon is sufficiently confused so that, when it ends five pages later, the reader is
satisfied, even though the text has not been entirely expounded word for
word and letter for letter. The author's controversy with himself proves,
among other things, that a boat is better for preaching than a tub: "He
should have preferred a Boate before a tub to make a pulpit of, for a
Boate is more primitive to preach out of, then a Tub or a Kinderkin." [3]

> **3.** *A full and compleat Answer against the Writer of a late volume set forth, entituled
> A Tale in a Tub, or a Tub Lecture: with a Vindication of that ridiculous name called
> Round-Heads . . . Also proving that it is far better to preach in a Boat than in a Tub.
> By Thorny Ailo, Annagram . . . 1642.* The doggerel vindication argues soberly that the
> roundheads have done all for England's good:
>
> > 'Tis manifest that we have done our best,
> > To bring all wit and learning in disgrace;
> > The Church and Church-men we do still molest,
> > In hope we each might have a Preachers place . . .

Again, in *An Apology for Private Preaching* (1642?), Taylor catches the spirit of the
zealot in a fantastic listing of the best positions for revealing God's word:

> *An Apology for Private Preaching.* In which those formes are warranted, or rather
> justified, which the malignant Sect contemne, and daily by prophane Pamphlets
> make ridiculous.
> > Preaching in a Tub.
> > Teaching against the backe of a Chaire.
> > Instructing at a Tables end.
> (Viz.) Revealing in a Basket.
> > Exhorting over a Buttery Hatch.
> > Reforming on a Bed side.
> > > or
> (Indeed) any place, according to Inspiration (since it is knowne) the Spirit moves
> in sundry places) . . .

The sermon begins:

> To you the Sanctified, Elected, Purified, Mundified, Justified, and Separated Breth-
> ren, I make this worthy and acceptable (although not Learned Apology) . . .

Other notable attacks on the Puritan sermons are *Love One Another: a Tub Lecture*
(n.d.); John Taylor's *A Swarme of Sectaries, and Schismatics* (1641), *An Honest*

Taylor's ironic sermon is centered on the single point that Puritanism is an anti-intellectual movement. The talented obscenity of the text repeats the old accusation that the Puritans are hypocrites.

Behind the parodies of the Puritan sermons are a number of the beliefs of the serious controversialists: the satirist by his attack on the world about him defends an order which he wishes to substitute for the one which he satirizes. And when Taylor and his fellows attack the Puritan sermon, they are reflecting many of the major objections to the whole Puritan movement; the Anglicans do, for instance, reflect their belief in their aristocracy of leadership. The Puritans support another aristocracy, one of quite different composition and intention. Among the Anglicans there is one order imposed from above: thus, the uneducated cleric who preaches without the authority of his king and the blessing of his bishop must be wrong; and his lack of education shows his wrongness, for he becomes ridiculous. Since the sectary, preaching, does not enforce the established order, he stands for misrule, for revolution. In registering this opinion in humorous terms, the satirists of the Puritan sermons simply echo what Whitgift, Hooker, and the skeptical Bacon had pointed out in their serious accounts. In the hands of dissenters the sermon was a major medium for communicating the most personal experiences, the most eccentric religious opinions, and the most highly individualized judgments. These personal feelings and opinions might be well enough: a John Donne telling of death's duel would overthrow no government, but a sectary might do great damage. The satirist attacking the sermon was doing no more than enforcing the contention of many serious Anglican writers: the Puritan movement was bred and nourished by the dissenting clergy and their inflammatory preaching.[4]

Answer (1642), and *The Brownists Conventicle* (1641). *John Taylor's Last Voyage* (1641), 32, makes fun of the theological pretensions of workers and beggars who want to preach.

4. The Puritan sermons and "prophesyings" were thorns in Elizabeth's side; Francis Bacon gives a good account of prophesying in *Certain Considerations Touching the Better Pacification and Edification of the Church of England* (1604), reprinted in *The Works of Francis Bacon,* ed. James Spedding *et al., 10* (1868), 119–20: ". . . that good exercise . . . commonly called prophesying, which was this: That the ministers within a precinct did meet upon a week-day in some principal town, where there was some ancient grave minister that was president, and an auditory admitted of gentlemen, or other persons of leisure; then every minister successively, beginning with the youngest, did handle one and the same piece of Scripture, spending severally some quarter of an hour or better, and in the whole some two hours; and so the exercise being begun and concluded with prayer, and the president giving a text for the next meeting, the assembly was dissolved. And this was as I take it a fortnight's exercise; which in mine opinion was the best way to frame and train up preachers to handle the word of God as it ought to be handled, that hath been practised." Clarendon, writing after the revolution, believes that the clergy and their sermons had more to do with stirring up discord than the Commons. He says in *The History of the Rebellion and Civil Wars in England* (Oxford, 1826), *3,* 230: "I must not forget . . . that this strange wild fire among the people was not so much and so furiously kindled by the breath of the parliament, as of their clergy . . ."

The characters, as they happen to attach themselves by subject matter to anti-Puritan satire, occupy a position close to and in respect to form and wit somewhat above the run of humorous pamphlets. The epigrams in turn come to be associated frequently with the characters: both are short forms, and both lend themselves to use in collections of prose and poetry, the miscellanies of varied tone and intent which appeared commonly in the seventeenth century.

Certain marked differences are to be observed between the diffuse prose and the popular poetry on the one hand, and the characters and epigrams on the other. Short both by tradition and intention, the character is necessarily more orderly than the average prose essay or discursive pamphlet: lacking order, the character will waste space and fail in the completion of its purpose within the short scope which convention allows it. The character is more concentrated, not only in respect to its content, where, for instance, repetition must be used chiefly for witty emphasis, but also in respect to its humor. In the character, the attack on the Puritan cannot afford the space to repeat one failing without striking variations of detail; and broad humor of situation, delivered with a leisurely account of events, is less native to the form than the twist of language such as the pun. In form and in content, the character shows affinities with court writing in general: the character might be called almost a royalist medium, like the flippant love song or the comedy of manners. In its polish and balance, the character would seem by its very nature to oppose the noisy zealot or the preaching sectary. The epigram, in turn, has a number of affinities with the character. Not markedly different from the character in intention—to amuse with a striking observation, and to do the job in a small space—the epigram is often in verse, and is short. Like the character, the epigram is commonly the tool of the royalist writer; it is generally of a highly conscious and sophisticated cast, and is opposed to the verbose, the casual, and the extreme. The course of the development of the anti-Puritan character and epigram follows roughly the prose pamphlet and the popular poetry.[5]

Until some time after 1600, the character writers pay little attention to the Puritans. The reasons are easy to find: for one thing, the character was not a common form before 1600, and for another, the Puritan did not come to receive much attention until the last quarter of the century and the period of the Admonitions. But around the turn of the century he does come to be commonly a figure of fun for the court wit and the Anglican, and begins to appear in prose and verse sketches. In several collections, there is no mention, favorable or unfavorable, of the

5. Benjamin Boyce, *The Theophrastian Character in England to 1642* (Cambridge, Harvard University Press, 1947), 315: "The theater, shut up in 1642, had-evil associations for the Puritans and so, no doubt, had the Character, for it was usually written from the Royalist and Anglican point of view, and one of its butts had been the zealot."

Puritan.[6] But by the beginning of James' reign the Puritan appears at least by indirection in a description of the ideal cleric who does not encourage sects in his church. By 1609 the character writers are attacking with relish and are making "Puritan" the synonym for assorted wiles and corruptions: a wicked woman is ". . . by birth commonly a bastard, by nature a canibal, by art a Puritan; in aluring a siren . . ." [7]

Among the 83 characters in the later editions of Sir Thomas Overbury's *A Wife* there are a number of satirical portraits of the Puritan.[8] The pictures present the familiar features of the hypocrite, the sanctimonious lecher, the thief, the noisy railer, and the precisian carping at the mention of Rome, or Latin, or the sound of organ music. But if it is the material of the ballads and the pamphlets, the presentation is quite different. It is more harsh, more exact in detail, more cruel than the parodies or the bawdy tales of the popular poetry, and it has a coldness which makes it closer to a polemicist like Bancroft than a satirist like Taylor. A precisian ". . . will not sticke to commit fornication or Adulterie, so it be done in the feare of God, and for the propagation of the godly; and can find in his heart to lie with any whore, save the whore of Babylon. To steale he holds it lawfull, so it be from the wicked & Aegiptians." [9] Other characters in the same collection center on the

---

6. Thomas Harman's *A Caveat or Warening* (1567), reprinted in *The Rogues and Vagabonds of Shakspere's Youth*, ed. F. J. Furnivall *et al.* (1880), 17–91, is a collection of serious descriptions of types common to the period. There is no account of the Puritan. There is similarly no mention of the Puritan in John Awdeley's *The Fraternitie of Vagabondes* (1575), reprinted in *The Rogues and Vagabonds of Shakspere's Youth*, 1–16. Joseph Hall's *Characters of Vertues and Vices* (1608), *Works, 6*, 89–125, describes "The Hypocrite" (106–8) as an extreme Anglican, but does not mention the Puritan.

7. W. M., *The Man in the Moone* (1609), reprinted in *Notices of Fugitive Tracts*, ed. James O. Halliwell (1849). Each tract is separately paged. In *A Poetical Rhapsody* (1608), ed. Hyder Rollins (2 vols. Cambridge, Harvard University Press, 1931), *1*, 239, there is a description of the divine:

> My calling is divine,
>   and I from God am sent,
> I will no chop-church be,
>   nor pay my patron rent . . .

8. *The Overburian Character*, ed. W. J. Paylor (Oxford, Oxford University Press, 1936), v: "The first twenty-two Overburian Characters which were added to the second impression of Sir Thomas Overbury's poem, *A Wife*, 1614, were the work of himself and 'other learned Gentlemen his friends.' The number was increased in later impressions to a total of eighty-three Characters by the contributions of other authors during a period of several years, until the Collection contained a series of widely varying portraits which inspired that luxuriant flourishing of Character writing in the seventeenth century."

9. *Ibid.*, 44. The bitterness of "A Puritane," 26, shows the hostility toward those who would not conform to Anglican practice:

A Puritane

Is a diseas'd peece of Apocripha, bind him to the Bible and he corrupts the whole text; Ignorance, and fat feede, are his founders, his Nurses, Raylings, Rabbies, and

contentiousness and carping of the Puritans. By the 1620's the theme
is well established, and the eccentric zealot appears a number of times.
The Interpreter (1622) attributed to Thomas Scott, is exceptional in
that in the three characters of the Puritan, the Anglican, and the Roman
Catholic, all virtues reside in the Puritan. He is honest, diligent, patriotic,
courageous, and loyal. John Taylor for once is equivocal in his treatment; in a character entitled "A Separatist" he admits that there can be
a good Puritan, or, perhaps that those who are virtuous and are called
Puritans really are not Puritans. Taylor begins with his usual denunciation: the Puritan is a lecherous hypocrite. But he allows for some
virtue:

> There are a sort of men which conscience make,
> Of what they say or doe or undertake:
> Who neither will dissemble, sweare, or lie,
> Who to good ends their actions all apply,
> Who keepe the Sabbath, and relieve the poore,
> According to their portions and their store:
> And these good people some men doe backbite
> And call them Puritanes, in scorne and spight,
> . . . I love and reverence onely beare to such . . .

Then Taylor returns to the attack and describes adulterous affairs among
dissenters; the sinners always rationalize their acts with pious references
to the Bible, to reform, and the spreading of the faith.[1] Owen Felltham
in 1628 offers a more calm appraisal: "I find many that are called
Puritans; yet few or none that will own the name . . . I suppose we
may call him a church-rebel . . . when a man in things but ceremonial,
shall spurn at the grave authority of the church . . . I shall think him
one of those whose opinion hath fevered his zeal to madness and dis-
traction." [2]

John Earle's *Microcosmographie* (1628) gives a striking description
of the silly Puritan woman and points out the folly of her hysterical worship: his chief point of argument is the virtue of moderation. The

---

round breeches; his life is but a borrowed blast of winde; for between two religions,
as betweene two doores hee is ever whisling . . . should the Church enjoyne cleane
shirts; hee were lousie . . . Shew him a Ring he runs back like a Beare; and hates
square dealing as allied to Caps, a paire of Organs blow him out o' th' Parish, and
are the only glister pipes to coole him.

Two other characters on the theme of preciseness and hypocrisy are "A Button-Maker
of Amsterdame," 61, and "A Meere Petifogger," 64.

1. *The Water-Cormorant His Complaint: against a Brood of Land Cormorants*
(1622), ed. *All the Workes of John Taylor* (1630). "A Separatist" is the second character. Items in the 1630 Folio are separately paged.

2. Owen Felltham, *Resolves* (1623), ed. 1840, "Of Puritans," 7–9.

superiority of the Anglican divine is in his devotion to reason and the strength of the Anglican position lies, as in Hooker's argument, in the fact that it holds the midpoint between two extremes of error.[3] But Earle is more moderate in his attacks than many of the character writers; if his Puritans are noisy and misguided, they seem also to be harmless.

After 1640, just as the tone of the serious polemics becomes more bitter and reconciliation appears impossible, so the anti-Puritan character has about it a savagery which often makes it little more than the denunciation of a traitor and a criminal; there is a marked loss of the wit and humor which enlivened the productions of some of the earlier writers like those of the Overbury collection.[4] John Cleveland serves as a sample of the new manner: "Thus they kill a man over and over, as Hopkins and Sternhold murder the Psalmes with another to the same; one chimes all in, and then the other strikes up, as the Saints-Bell . . . But Holy men, (like the Holy language,) must be read backwards. They rifle Colledges to promote Learning; and pull downe Churches for Edification. But Sacrilege is entailed upon him . . ."[5]

Inevitably when the epigrammatist dealt with the Puritan his findings agreed with those of the character writer. The epigrams do not examine Puritanism to any notable extent during Elizabeth's reign. In 1562 John Heywood anticipates the later attacks with a neat turn which makes fun of too-frequent grace before meals; but other writers before 1600 sometimes write epigrams which attack the very abuses the

3. John Earle, *Microcosmographie* (1628), ed. Harold Osborne (University Tutorial Press, 1933), 72, "A She Precise Hypocrite." In "A Grave Divine," 12, Earle says:

> He [the Anglican divine] has sounded both religions and anchored in the best, and is a Protestant out of judgement not faction . . . He shoots all his meditations at one butt; and beats upon his text, not the cushion, making his hearers, not the pulpit groan. In citing of Popish errors he cuts them with arguments, not cudgels them with barren invectives; and labours more to shew the truth of his cause than the spleen . . . In matters of ceremony he is not ceremonious, but thinks he owes that reverence to the Church to bow his judgement to it, and make more conscience of schism than a surplice.

4. Gwendolen Murphy in *A Bibliography of English Character-Books 1608-1700*, The Bibliographical Society (Oxford, 1925), "*Controversial Characters*," 97-117, lists anti-Puritan collections. Of the controversial collections, those which attack the Puritans are most common; there are some attacks on the Anglican clergy.

5. *The Character of a London Diurnall* (1642), reprinted in *The Works of Mr. John Cleveland* (1687), 83-92. The quotations are from 87-9. Cleveland's attacks on the Puritans are full of the bitterest invective. Notable are "The Character of a Country Committee-man," 72-8, and "The Puritan," 355-7. A large number of anti-Puritan poems, all written after 1642, appear in *The Poems of John Cleveland*, ed. John M. Berdan (New York, Grafton, 1903), 119-65. John Harris in *The Puritans Impuritie* (1641), 5, says: "A Protestant will deal uprightly, a Puritan will cozen his father, a true Protestant will love his enemy, a Puritan will hate every man, a true Protestant will serve God devoutly . . . a Puritan will make a zealous show of serving God . . . a Protestant will relieve the poor and fatherless, a Puritan will oppress the fatherless and Widdow . . ."

Puritans wished to reform.[6] The difficulty of classifying the author easily and certainly as a Puritan or Anglican appears here as in many of the serious reformers, and it is plain that a satirist can be a conforming Anglican in respect to polity and service, and a Puritan in respect to the ignorance and greed of the clergy. Around 1600 the anti-Puritan epigrams become fairly common. Thomas Bastard in *Chrestoleros* (1598) makes fun of the extreme piety of a man who sounds much like a Puritan; in addition, Bastard praises John Whitgift and attacks the presumption of tradespeople and menials who cause social disturbances by their ambitions.[7] Bastard's efforts echo the stock opinions in lines of verse which are as remarkable for their crudity as for their triteness. Francis Thynne writes of the sexual hypocrisy of the Puritan wife, the conceit of the elect, and the sectary's principle of one church for one member.[8] Samuel Rowlands in *Looke to It: for, Ile*

6. In *A Sixt Hundred of Epigrammes, John Heywoodes Workes* (1562), 276:

Of saying Grace

To say grace fair, and to say grace oft John,
From Grace church to Grantam thy like there's none.
At breakfast, at dinner, at supper, at all,
At sitting, at rising, have grace we shall.
There's no man alive, in house, street, or field,
That saith grace so oft, and showeth grace so seeld.

Robert Crowley's *One and Thirtie Epigrammes* (1550), reprinted in *The Select Works of Robert Crowley,* ed. J. M. Cowper (1872), contains, 8–17, attacks on alehouses, Sabbath-breaking, and bear-baiting; one epigram, 27–8, makes fun of the "Double Benificed Men." The tone of the collection is pro-Puritan.

Two good accounts of the epigram are T. K. Whipple's *Martial and the English Epigram, University of California Publications in Modern Philology, 10* (Berkeley, 1925), 279–414; and Hoyt H. Hudson's *The Epigram in the English Renaissance* (Princeton, Princeton University Press, 1947).

7. *Chrestoleros* is reprinted in *The Poems English and Latin of the Rev. Thomas Bastard,* ed. Alexander B. Grosart (1880). See 40:

Thymus is so enspirde, so mortifide
So pure a ghost, so heavenly spirituall:
That all things else to God he hath deny'd . . .

The praise of Whitgift is on 45. The attacks on the tradespeople and menials are on 62. *The Works in Verse and Prose of Sir John Davies,* ed. Alexander B. Grosart (3 vols. 1869–76), I, 321, has an epigram which charges the Puritans with gluttony. Davies' *Epigrammes and Elegies* probably appeared in 1590.

8. Thynne's *Emblemes and Epigrames* (1600), ed. F. J. Furnivall (1876), 59, 63. Of the schismatics, Thynne says, 81:

they sett upp churches twentie for their one,
for everie private house spirituallie
must bee their church, for other will they none . . .

John Weever in his *Epigrammes in the Oldest Cut and Newest Fashion* (1599), ed. R. B. McKerrow (1911), 87, complains of the violence of the Puritan attacks on the clergy:

Stabbe Ye (1604) sees faults on both sides: in the epigram, "Curious Divines," he finds, like Bacon, that a good part of the dispute is over elaborate theological distinctions of no importance.[9]

Through the years there is no marked development in the anti-Puritan epigram: it is never specifically moral or consciously instructive; wit is present when the writer has wit to put in it. The range is from crude libels without point to well-turned aphorisms of several lines, balanced and complete.[1] One epigram of Ben Jonson and several of Sir

---

> . . . lavish-tongu'd precisme will not spare,
> The chiefest pillars of our cleargie men,
> But to a cast of counters them compare . . .

On the other hand, Weever is able to lash out at the plural livings in one epigram, 70:

> Matho I 'm told that many do thinke much,
> Because I call you Piller of the Church:
> Matho, you bought a Deanry at best rate,
> And two church-livings now impropriate . . .
> And now hath got three livings at one lurch:
> Art thou not then a pillar of the Church?

9. Rowlands' *Looke to It: for, Ile Stabbe Ye,* The Hunterian Club, 6 (1871–72), 8.

1. Thomas Campion's *Observations in the Art of English Poesie* (1608), reprinted in *Campion's Works,* ed. Percival Vivian (Oxford, Oxford University Press, 1909), 48, offers the following:

> Drue feasts no Puritans; the churles, he saith,
> Thanke no men, but eate, praise God, and depart.

Epigrams by H.P. (1608), generally ascribed to Henry Parrot, attacks Puritan piety, F1:

> Silvanus is become so pure and holy
> As he accounts all mirth but idle folly,
> Aske him wherefore, he gives you ghostly reason,
> But then his whore comes never out of season.

John Heath's *Two Centuries of Epigrammes* (1610) describes, B4 verso, both Roman Catholics and Brownists as haughty and full of evil pride. There is, however, on C5, a pro-Sabbatarian epigram. It is well to remember that many of the collections of epigrams, like the character books, are not the product of one writer but of many. Some epigrams, for example, appear in three or four collections. John Davies of Hereford, *The Scourge of Folly* (1611?), reprinted in *The Complete Works of John Davies of Hereford,* ed. Alexander B. Grosart (2 vols, 1878), 2, 6, contains the following in a dedication:

> To the censorious precise . . .
> Nor that Geneva Doctor (most precise!)
> Who made the Hebrue Bible Latine talke . . .

Henry Parrot's *Laquei ridiculosi: or Springes for Woodcocks* (1613), G8, tells how a Puritan has learned a trick for cheating tenants and on P7 verso relates the story of the "fellow of the purer sect" who couldn't endure a surplice, but who was forced because of his sins to wear a white sheet in the chancel. A number of the epigrams in this collection appear also in *The Mous-Trap* (1606) and *Epigrams by H.P.* (1608). R. C., *The Times' Whistle* (1614?), ed. J. M. Cowper (1871), 10, speaks of

> . . . that pure seeming sect,
> Which now of late beginneth to infect
> The body of our land . . .

John Harington may be singled out as representative of the best, but
their qualities obviously depend less on the originality or truth of the
observations than on the arrangement, economy, and order of the lines.
Jonson writes on a Puritan preacher and the theater:

On Lippe, the Teacher.

I Cannot thinke there's that antipathy
  'Twixt puritanes, and players, as some cry;
Though Lippe, at Pauls, ranne from his text away,
  To inveigh 'gainst playes: what did he then but play? [2]

The Puritans are corrupting the English church with false holiness used to hide "bellie-
cheer and lust." Thomas Freeman's *Rubbe, and a Great Cast* (1614) has several epigrams on the stupidity and sexuality of the Puritans. One on Latin and the Puritans,
B3, reads:

> Gosling the Puritan held so excellent,
> Ner'e quoteth Father, ner'e speakes Latine sentence,
> Indeed the Scripture's all-sufficient,
> As he being ask't told one of his acquaintance,
> But wee who know him, know the cause was rather
> He ner'e learn'd Latine, never read a Father.

E4 verso, "In Hylam," tells the story of Hylas the Puritan. His wife beds with numberless men; he remains ignorant. I2 verso, "In Puritanum," describes the hypocrisy of the
Puritans.

   2. *Ben Jonson*, ed. C. H. Herford and Percy and Evelyn Simpson (11 vols. Oxford,
Oxford University Press, 1925–52), *8* (1947), 52. The epigram was first printed in
Jonson's 1616 folio. Epigrams around the time of the Jonson folio repeat the themes
of those at the turn of the century. Richard Brathwaite's *A Strappado for the Divell*
(1615), ed. J. W. Ebsworth (Boston, Lincolnshire, 1878), 109, tells the Puritan that
since he is too pure to read books, he must not read this one. There is also the old story
of the Puritan who killed his cat for mousing on Sunday. Henry Parrot's *The Mastive*
(1615), C4, tells of

> Luke that in Lattine lately scorn'd to looke,
> Would now read English, might he have his book.

Podrus who scorns Latin, D2, also sounds like a Puritan. William Goddard's *A Neaste
of Waspes* (1615) has a number of anti-Roman Catholic epigrams. Nicholas Breton's
Crossing of Proverbs (1616), reprinted in *The Works in Verse and Prose of Nicholas
Breton,* ed. Alexander B. Grosart (2 vols. 1879), *2*, 10, offers the following questions
and answers:

Q. What is most dangerous in a kingdome?
A. Civill Warre.
Q. What is most troublesome in a Common-wealth?
A. Sectes.

Breton says in *I Would and Would Not* (1614), *Works,* ed. Grosart, *1*, 11:

> I should be call'd but a Precizian:
> Or Formalist, and might goe preach alone,
> Unto my holy brother Puritan.

Henry Hutton's *Follies Anatomie* (1619), ed. E. F. Rimbault (1842), 35, takes a minor
dig at zeal:

> Purus doth sermons write, and scripture quote;
> And therfore may be tearm'd a man of note.

John Harington's *Epigrams Both Pleasant and Serious* (1615) was enlarged and republished as *The Most Elegant and Wittie Epigrams of Sir J. Harington* in 1618. They are to be dated, however, from about 1585 to 1603. Among them are a number which attack the Puritans with the economy of phrase which makes for a good epigram. Harington manages to cover many of the charges brought against the Puritans in the other forms of satire and in the serious writing: their hypocrisy, their hysterical fear of Rome, their overlong sermons, and the wild chatter of the female sectaries. One of the most pointed and least obviously indignant is "Of a Precise Taylor." The epigram tells the story of a Puritan tradesman: he is dishonest, is taken sick and reforms; then he listens to many sermons, keeps the Sabbath zealously, buys the Bible, and stops swearing. But he continues to cheat and steal. With that, the epigram ends. In 34 lines, rather more than average length, Harington has given a fairly detailed picture of the Puritan hypocrite with his excess of piety and great show of godliness.[3] The epigram, like

3. *The Letters and Epigrams of Sir John Harington,* ed. Norman E. McClure (Philadelphia, University of Pennsylvania Press, 1930), 52, dates the epigrams. "Of a Precise Taylor" is on 156. See also 155, "Of Blessing without a crosse"; 200, "Of a formall Minister"; 292, "Of certain puritan wenches"; 316, "Of a preacher and his Hourglass"; 317, "Of one that could not abide the crosse." *Certain Elegies, Done by Sundrie Excellent Wits* (1620), ed. Edward V. Utterson (1843), D6, has a good pun:

> Presbyter that of late his Parish crost,
> By his loose Living, hath his living lost . . .

One of the many versions of the Puritan, his cat and the Sabbath occurs in Richard Brathwaite's *Barnabees Journall* (1638?), ed. W. Carew Hazlitt *et al.* (1876), B2:

> To Banbery came I, O prophane one!
> Where I saw a Puritane-one,
> Hanging of his Cat on Monday,
> For killing of a mouse on Sonday.

It should be added, however, that Brathwaite also attacks the clergy for their ignorance (H7). John Taylor has some good lines on Puritan cats and Sabbath-breaking. Near the end of *The Praise of Hemp-Seed* (1620), *Workes* (1630), there is an extended anti-Puritan passage and the notable couplet:

> Suppose his Cat on Sunday killed a Rat,
> She on the Monday must be hang'd for that.

In *The Water-Cormorant,* "A Separatist," *Workes,* Taylor writes:

> Upon the Sabbath, they'l no Phisicke take,
> Lest it should worke, and so the Sabbath breake.

A similar quip appears in *The Distractions of Our Times* (1642). The literature, serious and flippant, on Sabbatarianism, is enormous.

Henry Peacham furnishes an example of the anti-Puritan epigram at its best. Peacham's epigram is quoted in *The Truth of Our Times* (1638), ed. Robert R. Cawley (Columbia University Press, New York, 1942), xviii:

> The Turkes hold this opinion very odde,
> That mad mens soules are talking still with God,
> And that to be an Ideot or a Vice,

that of Jonson on the preacher, gains in force by its shift from the general to the particular. The commonest tradition of the epigram and the character is the generalized statement. On the particular level, the two forms tend to merge in a single effect with better detail and color. One might call Harington's poem as accurately a character of one precisian as an epigram about a precisian.

In the years after 1640, the miscellanies came to be a chief medium for the dissemination of anti-Puritan characters and epigrams. Religion had been a fairly constant, although not major, theme in the characters and epigrams; in the miscellanies it had not commonly been treated. But in the later collections, Puritanism became a major subject. *Wits Recreations* (1640), for instance, a collection of epigrams, "Fancies and Fantasticks," and "Outlandish Proverbs," contains a good number of references to the Puritans. An assortment of popular reading, the book says nothing which is new: the Puritans are hot with zeal, hypocritical and factious. An epigram of two lines on the punishment of William Prynne, John Bastwick, and Henry Burton in 1637 rises above the average:

On Zelot.

Is Zelot pure? he is: yet see he wears
The signe of Circumcision in his ears.[4]

From about 1655 to the end of the century anti-Puritan verse flourished in the drolleries, collections devoted to making fun of the precisians.[5]

Is th'onely way to purchase Paradise:
If this be true their Alkarons relate,
Our Puritans were sure in happy state.

4. *Musarum Deliciae* (1656), *Wit Restor'd* (1658), and *Wits Recreations* (1640) are all reprinted in a two-volume collection (1817). "On Zelot" is in *2*, 131. Another, *2*, 30, repeats a theme which Ben Jonson had used:

'Tis not my person, nor my play,
But my sirname, Holiday,
That does offend thee, thy complaints
Are not against me, but the Saints;
So ill dost thou endure my name,
Because the Church doth like the same,
A name more awfull to the puritane
Then Talbot unto France, or Drake to Spaine.

See also *2*, 142, "On a Puritan"; *2*, 274, "An ancient Epitaph on Martin Mar-Prelate."

5. See Courtney D. C. Smith, "The Seventeenth-century Drolleries" (unpublished Harvard dissertation, 1944). Smith begins his account with *Musarum Deliciae* (1655) and ends with *Merry Drollery Complete* (1691). Anti-Puritan poetry continued, during and after the revolution, to appear in the miscellanies quite apart from the drolleries. See, for instance, *Parnassus Biceps* (1656), reprinted in an edition by G. Thorn-Drury in 1927, *3*, for an excellent anti-Puritan attack: "A Poem, In defence of the decent Ornaments of Christ-Church Oxon, occasioned by a Banbury brother, who called them Idolatries." Courtney D. C. Smith, "The Seventeenth-century Drolleries," *Harvard University Summaries of Theses 1943–1945* (Cambridge, 1947), 480, says: ". . . a drol-

A
SVVARME
OF
SFCTARIES, AND
SCHISMATIQVES:

Wherein is difcovered the ftrange preaching (or prating) of fuch as are by their trades
Coblers, Tinkers, Pedlers, Weavers, Sow-
gelders, and Chymney-Sweepers.

BY JOHN TAYLOR.

The Cobler preaches, and his Audience are
As wife as Moffe was, when he caught his Mare.

Printed luckily, and may be read unhappily, betwixt
hawke and buzzard, 1641.

In the variety of form and content, ranging from crude ballads and rhymes to the more sophisticated epigrams, the miscellanies continue the earlier tradition of anti-Puritan satire.

The average voice, serious or satiric, when it spoke against the Puritan, was often prejudiced either by passion or by the necessary distortion of humor. The baseless charges, such as hypocritical sexuality, are easily dismissed. But there is a residue of truth, and the residue is close to much which the serious writers had said. Figures as diverse as Donne, Harington, and John Taylor repeat the charge of immoderation among the Puritans; and the charge reflects Hooker's concern with the necessity for the use of reason in human affairs. That which endures from the satirists does connect in essential respects with the most important points of the serious writers.

Edmund Spenser and Puritanism

IN THE early years of the religious dispute, Edmund Spenser expressed in allegorical verse, satirical verse, and prose, opinions which are similar to those of the moderate Anglican. Bacon's impatience both with the corruptions of the right and with the extremes of the left suggests itself as Spenser writes on Puritanism in *The Shepheardes Calender* (1579); in *Prosopopoia. Or Mother Hubberds Tale,* a part of *Complaints* (1591); in *The Faerie Queene* (1590, 1595); and in *A View of the Present State of Ireland,* entered for publication in 1598.[1]

---

lery, in both intention and result, is an anthology of miscellaneous verse, never really dignified in nature, which was compiled by the Cavaliers for the sake of registering protest against the Puritans in a jocose, mocking and often frankly sensual fashion."

1. H. S. V. Jones, *A Spenser Handbook* (New York, Crofts, 1930), 377: "By internal evidence Spenser's *A View of the Present State of Ireland* may be dated 1594-1597 . . . On April 14, 1598, the book was entered for publication . . . the *View* was not published until 1633, when it appeared in Sir James Ware's *Historie of Ireland, Collected by Three Learned Authors.*" Frederick M. Padelford has discussed Spenser's religious opinions in a series of five articles. In "Spenser and the Puritan Propaganda," *Modern Philology, 11* (1913), 85–106, Padelford finds that Spenser was Low Church, but that he realized that the church was badly in need of reform. "Spenser and the Theology of Calvin," *Modern Philology, 12* (1914), 1–18; and "Spenser's Fowre Hymnes," *Journal of English and Germanic Philology, 13* (1914), 418–33, describe Spenser's theology as strongly Calvinistic, which is to say normally Anglican for the time. In "Spenser's Arraignment of the Anabaptists," *Journal of English and Germanic Philology, 12* (1913), 434–48, Padelford argues that Bk. v of *The Faerie Queene* contains a specific attack on the Anabaptists. "Spenser and the Spirit of Puritanism," *Modern Philology, 14* (1916), 31–44, makes the estimate that the poet was strongly sympathetic to much of the Puritan program, but that he was impatient of religious excesses. Virgil K. Whitaker in *The Religious Basis of Spenser's Thought* (Stanford, Stanford University Press, 1950), 7, says: ". . . all his works from the *Shepheardes Calender* on reveal the same religious viewpoint and that he apparently accepted the Elizabethan Settlement . . ." Whitaker, 69, agrees with other critics on Spenser and Puritanism: "For the Puritans Spenser has little sympathy except in so far as their demand for an honest and educated clergy agrees with his."

However, the frequency with which Spenser echoes the demand for the reform of abuses shows that he sympathizes with one section of the Puritan program. Specific charges of ecclesiastical corruption, so common in the controversial writing, appear in the May, July, and September Eclogues of *The Shepheardes Calender*. In the May poem, Piers and Palinode represent "two formes of pastoures or Ministers, or the protestant and the Catholique . . ." [2] In the argument between them on the nature and the function of the clergy, there is both a general agreement in favor of Puritan reform and specific support of one of the reformers. Piers speaks throughout the poem against ministers who neglect their parishes, who do not preach and teach, and who live in luxury. The imagery of the passage, centered around the neglectful shepherd, is too common in verse and prose, from Chaucer's parson on, to be anything but the stock description of ecclesiastical corruption; however, it is true that Milton echoed the tone of the passage and a good deal of the vocabulary and imagery both in "Lycidas" and the anti-prelatical writings: reforming Anglican and extreme Puritan can join hands without great difficulty. [3] Spenser, to a degree, looks to the ecclesiastical primitivism of the Elizabethan polemicists for his argument. He is not so simple as to say that anything which was not in the original church

2. *The Poetical Works of Edmund Spenser*, ed. J. C. Smith and E. De Selincourt (Oxford, Oxford University Press, 1924), *The Shepheardes Calender*, "May," 435.

3. *Ibid.*, ll. 43–50:

> Thilke same bene shepeheards for the Devils stedde,
> That playen, while their flockes be unfedde.
> Well is it seene, their sheepe bene not their owne,
> That letten them runne at randon alone.
> But they bene hired for little pay
> Of other, that caren as little as they,
> What fallen the flocke, so they han the fleece,
> And get all the gaine, paying but a peece.

This, and the context of the passage, were probably in Milton's mind in "Lycidas," ll. 123 ff.:

> . . . their lean and flashy songs
> Grate on their scrannel Pipes of wretched straw,
> The hungry Sheep look up, and are not fed . . .

In addition, the lines which follow:

> Besides what the grim Wolf with privy paw
> Daily devours apace, and nothing said . . .

are very similar to ll. 127–8 of the May Eclogue:

> There crept in Wolves, ful of fraude and guile,
> That often devoured their owne sheepe . . .

Milton quotes the Eclogue in *Animadversions* (*Works*, ed. Patterson, *3*, 166), and later (170) says:

> . . . they have fed themselves, and not their flocks, with force and cruelty have they ruled over Gods people . . .

cannot now be used (a trap which was later to ensnare John Milton), but Spenser does have Piers remind Palinode that the income of the church once came only from parishioners: lands and accumulated money have brought decay. The gloss to the passage plainly states that Piers is denouncing the corruption of the Roman Catholic church and of all clergy who live as parasities upon their charges; but the gloss also says that the passage contains no attack on the government of the Anglican church.[4] In a reference to Archbishop Grindal as Algrind, Piers reinforces the argument for virtue and simplicity in the lives of the clergy with a stricture from a man already in disgrace with the queen for his refusal to suppress the Puritan prophesyings.[5] The opinions in the May Eclogue are consequently neither those of a thoroughgoing Anglican opposed to all change, nor those of a Puritan who would raze and rebuild the church. Above all, Spenser would remedy ignorance and neglect: this is the chief burden of Piers' argument. In addition, Spenser believes that luxury corrupts and that the priest should seek virtue by simplicity of living. The reform of church government is undesirable, and on this question Spenser is clearly unsympathetic to a large section of Puritan thought. Although Milton later was to echo Spenser to the point of striking similarities of phrase in the description of clerical abuses, Spenser is so much the Anglican that in respect to polity he furnishes Milton with nothing. The traditionalist, writing in favor of an imperfect but working order, parts from the evolving Presbyterian out of patience with faults and sure of a church divinely ordered.

In the July Eclogue, Spenser again offers Grindal as the ideal of clerical virtue, makes further charges of corruption in the Anglican

4. Spenser, *Works, The Shepheardes Calender*, "May," ll. 103 ff.:

> The time was once, and may againe retorne,
> (For ought may happen, that hath bene beforne)
> When shepheards had none inheritaunce,
> Ne of land, nor fee in sufferaunce:
> But what might arise of the bare sheepe . . .
> Lulled the shepeheards in such securitie,
> That not content with loyall obeysaunce,
> Some gan to gape for greedie governaunce . . .

"Glosse," 440: "Some gan . . . Nought here spoken, as of purpose to deny fatherly rule and godly governaunce (as some malitiously of late have done to the great unreste and hinderaunce of the Churche) but to display the pride and disorder of such, as in steede of feeding their sheepe, indeede feede of their sheepe."

5. *Ibid.*, ll. 73 ff.:

> Ah Palinodie, thou art a worldes childe:
> Who touches Pitch mought needes be defilde.
> But shepheards (as Algrind used to say,)
> Mought not live ylike, as men of the laye . . .
> But shepheard must walke another way,
> Sike worldly souenance he must foresay.

church, and warns of the dangers of infection from Rome. The dialogue between the two shepherds is nominally over the worth of high land as opposed to low land for pasture; Thomalin, a good shepherd, defends low land as less dangerous and better for the sheep. In one speech, Grindal is applauded twice for having recommended humility and plain living; and the passage ends with a description of the luxury in which the Roman clergy live. The Eclogue ends with a reference to Grindal's sequestration, the story of the eagle which dropped a shellfish on Algrin's head and wounded him; presently he will recover. The emblem for Thomalin the good shepherd is: "In medio virtus." [6] The July Eclogue thus repeats the reforms proposed in the May Eclogue; it repeats the praise of Grindal; and it adds a warning of the dangers of Romish practices. Spenser plainly is again speaking in the manner of the moderate reformer: he is Low Church, he is for a purified church, but he is not for a revolutionized church. His suspicion of Romish elements is not hysterical, but he does regard overemphasis on form as dangerous in that it tends to belittle moral instruction, a prime concern of a vigorous faith. In the September Eclogue there is little more than the pretext of allegory; the poem is a statement of the wisdom of the shepherd who sticks to simple living and familiar ground for his sheep. Diggon has just returned from a trip which was intended to fatten the flock by giving it new pasturage; Hobbinol questions Diggon about the state of his flock and he launches into a denunciation of venality, ignorance, and pride in the clergy. The tone of the Eclogue is consonant with the others

6. *Ibid.*, "July," 444, ll. 99–105; 125 ff.; 173 ff.:

> And he that strives to touch the starres,
>   oft stombles at a strawe,
> Alsoone may shepheard climbe to skye,
>   that leades in lowly dales,
> As Goteherd prowd that sitting hye,
>   upon the Mountaine sailes . . .
>
> Such one he was, (as I have heard
>   old Algrind often sayne)
> That whilome was the first shepheard,
>   and lived with little gaine:
> As meeke he was, as meeke mought be,
>   simple, as simple sheepe . . .
>
> They bene yclad in purple and pall,
>   so hath their god them blist,
> They reigne and rulen over all,
>   and lord it, as they list . . .

The gloss to the passage reads: "In purple) Spoken of the Popes and Cardinalles, which use such tyrannical colours and pompous painting."
Ibid., ll. 229 ff.:

> . . . Ah good Algrin, his hap was ill,
>   but shall be better in time.

which deal with religion.[7] In addition, Thenot's tale of the oak and the brier in the February Eclogue clearly has some religious meaning: the oak is a form of the old church, or Roman Catholicism, and the brier is a new or Anglican church. But no detailed interpretation is possible; and there is no reason for connecting the passage specifically with Puritanism.[8]

The Puritan argument for reform is implicit in one section of *Mother Hubberds Tale,* but satiric indirection replaces the allegory of *The Shepheardes Calender.* The fox and the ape, traveling on the road, meet a priest. There follows a conversation in which the three of them talk about how to get a living and how to rise in the church; in the course of the account of the way to preferment Spenser uses the standard devices of irony, wit, and exaggeration to portray the evil state of the clergy. The priest who is speaking is illiterate; but ignorance is best, for learning only gives rise to religious dissension. By natural wit, the priest counsels the travelers, a man can reach great heights in the church. When the ape objects to the responsibility involved in feeding souls, the priest points out that the only requirement is that the spiritual pastor should place the food before the sinner; all duty is then fulfilled. As for advancement in the church, the aid of a nobleman, or cringing sycophancy at court helps: the man of God will get an easy living and perhaps a position of importance. Through the priest's good advice, the ape is ordained, the fox is his clerk, and the two get a benefice. Unfortunately, they are so riotously corrupt that they get into trouble with the ecclesiastical authorities and have to skip out, after having sold their living to the priest next door.[9] The passage is religious satire at its best: there is no

---

7. *Ibid., The Shepheardes Calender,* "September," 452. Diggon's speech begins with l. 25. He says of the shepherds:

> They setten to sale their shops of shame,
> And maken a Mart of their good name.
> The shepheards there robben one another,
> And layen baites to beguile her brother.

James J. Higginson in *Spenser's Shepherd's Calender* (New York, Columbia University Press, 1912), 71–162, discusses the eclogue in detail. Of the May, July, and September Eclogues, Padelford in "Spenser and the Puritan Propaganda," 19, says: "There can be no question that in these eclogues Spenser condemns in strongest terms the pomp and greed of worldly-minded ecclesiastics, their love of office for its own sake, of soft living, of fat benefices, of fine linen and robes . . ."

8. Thenot's tale in the February Eclogue is from ll. 98 to 239 (*Works,* ed. Smith and De Selincourt, pp. 425–6). See Whitaker, *The Religious Basis of Spenser's Thought,* 11.

9. Spenser, *Works, Mother Hubberds Tale,* 498–501, ll. 383 ff.:

> . . . Ne tell a written word, ne write a letter . . .
> Of such deep learning little had he neede,
> Ne yet of Latine, ne of Greeke, that breede
> Doubts mongst Divines, and difference of texts,
> From whence arise diversitie of sects . . .
> For they must feed themselves, doo what we can.

angry protest at the condition of the church; but in the accumulation of ironic observations the corrupt priest gives the animals advice on how to succeed in a thoroughly unchristian establishment. If the ape turns out to be a bit too evil even for a priest, he at least has no trouble in disposing profitably of his cure before he leaves for his next adventure.[1] The satire obviously complements the allegory of *The Shepheardes Calender,* and *The Shepheardes Calender* in turn approves a part of the reform program of the two Admonitions; at the same time, Spenser is to furnish Milton, the reforming Presbyterian of the early 40's, with a part of his program.

But there is still another side to Spenser's opinion of Puritanism. If Spenser agrees with Cartwright on the reform of abuses, several passages in *The Faerie Queene* and in *A View of the Present State of Ireland* plainly disapprove of haughty preciseness, excessive religious dissension, and violence in pronouncements on doctrine. In *The Faerie Queene,* ". . . that ungracious crew which faines demurest grace . . ." seems plainly a pejorative reference to the Puritans, their zeal, and their traditional hypocrisy.[2] The sour Elissa, scorning worldly entertainment and sitting in stony immobility, is the embodiment of the Aristotelian evil of the extreme of "too little." But in addition, she frowns on pleasure, and with her suitor Sir Huddibras, described as "Sterne melancholy" and the "Malecontent," the pair have many of the characteristics of the dourest of the stock Puritans.[3] In the story of Artegall,

---

> We are but charg'd to lay the meate before:
> Eate they that list, we need to doo no more . . .

1. Padelford in "Spenser and the Puritan Propaganda," 10, says of the satire of *Mother Hubberds Tale:* "Spenser is thus found to voice the general Puritan complaint of the prevailing ignorance of the lower clergy, of the subordination and neglect of preaching, of vestments, of impropriations and advowsons, and of plural livings . . . he must be classed with the Low Churchmen of the type of Grindal, Jewel, and Pilkington, bishops who accepted the organization of the church, preferred that vestments should not be used—though they yielded this point for the sake of harmony—and steadily strove to correct those abuses in the church that sprang from ignorance or worldliness."

2. Spenser, *Works, The Faerie Queene,* 403, Bk. vii, Canto vii, stanza 35:

> And after her, came jolly June, arrayd
> All in greene leaves, as he a Player were;
> Yet in his time, he wrought as well as playd,
> That by his plough—irons mote right well appeare:
> Upon a Crab he rode, that him did beare
> With crooked crawling steps an uncouth pase,
> And backward yode, as Bargemen wont to fare
> Bending their force contrary to their face,
> Like that ungracious crew which faines demurest grace.

3. *Ibid., The Faerie Queene,* 79, Bk. ii, Canto ii, stanza 35:

> Elissa (so the eldest hight) did deeme
> Such entertainment base, ne ought would eat,
> Ne ought would speake, but evermore did seeme
> As discontent for want of merth or meat . . .

Talus, and the giant, there is at least an attack on the political and economic theories of radical groups, and possibly an attack on the Anabaptists. Artegall comes upon a giant who is haranguing a mob; the mob is being misled by his promises of benefits and uncontrolled freedom, and Artegall denounces the giant for misleading the people.[4] Whether or not Spenser is attacking the Anabaptists is of little consequence; if he is, everyone from archbishops to Brownists attacked the Anabaptists: the word was a synonym for riot and rebellion. But as an attack on the sects in general, the passage does indicate once more that Spenser was opposed to the violent destruction of established social and political patterns. Later in the narrative, the Blatant Beast is, like the giant, noisy, and Jonson believed that in the Blatant Beast ". . . the Puritans were understood . . ." The beast's activities make it clear that he is the sin of calumniation.[5] Recent critical opinion has not generally supported Jonson, although calumniation could certainly be charged against the Puritan extremists. Thus, with exceptional uniformity, Spenser's allegory aligns him with the Anglican apologists from Whitgift on, although Spenser offers no divine justification for the order as does Whitgift, nor the justification of human reason, as does Hooker. The dominant tone of *A View of the Present State of Ireland,* despite passages of harshness, is of conciliation and mildness. Indeed, part of Spenser's program is the restoration of ruined Roman Catholic churches in Ireland, since outward appearance impresses simple worshipers. The recommendation is scarcely that of an extremist, Anglican or Puritan.[6]

For a discussion of her as the personification of Moral Deficiency or "too little," see *The Works of Edmund Spenser: A Variorum Edition,* ed. Edwin Greenlaw *et al.* (10 vols. Baltimore, Johns Hopkins Press, 1932–49), *2,* 201. Sir Huddibras, who supplies the name for Butler's Puritan hero, is described in Bk. II, Canto ii, stanzas 17 and 37. In Spenser, Huddibras particularly represents the extreme of rashness. See *A Variorum Edition, 2,* 198.

4. *Ibid., The Faerie Queene,* 284–6, Bk. v, Canto ii, stanzas 32–54. Stanza 33 marks the passage clearly as being directed against revolutionary teachings:

> Therefore the vulgar did about him flocke,
> And cluster thicke unto his leasings vaine,
> Like foolish flies about an hony crocke,
> In hope by him great benefite to gaine,
> And uncontrolled freedome to obtaine . . .

5. *Ibid., The Faerie Queene,* Bk. VI, Canto vi, stanza 12:

> . . . This hellish Dog, that hight the Blatant Beast;
> A wicked Monster, that his tongue doth whet
> Gainst all, both good and bad, both most and least . . .

The beast appears at the end of Bk. v and throughout VI. Jonson's opinion is in *Ben Jonson,* ed. C. H. Herford and Percy Simpson, *1* and *2, The Man and His Work* (Oxford, Oxford University Press, 1925), *1,* 137. For a discussion of the Blatant Beast, see the *Variorum Edition, 6,* 382–3.

6. *A Variorum Edition, 10, Spenser's Prose Works,* 221–3: ". . . in plantinge of religion thus muche is nedefull to be observed that it be not soughte forciblie to be im-

Spenser is like Bacon in many respects, although Bacon is obviously less interested in what is religiously right than in what is socially convenient. The end and aim of Spenser's program is Christian virtue, and that virtue is best attained by moderation and a regard for religious and social order within the Anglican establishment. Excessive zeal in the display or practice of virtues, and devotion to overelaborate worship are equally violations of the motto of the good shepherd Thomalin. Spenser speaks as the reforming Anglican on the ordering of the church and the teaching of the people.

---

pressed into them with terrour and sharpe penalties as now is the mannour, but rather delivered and intymated with mildenes and gentlenes soe as it maie not be hated before it be understode . . . nexte Care in religion is to be builde upp and repaire all the Ruined Churches wheareof the moste parte lie even withe the grounde . . . for the outwarde shewe asure your selfe dothe greatlye drawe the rude people to the reverensinge and frequentinge thearof what ever some of our late too nice foles saie that theare is nothinge in the semelye forme and Comelye order of the Churche." Jones in *A Spenser Handbook*, 384, says: "In the *View* Spenser is both tolerant and uncompromisingly ruthless, both critical and credulous."

3. The Puritans and the Stage

The Puritan Attack on the Stage

THE TRADITION of Puritan hostility to the stage was based on a long series of attacks from pamphleteers, writers of books, and preachers; the attacks, generally dull and undistinguished, came from men who could often be branded as Puritan, or from sympathizers with various elements of the Puritan program of reform.[1] By comparison, the Anglican clergy have little to say against the theater. An amount of disapproval is apparent, but there is none of the heated denunciation which is found in a number of Puritan writers. Launcelot Andrewes, for instance, mildly rebukes the Sunday playgoers with a quotation from St. Augustine, and the chief objection is plainly that the theater is open on Sunday.[2]

However, there appears to have been no very early union of Puritan forces against the stage, nor, on the other hand, of the dramatists against the Puritans. The play *Lusty Juventus* (1550) supports justification by faith and is bitterly anti-Roman, but *Respublica* (1553) supports the Roman Catholic church. The variety of opinion which had appeared on the stage indicates at least that there was no unanimity of religious feeling.[3] By 1577, however, a notable attack was made on the stage

1. Detailed analyses of the attack on the stage are given in E. N. S. Thompson, *The Controversy between the Puritans and the Stage* (New York, Holt, 1903), "The Puritan Attack on the Stage," 9–191; in J. Dover Wilson's article, "The Puritan Attack upon the Stage," *CHEL, 6*, 421–61; and in William Ringler's *Stephen Gosson* (Princeton, Princeton University Press, 1942), "The Attack on the Stage," 53–82. Thompson and Wilson both see the attack as something which came from Puritanism. Ringler, on the other hand, says, 80: "It is unfortunate that scholars have labelled this early attack on the stage 'the Puritan attack,' for such a label obscures some of the fundamental issues involved."

2. *A Patterne of Catechisticall Doctrine* (1630), 244.

3. The dates of plays are of the first performances as recorded or estimated in Alfred Harbage's *Annals of English Drama* (Philadelphia, University of Pennsylvania Press, 1940). The plays were edited by John S. Farmer in 1907, 1908, and 1907, respectively. The diversity of religious opinion expressed by the stage is discussed in E. N. S. Thompson's *The English Moral Play, Transactions of the Connecticut Academy of Arts and Sciences, 14* (New Haven, 1910), 291–413. Thompson lists, 365–71, Puritan, Roman Catholic, and anti-Roman Catholic plays in the sixteenth century. C. F. Tucker Brooke says in *The Tudor Drama* (Boston, Houghton Mifflin, 1911), 83: "The religious controversy of the later years of Henry VIII and the animosities incident to the reigns of Edward VI and Mary were prolific of dramas which, under cover of abstract figures, supported one or another of the factions in Church and State." Brooke lists, 100–1, *John, King of England* (1536), *John Baptist's Preaching in the Wilderness* (1538), *God's*

by John Northbrooke, a conforming divine, who disapproved in particular the abuse of the Sabbath: *"A Treatise wherein Dicing, Dauncing, Vaine playes, or Enterluds, with other idle pastimes, &c., commonly used on the Sabboth day, are reproved by the Authoritie of the word of God and auntient writers . . ."* [4] The treatise consists of a dialogue in which Age, speaking to Youth, condemns immoral, obscene, and profane plays, as well as the presentation of plays on Sunday. At one point in the discussion Age proposes that the plays be preserved in the schools for instruction in music and poetry. But the author believes that the evils attendant on the public gatherings where plays are given are so serious that the theaters should be closed.[5] If by 1577 a section of opinion favored the closing of the theater, later years saw the spread of that opinion: the objections to the theater remained the same. Stephen Gosson, the reformed playwright, furnished in 1579 a more voluminous account of the sins of the stage, and ended like Northbrooke with the recommendation that the drama be suppressed. *The Schoole of Abuse, Conteining a plesaunt invective against Poets, Pipers, Players, Jesters, and such like Caterpillers of a Commonwelth* is written with a touch lighter than Northbrooke's, but there are the same old charges. For his attack, Gosson draws less on classical authority and the church fathers and more on the common reputation of the theater. The argument of moral instruction has no validity to Gosson, for there are preachers to teach, and the representation of vice does not cure vice. The whole stage and its environment have degenerated to a point where they are a breeding place of immorality. Decent folk, Gosson concludes, will shun the theater.[6]

A Reply to Stephen Gosson's School of Abuse (1580?), also known as *A Defense of Poetry, Music, and Stage Plays,* is an answer from Thomas Lodge.[7] The pamphlet is moderate, and considers in a calm man-

---

Promises (1538), *The Temptation of Our Lord* (1538), *New Custom* (1563), *Robin Conscience* (1550) and *John Bon and Mast Parson* (n.d.). The dates of production are from Harbage.

4. Ed. John P. Collier (1843). Brooke, *The Tudor Drama,* 427–8, says: "A sermon preached at Paul's Cross by one Thomas White, December 9, 1576, denounces the 'sumptuous theatre houses, a continual monument of London's prodigality and folly,' and the distinctive names of the original playhouses, The Theatre and The Curtain, are mentioned both by John Northbrook in his Treatise against 'Dicing, Dauncing, Vaine playes, or Enterluds, with other idle pastimes,' licensed in 1577, and in a sermon delivered by John Stockwood in 1578."

5. *A Treatise,* 86, 104.

6. *The School of Abuse,* ed. Edward Arber (1868), 31; 35–6. Gosson's *The Ephemerides of Phialo* (1579) and *An Apologie of the Schoole of Abuse* (1579), ed. 1868, continue the attack without the addition of new arguments. Ringler in *Stephen Gosson,* 80, points out that Gosson was not a Puritan.

7. The pamphlet is reprinted in *The Complete Works of Thomas Lodge,* ed. E. W. Gosse, the Hunterian Club (4 vols. Glasgow, 1883), *1.* Items in the edition are separately paged.

ner the arguments on both sides. There is a sound attack on the position
that classical authorities disapproved of the theater; drama, the pamphlet
concludes, can be a great force for good, and if the modern theater is
evil, it is reform which is needed, not suppression.[8] Gosson produced a
sour rebuttal: *Playes Confuted in Five Actions* (1582). A cast of
earnestness has come over Gosson's style: he calls on classical authority, and the church fathers are mentioned more frequently than in
the *Schoole of Abuse. Playes Confuted* repeats the old arguments; in
addition, the author now objects to the boys dressed as women and
concludes that the plays are a relic of heathen worship. Gosson's attack
was ended. However, the anonymous *Pleasant Quippes for Upstart New-
fangled Gentlewomen* (1595), possibly by him, contains several slurs at
the actors and the stage.[9] Lodge withdrew from the dispute in the
dedication of his *Alarum against Usurers* (1584).[1] Northbrooke had
crystallized the traditional attack on the stage; Gosson had echoed
Northbrooke. Lodge had supported moderation, but moderation was not
to be practiced either in the attacks or in the answers which came from
the dramatists.[2]

The general subject of English morality furnishes occasions for denunciations of the plays. Philip Stubbes' *The Anatomie of Abuses in
England* (1583) [3] is a compendium of Elizabethan follies, among which
the theater is numbered. In the entire book, only a few pages deal with
the corruptions of the plays, but these pages review the old charges with
vigor and end with the threat of suppression. The preface to the first
edition makes an allowance for the drama: many plays have worth
through their moral examples.[4] But this preface is later omitted,[5] and at
any rate the section of the text on the drama is entirely at variance with
the preface. The few pages headed "Of Stage-playes, and Enterluds, with
their wickednes" is a thoroughgoing curse on all actors and acting. Plays

8. William Ringler, "The Source of Lodge's *Reply to Gosson,*" *The Review of English Studies, 15* (1939), 164–71, demonstrates that almost every important statement in the
pamphlet had been plagiarized. Lodge's pamphlet is reprinted as "A Defence of Poetry"
in *Elizabethan Critical Essays,* ed. G. G. Smith (Oxford, Oxford University Press,
1904), *1,* 61–86. The confusion in titles is due to the fact that the title page is missing
from the two known copies of the original edition.

9. The pamphlet has been edited by E. J. Howard (Oxford, Ohio, Anchor Press,
1942). Howard points out that the ascribing of the pamphlet to Gosson is the result of a
Collier forgery.

1. *Works,* ed. Gosse, *1.*

2. Two anonymous attacks, *News from the North* (1579) and *A Second and Third
Blast of Retrait from the Plaies and Theatres* (1580) repeat the Sabbatarian argument
and the general charge of immorality. They add nothing new to Gosson's denunciation.
J. O. Halliwell-Phillipps, *Outlines of the Life of Shakespeare* (6th ed. 1886), *1,* 344,
contains an extract from *News from the North.*

3. Ed. F. J. Furnivall (1879).

4. *Ibid.,* x.

5. In the editions of August, 1583; 1585; and 1595.

which treat of profane subjects corrupt the onlooker; plays which treat of sacred subjects are blasphemous. The drama has no value as instruction, and the environment of the playhouse is such that the actors and the audience are alike infected.[6] There is the usual objection to the violation of the Sabbath, and the reader is finally warned: ". . . avoid all the vanities and deceivable pleasure of this life . . . it is unpossible to wallowe in the delights and pleasures of this World, and to live in joy for ever in the Kingdom of Heaven." [7] A number of minor attacks were made in the tone and spirit of Stubbes. George Whetstone's *An Addition: or Touchstone for the Time* (1584) repeats the Sabbatarian argument,[8] and William Rankins' *The Mirrour of Monsters* (1587) describes plays as ". . . the subtile slights of Sathan, making them his instruments." [9]

Far above the level of the repetitious invective against the stage is Sir Philip Sidney's *The Defense of Poesie* (1595). *The Schoole of Abuse* had been dedicated to Sidney, and sections of the *Defense* may have been written as a refutation of Gosson's opinions.[1] However, Sidney's essay is concerned only slightly with the denunciation of the theater. He believes in the moral power of tragedy and deplores the fact that comedy has come to "stirre laughter in sinfull things." The faults could be mended if the authors would return to the classical ideals of dramatic writing.[2] Gabriel Harvey, by contrast, writes patronizingly of "malconceived comedie," but he gives no detailed account of abuses and he suggests no cure.[3]

To a slight extent, Martin Marprelate furthered the attack: in *Martin Junior's Epilogue,* attached to the *Theses Martinianae* (1589), the players are denounced for not earning an honest living, and are cursed with ". . . the crowne of Canterburie . . . these prelates, these popes, these devils . . ." [4] The invective may be an answer to attacks on Martin from the stage. Thomas Heywood's *An Apology for Actors* (1612) called forth a Puritan answer in *A Refutation of the Apology for Actors* (1615). The pamphlet consists of an elaborate diatribe against the players and the lines they speak; nothing new is added to the old objections. The

6. *The Anatomy of Abuses,* ed. Furnivall, 140–6.
7. *Ibid.,* 191.
8. In *A Mirour for Magistrates of Cities* (1584).
9. Quoted in Thompson, *The Controversy between the Puritans and the Stage,* 88. See G. G. Smith's *Elizabethan Critical Essays, 1,* 61–3, for a summary of the earlier documents in the dispute.
1. Sir Philip Sidney, *The Defense of Poesy,* ed. Albert S. Cook (Boston, 1890), xiv.
2. *The Complete Works of Sir Philip Sidney,* ed. Albert Feuillerat (Cambridge, University Press, 1923), *3,* 38–41.
3. *The Works of Gabriel Harvey,* ed. Alexander B. Grosart (2 vols. 1884–85), *1* (1884), 125.
4. *The Marprelate Tracts,* ed. William Pierce, 328, 330.

attack is perhaps representative in that it sums up all that has been said and ends with the usual plea that the theaters be closed.[5] John Rain lds in *Th' Overthrow of Stage-plays* (Middleburg, 1599), quotes classical authority for the damnation of the theater; the discussion of the boy actors is extensive and makes specific charges.[6] *The Rich Cabnit Furnished with Varietie of Descriptions* (1616) finds that the drama has lost its high moral purpose.[7] *A Short Treatise against Stage-Playes* (1625) is an orderly array of scriptural arguments against the stage; in addition, the unknown author asserts that the drama started with pagan rites, passed to the Greeks and Romans, and finally through the Roman Catholic church to England. Vice in London is the general subject of Richard Rawlidge's *A Monster Lately Found out* (1628), but the plays are marked as a special sin.

During the years of attack from the pamphlets and books, the Puritan pulpit had not been silent. The clergy were not preoccupied with the suppression of the drama, yet they did speak on the subject often enough to leave no doubt about their sympathies. Their denunciations are marked generally by immoderate terms and by a uniform desire to see the theaters closed and plays, private and public, forbidden. William Perkins in a sermon printed in 1606 found the plays evil because of the boy actors, the profane use of sacred subjects, and the frivolous display of human vanity.[8] The complaints are numerous and follow consistent

5. Reprinted in Thomas Heywood, *An Apology for Actors,* ed. Richard H. Perkinson (New York, Scholars' Facsimiles, 1941).

6. Most writers are content to say that the practice is contrary to Scripture. Rainolds, 8–19, is blunt enough to say that boys dressed in women's clothes encourage homosexuality in the theater. J. Dover Wilson, "The Puritan Attack upon the Stage," *CHEL, 6,* 421–61, says (449–50): "When therefore, William Gager of Christ Church, a well known Latin dramatist, and John Rainolds, an eminent theologian, afterwards president of Corpus Christi, crossed swords, in 1592, on the subject of the propriety of the academic play, they were fighting over old ground . . . Gager sent his opponent a printed copy of his *Ulysses Redux* . . . *Th' Overthrow of Stage-Playes* printed at Middleburg in 1599, attacks both this and a comedy by Gager known as *Rivales,* at the same time setting forth at full length his objections to all forms of dramatic representation. Gager, like other stage apologists, had appealed to antiquity: Rainolds refers him to a Roman praetor's decree against actors. Gager's performers, moreover, had twice broken divine law, first in playing on the Sabbath and, secondly, by donning women's clothes. The latter point, a stock argument in the puritan portfolio, is treated with overwhelming fulness. Gager's elaborate reply . . . is claimed as one of the most graceful and convincing of the treatises in answer to the puritan attack . . . Rainolds was in no mind to allow his adversary the last word. After a delay occasioned by sickness, he produced, on 30 May 1593, a very lengthy reply in which, however, he did little more than recapitulate and enlarge his previous arguments." A footnote to the last sentence adds: "This is also to be found in *Th' Overthrow of Stage-Playes.*"

7. Extracts are reprinted in *The English Drama and Stage,* ed. William C. Hazlitt (1869), 228–30. Of William Vaughan's book, *The Golden-grove, Moralized in Three Books* (1600), Smith, in *Elizabethan Critical Essays, 2,* 325, says: "Book i, chap. 51, entitled 'Whether Stage Playes ought to be suffred in a Commonwealth?' is a diatribe against plays as mere folly and wickedness: the literary problem is not discussed."

8. William Perkins, *The Whole Treatise of the Cases of Conscience* (1606), ed. 1651, 343–4.

patterns.[9] The divines have two principal objections to the stage: the violation of the Sabbath, and the actors dressed in women's clothing. On the first count, the writer usually describes the theaters as cesspools of sin, but the sins are Sunday sins. Almost never does the preacher denounce the theaters only for their weekday trespasses. The explanation may be that the Sabbatarian argument was a sound point for the opening of the indictment; the rest followed easily. On the question of men in women's clothing, there is a general disinclination to discuss the practice in terms more specific than those of biblical prohibitions; John Rainolds is exceptional in that he says that the practice is bad and gives reasons. From the scriptural objections there foll ow the moral objections to drunkenness, disorderly conduct, lewd actions, and extreme levity. The sermon agrees with the tract, while the books and pamphlets from writers of unknown religious leanings fortify a cause easily associated with the asceticism of one part of Puritan thought.

The attacks on the theater received the reinforcement of the heaviest artillery with the publication of William Prynne's *Histrio-Mastix. The Players Scourge* (1633). The book is divided into two parts or "tragedies," and it repeats to tedium every argument which had been arrayed to prove that the English stage was an evil damned by scriptural and classical authority alike. The plays are the work of the devil and their subject matter is filthy and profane. The actors are no better than what they play; their lives are the model of immorality, while the audiences are no better than the actors. All is enforced with marginal notes consisting of laws and opinions, ancient and modern, holy and profane, against the theater. The second section of *Histrio-Mastix* is for the most part a repetition of the first and a refutation of possible arguments in favor of the theater. Despite the great length of the book, there is no contribution to the attack; the volume is rather another copy of all that has come before. Its faults are the intolerance which forbids serious acceptance of its arguments, and its naïve ignorance of the drama; others had written with less copiousness, but more convincing detail, on the sins of the stage. Prynne's attack is almost sufficient reason alone for the hatred between the stage and the Puritans. The book is singularly unfair in its presentation of evidence and opinion: the faults of the drama are numbered over, but little is said of its virtues. Prynne's central

9. Typical attacks on the stage occur in John Norden, *A Progresse of Pietie* (Oxenbridge, 1596), ed. Cambridge, England, 1847, 177; Thomas Beard, *The Theatre of Gods Judgements* (1597), ed. 1643, 147, 150; Robert Bolton, *A Discourse about the State Of True Happinesse* (1611), ed. 1614, 73, 74; Lewis Bayly, *The Practise of Pietie* (1613), ed. 1792, 169; and Daniel Dyke, *Two Treatises. The One, of Repentance, The Other, of Christs Temptations* (1616), 216. The texts most commonly quoted in the denunciations of the theater are Exod. 20:8: "Remember the sabbath day, to keep it holy," and Deut. 22:5: "A woman shall not wear that which pertaineth unto a man, neither shall a man put on a woman's garment: for whosoever doeth these things is an abomination unto the Lord thy God."

objection is that of his contemporaries: the theater is an evil force in English life both because of the contents of the plays and the environment of the playhouse. In addition, there was in the attack an element which skirted the edge of sedition, a tactless slur on the king and queen in the strictures against lovers of private theatricals.[1] The queen was interested enough in the drama to have acted in a play just before or just after the appearance of *Histrio-Mastix,* and Prynne damned women on the stage.[2]

Laud brought the offending writer before the Star Chamber; the attitudes of all those concerned with the trial demonstrate that the dispute between the Puritans and the stage now had overtones at least as important as the original theme of reform. Prynne was charged with libel, but the stage was not defended at all: the chamber admitted that the corruption and license of the theater was extreme.[3] Prynne's fault was in the slur on the royal name. The accusers observed of the writer: ". . . there never arose such a pestilent, factious, seditious person, both in Church and State, and soe great an enemy to both."[4] He was convicted of sedition. Nowhere does it appear that the prosecution feels the attack on the theater immoderate; nor, certainly, could immoderation have been a fault sufficient to bring the miscreant before the Star Chamber. Prynne had simply ventured into areas where politics, religion, and public morals became one. Insofar as the crown was involved in supporting the theater, or in participating in the plays, an attack on the theater could well be seditious. For the Puritan, the stage was connected with the question of Christian morality: could the Christian church approve of the corrupt stage? The stage was likewise connected with the question of scriptural authority: do the Scriptures allow stage performances? And the Puritan was compelled ultimately to ask: what is the virtue of a crown and a government which support a stage forbidden by God?

The tradition of hostility, enforced through the long series of attacks, was attended by casual elements which increased the friction.[5] The dramatists, for example, had a living to make, and could scarcely love a group which wanted to deprive them of their livelihood. Again, great support for the theater came from the government, a group which opposed the Puritans. Players acted before the sovereigns, while the average audience in the playhouse was scarcely composed of Presby-

---

1. *Histrio-Mastix* (1633), 708: "It is infamous . . . for Emperors or persons of quality to dance upon a Stage or Act a Play."

2. *Ibid.,* 414: ". . . impudent, shamefull, unwomanish, gracelesse, if not more than whorish attempt."

3. *Documents Relating to the Proceedings against William Prynne in 1634 and 1637,* ed. S. R. Gardiner (1877), 2, 22.

4. *Ibid.,* 33.

5. Mary G. M. Adkins in "The Genesis of Dramatic Satire against the Puritan," *The Review of English Studies,* 22 (1946), 81–95, argues that anti-Puritanism on the stage originated in the medieval tradition of making fun of the corrupt clergy.

terians. Thus, the lines of the plays would necessarily reflect not only what the government would allow, but what it wanted. Needing a butt for his wit, the writer would encounter no difficulties if he dealt harshly with religious eccentrics and extremists who incessantly disturbed the order of church and state and who, with their dreary and repetitious pamphlets, plainly hoped to close the theaters. The dramatic satirist had before him a field ripe for cultivation : he did not let it lie fallow.

The Stage Puritan as a Stock Figure

FOR MANY YEARS the English drama concerned itself intermittently with religious controversy, and the Puritan, one particular figure in the religious picture, came to be a stock in trade of the playwright. Quite aside from the fact that the stage and its support, the court, had good reasons for hating the Puritan, he did lend himself in an obvious manner to comic caricature with material as rich and as rewarding as the old vice. It is thus not surprising that stage satire of the Puritan reaches, in richness of detail, variety of character, and wealth of situation, a position often superior to that in prose or nondramatic verse.

Religious dispute had been native to the English drama from an early date : in the anonymous *New Custom,* printed in 1573 but written perhaps as early as 1559, there is a discussion of Protestantism as a force in opposition to Roman Catholicism. The play has slight value as dramatic argument : the author generally fails in his intention to make fun of the opposition to the crown, but he does at least succeed in presenting an unfavorable picture of the group which resists reform away from Rome. Two of the characters, Ignorance and Perverse Doctrine, explain that the church is in a state of decline because of the changes which are being imposed : vestments, beads, incense, and crosses are no longer esteemed, and English is to be the language of the service.[1] The essence of their objections is that the church is moving toward simplified practices and away from old patterns. In an elementary way, the dialogue shows a satirical intention since the ideal of Roman Catholicism is offered ironically : the author sides with reform, and he tells his audience obliquely that the changes in the church are all for the better. It is notable that in

---

1. All plays are dated by their first production as recorded or estimated in Alfred Harbage's *Annals of English Drama.* References to the plays are by act, scene, and page of the edition listed in the bibliography.

New Custom, I, i. 11 :

> . . . Surplices are superstition : beads,
> paxes, and such other gear,
>
> Crosses, bells, candles, oil, bran, salt,
> spettle, and incense,
>
> With censing, and singing, he accounts
> not worth three-halfpence.

the indirect presentation of his argument he centers attention on one of the chief points of early Anglican reform, a point which the Puritans were presently to appropriate to their own uses and present once more to the English people on the ground that it had been neglected. The argument is in the writings of Hooper; it appears here in a Protestant play supporting the government; a generation later, the argument comes from the Puritans, while the Anglican stage finds it a perverse innovation sought only by religious zealots.

When the dramatist turned to the examination of the Puritan, the result was almost invariable; as in *New Custom,* the writer supported orthodoxy and deprecated religious forces which opposed the government. The nonconformist was subjected to examination in all of his waking hours: there were his clothing, his speech, his manners, and his morals.[2] And from the 1590's until the outbreak of fighting in 1642, and indeed, at the Restoration in 1660, the commonest barb hurled from the stage at the reformers had to do with their ways of worship. These quips were particularly common around 1600, and they make up the burden of the charge to the closing of the theaters. There is no evolution: in the later years the details of the religious picture conform to those of the earlier; but the accumulation of weight is impressive. The indictment, even though it occurs in snatches of a few lines or in a phrase, manages to cover most of the details of the Puritan program, from his adoration of the Bible to the fissiparous tendencies of the nonconformist forces.

In the Puritan's worship, prayers and sermons were, as in his writings, easy marks to aim at. The same objection comes frequently from the serious controversialists: the Puritans improvise, they discard Anglican forms of service; on the one hand they worship with ravings undignified or seditious, and on the other they have rites barren and cold. The serious arguments of the polemicists take on humor and point when presented on the stage. The Puritan did depart from conventions accepted by large numbers of people, the departures were in the direction of extremes of one sort or another, and it was not difficult to make the new ways seem ridiculous. By the standard device of exaggeration, the zealots and the eccentrics could be made typical of the whole movement, and the intentions of reform could be omitted since they would lessen the satiric force. Thus, according to the stage writers, strife, noise, and

2. Two extensive compilations of references to the Puritans in the drama have been made in E. N. S. Thompson's *The Controversy between the Puritans and the Stage* and Aaron M. Myers' *Representation and Misrepresentation of the Puritan in Elizabethan Drama* (Philadelphia, University of Pennsylvania Press, 1931). Thompson surveys the dispute between the Puritans and the stage, the pressure brought by the Puritans and the reforming Anglicans for the closing of the theaters, and the development of the anti-Puritan attack from the dramatists to about 1642. Myers lists the allusions to the Puritans, for the most part chronologically, from about 1572 to 1642.

confusion were the basic elements of any Puritan service. Prayers, sermons, and psalms were delivered in a high, nasal tone, and the overpious manner enforced the delivery. The result was a most unattractive performance, ". . . hoarse midnight lectures preached by wives of comb-makers, and midwives of Tower-wharf." [3] The ignorant deliver long, noisy sermons; subtle arguments too abstruse for human understanding are carried on by means of a complex vocabulary of theological hair-splittings; and the prayers are like the sermons. The accounts are burlesque versions of Bacon's, ". . . a thing rather ingenious than substantial." [4]

The titles of the devotional writings were not hard to make fun of. Thomas Becon's *The Sicke Mans Salve* (1561) could give the dramatist a starting point, and then one of the zealots on the stage could make a fool of himself with a parodied list and a concluding comment on the superiority of Puritan thought:

> . . . A pill to purge phlebotomy,—A balsamum
> For the spiritual back.—A lozenge against lust;
> With divers others, sir, which, though not penn'd
> By dull platonic Greeks, or Memphian priests,
> Yet have the blessed mark of separation. . . .[5]

Throughout the plays there are casual, passing references to the chatter which goes on in the reformed meetinghouses; there are detailed accounts of sins more heinous than dullness, stupidity, and noise redundancy. In the accounts of the sermons and the prayers the stage writers usually avoid the direct representation of the event, and extract humor from a distorted report, told at second hand, of the chaos of Puritan worship. "This was never penn'd at Geneva; the Note's too sprightly." [6] The dramatist is not only making fun of Puritan dullness; he is also calling up one of the stock responses upon which he had come to depend.

The stigma of a foreign doctrine, alien to English good sense, was easily attached to those who praised the reformed churches on the Continent. The dramatist likes to suggest to his audience an English church, uncorrupted by external influences since Henry VIII, and sullied

---

3. D'Avenant, *The Wits* (1634), IV, ii, 199. In Dekker's *West-Ward Hoe* (1604), I, i, 292, are the lines: "Talke and make a noise, no matter to what purpose, I have learn'd that with going to puritan Lectures." One man mentioned in Webster's *The Duchess of Malfi* (1614), IV, ii, 96, aids the dissenters' cause in his own way: ". . . he makes allom of his wives urin, and sells it to Puritanes, that have sore throates with over-straining."

4. The phrase is from "Of Unity in Religion," *Works,* ed. Spedding, 6, 383. Fletcher, *The Woman's Prize* (1611), II, vi, 36–37, makes fun of the sermons. Jonson parodies Puritan pulpit oratory in the lines of Zeal-of-the-Land Busy in *Bartholomew Fair* (1614), discussed below.

5. D'Avenant, *The Wits* (1634), II, iii, 159. The lists of dull sermons and pamphlets are common.

6. Beaumont and Fletcher, *The Elder Brother* (1625), IV, iv, 44.

only in recent years by the Puritans who had imported ideas from which all decent people would shrink. And the dangerous importations had come largely from the three centers of Amsterdam, Rotterdam, and Geneva. The first two were symbols of sects devoted to outlandish practices; the last was inevitably the focus of a doctrinal infection which had made England unwell. Usually the dramatists in their satire admit no debt which Anglicanism owed to Calvin, and so no good word is said for Geneva. The "little ruff'd Geneva-man" is the quintessence of hypocrisy and carping precision in church matters and the phrase "Geneva print" comes to mean writing which is full of a false piety to trap the unwary.[7] Amsterdam spreads confusion, falsehood, and dullness, and furnishes the models for the English sects.[8] There is, according to the plays, a direct connection between the services of the English dissidents and the teachings of the foreigners: had it not been for Holland and Switzerland, England would not be cursed with the Puritans.[9] In his account of the foreigner, the satirist chooses to depict a depravity which is the product of evil religion and an intellectual confusion which is the product of ignorance. There is no detailed account of what the Dutch or the Swiss are like or even much of what they believe; it is rather that they are foreign, and that the sects in their cities have given comfort to the same groups in England. With no detailed picture, the writers still manage to make the place names symbols of all that is most sinister in alien ideas. Like the Rome of earlier days, Holland and Switzerland become a stock curse.[1] The dramatists have again echoed one part of the

7. Beaumont and Fletcher, *The Chances* (1625), III, i, 210.
8. D'Avenant, *News from Plymouth* (1635) 4, 170:

> . . . Rome is taken
> By the ships of Amsterdam, and the Pope himself
> To save his life, turn'd Brownist.

Shirley, *The Gentleman of Venice* (1639), III, i, 37:

> . . . if I live, I will to Amsterdam
> And add another schism to the two hundred
> Fourscore and odd. I am resolved. . . .
> To cry down all things
> That hang on wit, truth or religion.

9. Beaumont and Fletcher, *Fair Maid of the Inn* (1626), IV, i, 195:

> *Pedant:* I am a school-master sir,
>   And would fain confer with you
>   About erecting 4 new sects of religion
>   at Amsterdam.
> *Forobosco:* What the Divell should
>   New sects of religion doe there?
> *Pedant:* I assure you I would get
>   A great deal of money by it.

1. Middleton, *The Witch* (1615), I, i, 361. The references to the three cities are extremely common. Amusing quips occur in Shirley's *The Bird in a Cage* (1633), IV, i,

controversy and have omitted another for the good reason that it does not well lend itself to dramatic treatment: doctrine is too impersonal and, on the stage, is unusable until it is attached to a character or can be brought to life by dramatic action.

Thus, if in *New Custom* the author argued for reform away from the old ways and in the direction of Protestantism, the later writers speak for a reversal of the trend, or at least a halt in the march toward starkly simple worship. The forms and furnishings of the church, the dress of the clergy, the ritual, all the things which were argued over so seriously, served as comic material when the dramatists had sufficiently exaggerated the terrors which the Puritan felt at the supposed sight of the rags of Rome.[2] At the mention of bells or crosses, or the word *Christmas*—compounded of *Christ* and *mass*—the stage Puritan will panic: the pope is at his heels.[3] The precisian's terror is plainly over dangers which no longer exist, and his hysterical anti-Romanism adds a ridiculous quality to the conventional portrait of ignorance and superstition. In a sense, the basis for the fun is just the opposite of the sneers at foreign influences. The fear is, the satirist suggests, really the shunning of things which are as native to England as honest virtue. The church has always had vestments, crosses, bells, and colored windows: those who object are urging changes which would make the church un-English.[4] One small item makes clear the interplay of nationalism and the Puritan's refusal to conform: that is the question of when to eat fish. The reformer (according to his stage tormentors) refused to eat fish on Fridays simply because Roman Catholics were forbidden to eat meat on Fridays. On the other days of the week, the Puritan might eat fish; on Fridays he might not. But Englishmen had always eaten fish on Fridays; it was

428, and in Middleton's *The Mayor of Queensborough* (1618) v, i, 96. In Middleton's *Anything for a Quiet Life* (1621) II, i, 264, it is reported that the Familists of Amsterdam say that adultery ". . . may be done with a safe conscience." Marston, *Parasitaster; or the Fawne* (1605), II, i, 152, and Massinger, *The Renegado* (1662), I, i, 127, speak of Amsterdam and Rotterdam as centers of Puritan infection.

2. Shackerley Marmion, *A Fine Companion* (1633), v, ii, 188: "But the most dangerous of all was a Puritan chandler, and he run mad with illuminations . . . he thought a man in a surplice to be the ghost of heresy, and was out of love with his own members, because they were called organs."

Thomas Jordan, *The Walks of Islington and Hogsdon* (1641) IV, i, F1 verso: ". . . here comes my white Knight in his Lawn sleeves, now if a Quaker saw him he would take his shirt for a Surpless, and condemn it for a Babylonish Garment, or in good sooth and verily a wicked and superstitious remnant of that foul slaps the whore of Babylon."

3. Brome, *The Covent-Garden Weeded* (1633), I, i, 8: ". . . he has spied the little Crosse upon the new Church yond, and is at defiance with it." Other references occur in II and IV.

4. Middleton, *The Inner-Temple Masque* (1619), 201 ff., contains a large amount of pointed satire of the Puritans' fears, particularly on ritual, and their refusal to observe fasting days. *The Parson's Wedding* (1641), by Thomas Killigrew has, III, v, 521–2, an amusing passage on Romish things, bishops, and lawn sleeves.

an accepted part of the national diet, and the government was at pains to
encourage the habit both because of the commercial and the maritime
importance of the fishing industry. The satirist on the stage was furnished with an exploitable situation. His Puritan, refusing to eat, was
against the nation; he was trembling with terror at Rome when Rome
was nowhere in sight; he was shying at a fish.[5]

Like the fear of Roman Catholicism, the Puritan's love for the Bible
laid him open to attacks on the counts of hysteria, immoderate zeal, and
lack of good sense. In the serious controversy, the Puritan turned sooner
or later to Holy Writ for authority, and the Anglican in turn frequently
found approval for his theories in the same book and the same text. Both
sides came to admit that the Bible was insufficient as a complete guide to
life: interpretation complicated the proposal of a purely scriptural order.
However, it is true that for the Puritan the Bible remained through the
years a particularly living and personal source for instruction, inspiration, and pleasure. Quoting it, reading it frequently, casting his speech
and his writing in its mold, he became the easy mark of the satirists'
parodies. Lofty models are dangerous, and the dangers increase with the
seriousness of the subject. The dramatists pick out the things which are
ludicrous about the bibliolatry of the Puritans, their love of Old Testament names, the snatches of Scripture common in their talk, and the
absurd use of a biblical style of speech in dealing with everyday situations. In the portrayal there is the usual exaggeration indispensable to
parody. The names for the stage Puritan are generally virtues, particularly those with Job-like overtones of suffering: ". . . Tribulation,
Persecution, Restraint, Long-Patience and such like. . . ."[6] and are
calculated not only to spread false gloom but also, within the context of
the scene, to suggest infinite hypocrisy and corruption. Another Puritan
may complain because he was baptized Credulous and not: ". . . Trib-

5. Massinger, *The Renegado* (1624), I, i, 127:

> . . . nor do I like
> The other, that allows us to eat flesh
> In Lent, though it be rotten, rather than be
> Thought superstitious; as your zealous cobler,
> And learned botcher preach at Amsterdam . . .

In Middleton's *The Inner-Temple Masque*, 201–2, the character Fasting-Day says:

> O, sweet doctor Almanac,
> I've lost a dear old master! beside, sir,
> I have been out of service all this Kersmas;
> Nobody minds Fasting-Day;
> I've scarce been thought upon a' Friday nights;
> And because Kersmas this year fell upon't,
> The Fridays have been ever since so proud,
> They scorn my company . . .
> Nay, Fish-street loves me e'en but from teeth outward . . .

6. Jonson, *The Alchemist* (1610), III, ii, 345.

ulation, Nor holy Ananias . . ."⁷ The name which he has can inspire no one to gloom and dissent.

The biblical chatter of the Puritans enforces the pretentious names and makes the zealot doubly ridiculous. Ordinarily, the dramatist does not put a quotation from Scripture in the mouth of the comic character; the technique is rather to involve the zealot in some trivial or silly topic which he discusses in English suggestive of the majestic periods of the Geneva Bible.⁸ Thomas Randolph's *The Muse's Looking Glass* (1630) has two overpious characters, Bird, a feather man, and Mrs. Flowerdew, the wife of a haberdasher; Bird and Mrs. Flowerdew go to a play and their outraged talk about what they see is in spirit a blend of Job, Jeremiah, and the preacher of Ecclesiastes:

> *Mrs. Flowerdew:* See, brother how the wicked throng and crowd
>   To works of vanity! Not a nook or corner
>   In all this house of sin, this cave of filthiness,
>   This den of spiritual thieves, but it is stuff'd,
>   Stuff'd, and stuff'd full, as is a cushion,
>   With the lewd reprobate.
> *Bird:* Sister, were there not before inns,
>   Yes, I will say inns, (for my zeal bids me
>   Say filthy inns,) enough to harbour such
>   As travell'd to destruction the broad way;
>   But they build more and more, more shops of Satan?
> *Mrs. Flowerdew:* Iniquity aboundeth, though pure zeal
>   Teach, preach, huff, puff, and snuff at it; yet still,
>   Still it aboundeth. . . .⁹

The rhythm, the structure of the sentences, and the vocabulary are juggled with considerable skill. The verse has sufficient dignity to be the proper medium for serious ideas; and indeed, to a point, the ideas are serious. The figures at the beginning of Mrs. Flowerdew's denunciation are solemn enough. She mentions vanity, and then she delivers herself of some metaphors worthy of corruption and decay. But at the climax of her speech she takes a rhetorical fall: she repeats "stuff'd" too many times, and ends with the trivial word *cushion* to describe sin, when she started with the strong figure, *cave of filthiness*. Bird lacks his companion's command of synonyms: he repeats "inns" and "more" three times

7. Cartwright, *The Ordinary* (1635), IV, i, 280.
8. Field, *Amends for Ladies* (1611), III, iii, 132:

> *Widow:* Precise and learned Princox, dost not thou go to Blackfriars?
> *Bold:* Most frequently, madam, unworthy vessel that I am to partake or retain any
>   of the delicious dew that is there distilled.

Bold is parodying the biblical talk of the Puritans.
9. Randolph, *The Muse's Looking-Glass* (1630), I, i, 145–146.

each, perhaps in the belief that noise will compensate for lack of variety. Mrs. Flowerdew's last three lines are a good blend of scriptural phrase and silly cant. The decline is from "iniquity aboundeth" to "huff, puff, and snuff." Randolph has convincingly satirized the bibliolatry of the Puritans: the simplicity and strength of the English Bible become, in the mouths of his characters, noisy trivialities.

The divisions and subdivisions within the Puritans' ranks are another phase of the reforming movement which furnished worthy material for the satirist's dialogue. Conservative reformers, both among the Puritans and the Anglicans, had always disliked the sects, and indeed the sects themselves usually hated all except one: Gibbon observed that the appellation of heretics has always been applied to the less numerous party. But the stage did take particular advantage of the evil reputation of some eccentric groups, showed them no mercy, and made them the equivalent of more conservative elements, or, still more inaccurately, of that fictitious entity, the typical Puritan. It is useless, however, to look for any clear line of development in satire against particular groups for, making no distinction among the teachings of the various minorities, the dramatist usually threw out to his audience the names which would stir the most laughter or indignation: ". . . Papist, Protestant, Puritan, Brownist, Anabaptist, Millenary, Family-o'-Love, Jew, Turk, Infidel, Atheist, Good-Fellow. . . ."[1] If the speaker had been questioned, he would have made a difference between a Protestant and a Roman Catholic, but probably none between an Anabaptist and an atheist; sectary, Puritan, and foreign innovator would have been synonymous.[2]

It is, however, true that of the "old dissent" the Presbyterians and the Congregationalists or Independents commonly fare better than the later groups: established dissenters had taken on respectability and lacked in addition the spectacular features of worship which could make them suited to the stage: they suffer occasional quips at their advanced views.[3] On the other hand, the Anabaptists were no less an abomination to the

1. Chapman, *Eastward Ho* (1605), v, ii, 523.

2. Glapthorne, *Wit In A Constable* (1639), ii, i, D1:

> . . . I will bring
> Sects of Philosophers and queint Logicians,
> Weel Procreat by learned art, and I
> Will generate new broods of Schollers on you,
> Which shall defend opinions far more various
> Then all the Sectaries of Amsterdam
> Have ever vented.

3. As in Brome's *A Jovial Crew* (1641), ii, ii, 390:

> . . . We of our Ministery,
> As well as those o th' Presbyterie,
> Take wives and defie Dignitie.

dramatist than to John Taylor or Queen Elizabeth; the stage references are myriad and uniformly unfavorable.[4] Jonson, for instance, speaks of the sect a number of times and in one of his masques he puts the ultimate curse upon the "Doppers": they are not allowed "to prophecie, or start up upon stooles to raise doctrine."[5]

The Family of Love furnished the dramatist with one of the richest veins of ore: lines about their practices could titillate and outrage at once.[6] The satirist necessarily concentrates on those elements which will be most successful on the stage and neglects attitudes and habits which are not good material for humorous distortion: one of the most important questions in the serious dispute, church government, receives very little attention. In general, the objection to bishops is unmentioned simply because it offers slight opportunity for humor. When ecclesiasts are spoken of, *fathers* is a more convenient term, and the audience is allowed to make its own choice of *minister, priest, bishop, archbishop,* or all four. Then the lines are less relevant to reform than to the fear of Romanism within the English church, and the writer has collapsed on one of his old and easy themes. Indeed, so thin is the material on polity and the orders of the clergy as viewed through Puritan eyes that the satirist will with even hand write lines making fun of the reformers for their excess of zeal and then turn on the orthodox clerics for their sybaritic ways.[7] The infrequency with which quips on specific points of doctrine occur perhaps suggests also the essential agreement apparent

4. Shirley, *The Wedding* (1626), I, iii, 374:

> *Justice Landby:* . . . wer't ever christen'd?
> *Camelion:* Yes, twice; first, in my infancy, and the last time about a year ago, when I should have been 'prentice to an anabaptist.

John Day, *Law Trickes* (1607), II, 33: ". . . but chast, and poore, as singuler and rare as Conscience with the Anabaptist."

5. Jonson, *News from the New World* (1621), 519. In *The Staple of Newes* (1625), III, ii, 332, he speaks of a sect which looks forward to the birth of a messiah. The story was a common one about the Anabaptists.

6. Shirley, *The Lady of Pleasure* (1635), I, i, 9:

> And ladies, thither bound by a subpoena
> Of Venus, and small Cupid's high displeasure;
> 'Tis but the Family of Love translated
> Into more costly sin!

The general tradition of immorality and atheism was strong. See also Chapman's *Sir Giles Goosecap* (1603), II, i, 630.

7. D'Avenant, *News from Plymouth* (1635), IV, 170:

> *Trifle:* From Florence:

> All the silk-worms are dead, and an edict made
> Unbenefic'd ministers must give o'er their satin,
> And damask cassocks, and wear friars' habits;
> Punks must not trade in taffetas . . .

in the debate of Whitgift and Cartwright on most questions of belief.[8]
But the dissenters' noisy devotion to salvation by faith, particularly in
the later years when good work had regained its old prestige, could be
turned for a fantastic account of Puritan extremism:

> I say no works are good;
> Good works are merely popish, and apocryphal.[9]

The dramatist has made his character funny by tangling his doctrinal
fingers in the flypaper of Romanism; and the scorn of good works echoes
a devotion to salvation by faith too extreme for the time when the lines
were written.

Scattered throughout the plays, these casual references, principally to
the practices and religious quirks of the Puritans, form a base of operation. Ideas in themselves could less easily be distorted and parodied on
the stage; and the playwrights consequently picked eccentricities which
could amuse and at the same time suggest the ideas indirectly. Since
the Puritan violated convention in his worship, in his preaching, in his
attitude toward the Bible, and in his daily conversation, he easily became a clownish parody of the religious reformer. Stripped of virtue,
his vices magnified, he was offered on the stage as a fanatic who would
destroy religion. The dramatist is not, however, concerned with a sober
indictment of the Puritan for his beliefs. The casual lines are scarcely
protests; they rather add up to a witty picture of fools who have gone
mad on religion. In the picture there is usually little of John Taylor's
bitterness and certainly none of the fury of some of the serious polemicists. With their quips, the dramatists offer a figure of fun who will
brighten lines, enliven situations, and evoke from the audience predictable
responses.

The account of the Puritan's religious activities suggests a second
group of charges, more inclusive, more detailed, and more serious. This
group appears, like the indictment of rite and practice, in scattered
references in many plays and over a considerable period of time; it is
most completely expressed in a number of highly developed accounts of
the Puritan around 1600. Instead of centering on the Puritan in church,
the second account examines him in the world of affairs: it considers
his attitude on learning, his assorted sins against mankind, his manners

---

8. Marmion, *A Fine Companion* (1633), v, ii, 188:

> *Aurelio:* Ay, and held very strange positions, for he counted Fathers to be as un-
> lawful in the church, as Plato did poets in his commonwealth, and thereupon
> grounded his conclusion for the lawfulness of whoredom. . . .
> *Fondling:* How did you heal him, sir?
> *Aurelio:* Why, lady, with certain pills of sound doctrine, and they purg'd his ill
> humours.

Aurelio uses *doctrine* to mean *polity*.

9. Randolph, *The Muse's Looking Glass* (1630), i, i, 146.

and his conduct in society. The techniques of portrayal are unchanged: there is the exaggeration and distortion of failings in order to portray vices; and there is the elimination of all good or all dignity to produce a vicious or farcical figure.

For one thing, the Puritan was, according to the dramatist, an ignorant fool. The picture was a common one both among the serious writers and the satirical pamphleteers. His foolishness showed itself in the eccentricities of his conduct; his ignorance was revealed in his conversation and his opinions. And it is undeniably true that some Puritans furnished a handle for the satiric ax: they commonly opposed the stage with narrow and bigoted arguments; they sometimes condemned secular learning; they often held to a narrow and literal morality; and they were inclined to extol the superior insight of the simplest mind.

The general accuracy of the judgment was, certainly, of no interest to the dramatic satirist. It is thus common for the Puritan to carp whenever he encounters, in the course of a scene, something which is intelligible to the ordinarily literate man. One of the favorite tricks is to infuriate and puzzle him with Latin or Greek, and the force of the device must have been considerable in an age when every boy who had been to a grammar school knew something of the classics. At the same time, when the Puritan cried out in horror at the very sound of Latin, he was once more showing his silly fear of Rome. On the wittiest level, these references to ancient languages involve a gibe which is more complex than the objection of an ignoramus to a literature which he knows nothing of:

> *Ananias:* I understand no heathen language, truely.
> *Subtle:* Heathen, you Knipper-Doling? Is Ars sacra,
>   Or Chrysopoeia, or Spagirica,
>   Or the pamphysick, or panarchick knowledge,
>   A heathen language?
> *Ananias:* Heathen Greeke, I take it.
> *Subtle:* How? heathen Greeke?
> *Ananias:* All's heathen, but the Hebrew.[1]

The passage is a better-than-average sample of the traps into which the Puritan was led. Ananias has begun by admitting that he is not an educated man; he knows no "heathen language." But then he proceeds to judge Subtle's alchemical hogwash. The Puritan begins pretentiously; he ends by making his taste and judgment seem even worse by his remark on Hebrew. He has thrown out Greek and Latin literature and has said in effect that out of the past only the Old Testament is worthy of consideration.

A fairly developed portrait of the Puritan as the enemy of learning

1. Jonson, *The Alchemist* (1610), II, v, 334.

occurs in *The Pilgrimage to Parnassus,* a drama both thin and dull, which was "performed in St. John's College Cambridge 1597–1601." [2] The play is of interest since it is the product of a university environment, and contains a character who is both a Puritan and opposed to learning and the arts. In him is summed up most of the tradition of anti-intellectualism which had come to be attached to the dissenters. The plot of the play is of the simplest sort: it operates in the tradition of the interlude, and has no particular bearing on Puritanism. Among the virtues and vices assembled is Stupido, the essence of all that the educated man should not be. He is, first of all, dull; he is also a devout precisian. In his simple lines he reveals himself as a man who not only hates liberal learning and the arts, but who has a perverse love for theological cobwebs. As he talks, he mixes a number of the old prejudices of the Puritan with ill-considered opinions on literature and philosophy; the picture which results, although it is not lively, is the sum of the anti-intellectual charge. For all the limitations of the playwright's skill, he has managed to present his character not merely as an ignorant man but as an ignorant man who is proud of his ignorance and who, in addition, opposes all learning which does not directly contribute to his particular brand of religion. Stupido can praise a Calvinist theologian or Martin Marprelate; but poetry is evil because it leads no soul to Geneva.[3] A crude denunciation from Philomusus (who necessarily speaks poetry in contrast to Stupido's prose) sums up the author's opinion of the dissenter: he is a philistine beyond redemption.[4]

2. *The Pilgrimage to Parnassus* (1599), ed. William D. Macray (Oxford, 1886), title page.

3. *Ibid.,* III, 11–12:

> Welcome, my welbeloved brethren! trulie (I thank God for it!) I have spent this day to my great comfort. I have (I pray God prosper my labours!) analised a peece of an hommelie according to Ramus, and surelie in my minde and simple opinion Mr Peter maketh all things verie plaine and easie . . . I have a good man to my uncle, that never wore capp nor surples in his life, nor anie suche popishe ornament, who sent mee yesterday a letter . . . and the same counsell that he gave mee I, as I am bounde in charitie, will give you. 'Studie not these vaine arts of Rhetorique, Poetrie and Philosophie; there is noe sounde edifying knowledg in them.' Why, they are more vaine than a paire of organs or a morrice daunce! If you will be good men indeede, goe no further in this way; follow noe longer these profane artes that are the raggs and parings of learning; sell all these books, and by a good Martin, and twoo or three hundreth of chatechismes of Jeneva's printe, and I warrant you will have learning enoughe. Mr Martin and other good men tooke this course. . . . Artistes, fools; and that you may knowe by there undecent apparell. Why, you shall not see a Rhetorician, a rimer (as poet as you call it) but he wears such diabolicall ruffs and wicked great breeches full of sin, that it would make a zealous professor's harte bleed for grife . . .

4. *Ibid.,* IV, 14:

> . . . Stupido, that plodding puritane,
> That artless ass, and that earth-creeping dolt,
> Who, for he cannot reach unto the artes,

According to the almost universal judgment of the playwrights, the morals of the Puritan in society were no better than his learning. The vices which he practiced included all those which could furnish the writers with material for comedy : adultery would tickle an audience, so the Puritan was a habitual adulterer; and if he was not a murderer, it was only that crimes of blood offered no chance for the satirist's art. It is patently absurd to discuss the validity of the charges. The proposal that Presbyterians were thieves but Anglicans were honest can scarcely be supported. However, it should be remembered that the portrayal of corruption can give the audience a feeling of superiority when the corruption comes from a religious group which has put special stress on its purity, and thievery among Puritans has ironic humor simply because they are so very pure. In addition, the Puritan with his talent for theological word-spinning could, in the midst of his sin, explain that what he was doing was not wrong, but was really in accord with good morals and sound religion.[5]

One of the stock figures of sexual hypocrisy is the wife. Cheating her husband, she is in no danger from him or from God, provided she preserves appearances. Another stock figure of hypocrisy at its most pleasing is, inevitably, the clergyman. There is Jonson's pastor who has no objection to counterfeiting, there is Tourneur's corrupt Snuffe, "a Puritane; Chaplaine to Belforest," and the cleric in *A Merry Knack to Know a Knave*. The cleric speaks for them all: they will not swear an oath, they talk much of original sin, and so with excess of piety they trick the world into believing that they are pure.[6] In the course of the

---

> Makes showe as though he would neglect the artes,
> And cared not for the springe of Hellicon . . .

Myers, *Representation*, 120–1, discusses the play. See also Thompson, *Controversy*, 201–2, and Macray's preface to his edition of the play.

5. Dekker, *The Wonder of a Kingdom* (1623), I, i, 227 :

> *Alphonsina:* Walls of chastitie? Walls of wafer-cakes, I have
> Knowne a woman carry a fether-bed, and a man in't
> In her minde, when in the streete she cast up the white of
> Her eye like a Puritane.

6. *A Merry Knack to Know a Knave* (1592), 519 :

> And I, among my brethren and my friends,
> Do still instruct 'em with my doctrine,
> And Yea and Nay goes through the world with us.
> Fie, not an oath we swear for twenty pound:
> Brethren, say we, take heed by Adam's fall;
> For by his sins we are condemned all . . .
> Thus do we blind the world with holiness,
> And so by that are termed pure Precisians.

See also Jonson's *The Alchemist* (1610). For Tourneur's "Snuffe, a Puritane," see *The Atheist's Tragedie* (1609). Myers, *Representation*, 122, discusses the character at some length.

same play, a beggar asks the priest for some money; the answer is a piece of theological web-spinning typical of the stage precisian when he would get himself out of a generous deed: the spirit does not move the priest to give, and anyhow, good deeds do not justify. In his answer there is a good mixture of ironically perverted private judgment, the private judgment which Hooker found so dangerous, and the old habit, not exclusively Puritan, of extolling grace over works with the result of slight incentive to virtuous acts.[7]

Among the assorted evils, fornication and adultery are among the most pleasing to the audience. Cheating, hard-dealing, lying, and drunkenness are frequently on the list, but the sins of the Puritans are without number. There is the general tradition that the devil is a Puritan, that is, that any sort of bad deed from a dissenter indicates that the spirit of Satan, or of true dissent, is within him; hardheartedness and cruelty are his marks, and "the devil turned precisian" simply means vice compounded.[8] Among the various transgressions, drunkenness furnishes the dramatist with fine opportunities for satire. The Puritan in his cups is funny enough, but if he preaches and "reveals," so much the better.

7. *A Merry Knack to Know a Knave*, 579:

> *Priest:* Why, I tell thee no, for the Spirit doth not move me thereunto. And in good time, look in the blessed Proverb of Solomon, which is, Good deeds do not justify a man; therefore, I count it sin to give thee anything.

Honesty, another character, remarks:

> See how he can turn and wind the Scripture to his own use . . .

The indignant denunciation of the Puritan is extremely common. Shirley's *The Grateful Servant* (1629), II, i, 36, has the phrase, "methodicall an hypocrite." In *The Pedlers Prophecy* (1561), D2 verso, there is the following:

> *Marriner:* . . . we bring in none but Gospellers,
> And such as we know to be very good Christians.
> *Pedler:* Oh holy Ghospell, o tidings of health most pure,
> Thou art made a cloake to all abhomination . . .

In Middleton's *Your Five Gallants* (1607), I, i, 135, the scoundrel Frippery asks: "Can you carry yourself cunningly, and seeme often holy?" Novice answers: "O, fear not that, sir! My friends were all Puritans." The dramatists do occasionally betray themselves. In Tourneur's *The Atheist's Tragedie* (1609), II, iv, 204, there is this conversation:

> *Borachio:* Then the Precisian to be ready, when
> Your brother spake of death, to move his Will.
> *D'Amville:* His businesse cal'd him thither; and it fell
> Within his office; unrequested to 't.
> From him it came religiously; and sav'd
> Our project from suspition . . .

Here is the plain statement that precisians had a reputation for honesty and piety.

8. Massinger, *A New Way to Pay Old Debts* (1625), I, i, 493. Middleton, *A Trick to Catch the Old One* (1605), IV, iv, 322:

> *First Creditor:* Do you call us devils? you shall find us Puritans—Bear him away; let 'em talk as they go.

Combine the preaching with a conversion, and the conversion with a seduction, and there is a rewarding situation for farce:

Crosse: Will he be drunke?
Ball: Most swine-like, and then by the vertue of his good liquor hee's able to convert any Brownisticall sister.

Convert involves the Latin meaning; and the conversation is about a sectary, Joshua, who has already delivered himself of a pun:

"I . . . doe fructifie among the brethren. . . ." [9]

The cheating Puritan accompanies the drunken whoremaster; the thievery is used for producing both simple indignation and ironic pleasure at the hypocrisy of the character. Frequently, the Puritan shows himself as a cozener and another character, transparently dishonest, exclaims with disgust at the false piety. In Strode's *The Floating Island,* for instance, Melancholico, by his name a stock precisian, persuades the villainous Desperato to cheat the sick out of their money. Desperato gives the standard answer:

This is a verier rogue than I myselfe.

In the same play, a "sister" turns up the white of her eye to heaven and another character says:

The white's pure, the black as full of Adultery
As thou art of Hypocrisy. . . .[1]

Adultery and indiscriminate sexuality turn out to be usually rather genial charges from the satirists. Puritan wives are eager to be seduced, providing only that the seducer will put up with an amount of protest mixed with theological dalliance. The husbands likewise bed when the opportunity occurs, and just as the Puritan can explain away thievery, so adultery disappears when one of the saints uses the right words.[2] The accounts are written almost entirely with good humor; there is scarcely

9. William Sampson, *The Vow-Breaker* (1625), v, i, 66; i, ii, 14. It might be noted that Joshua is one of the many Puritans who killed their cats for catching mice on Sunday. The story is told on the same page.
1. William Strode, *The Floating Island* (1636), iv, ii–iv, D4, D4 verso.
2. Dekker, *North-Ward Hoe* (1605), i, 3: ". . . his wives puritanicall coyness." In Tourneur's *The Revenger's Tragedie* (1606), ii, ii, 105, Vindice says:

> . . . I durst undertake
> Upon the pawne and forfeit of my life
> With half these words to flat a Puritanes wife . . .

Marston's *The Malcontent* (1604), v, ii, 298–9, has the line, ". . . a precisian's wife is very flexible." Maquerelle then says: ". . . I have heard of a sect that maintained, when the husband was asleep the wife might lawfully entertain another man, for then her husband was as dead . . ."

any of the indignant protest which occurs in the stories of the Puritan's cruelty and greed. No one suffers; no home is wrecked; the lewd tale is satire and not invective. From the conversations of bawds and rakes and their lists of sexual misdemeanors, the writer often produces his most pleasing scenes of Puritan deviltry; and by a twist of context, the word *Puritan* comes to mean *prostitute;* [3] at its best the dialogue is a clever blend of obscenity and biblical phrase. The ideal climax to the carryings-on comes when an outsider—preferably a licentious man-about-town—collects his evidence, then lines up the pious miscreants and numbers their sins over for the audience:

> *Gerardine:* Silence! The first that marcheth in this fair rank is Thrum the feltmaker, for getting his maid with child, and sending his 'prentice to Bridewell for the fact; Whip the beadle, for letting a punk escape for a night's lodging and bribe of ten groats; Bat the bellman, for lying with a wench in a tailor's stall at midnight, when 'a should be performing his office; and Tipple the tapster, for deflowering a virgin in his cellar; doctor Glister, his wife, Maria, mistress Purge. . . . [4]

The speech is full of good humor. There is no sour resentment toward the sectaries. They have been caught in their sins, but the evil deeds are ones which ordinary men commit and which are now more amusing because they have been done under a cloak of piety. If it was cruel to send the apprentice to Bridewell, he was perhaps as chargeable as his master, and did not have the wit to know that paternity is difficult to prove. The satirical quality of the speech comes not simply from the lewd conduct, but from the contrast between the claim of the Puritans to great virtue and their collective performance; the dramatist has delighted his audience with his picture of folly.

Aside from the larger social sins of the Puritan, there are a number of items which the dramatist habitually uses to give consistency and familiarity to the stage Puritan: through these the audience recognizes the traditional figure. These traits fall under the general heading of manner; they are matters of dress, speech, and taste, all of which go to make up the distinctive personality of the character. If they seem to include disparate elements, they are surprisingly uniform in the way in

3. Marston, *What You Will* (1601), III, iii, 383:

> *Bidet:* . . . Stand forth, page of the placket, what is your mistress?
> *Slip:* A kind of puritan.
> *Bidet:* How live you?
> *Slip:* Miserably, complaining to your crackship: though we have light mistresses, we are made the children and servants of darkness . . .

Marston's *The Malcontent* (1604), v, ii, 305, has the sentence: ". . . your whore went down with the stews, and your punk came up with your puritan."
4. Middleton, *The Family of Love* (1602), IV, iv, 91-2.

which they contribute to a coherent picture. Less striking than adultery in the midst of divine worship, the small details do lend realistic depth.

By and large, the manner of the stage Puritan is calculated to irritate —but not to bore—the onlooker. If the dramatists sometimes admit that nasal piety is not the essence of Puritanism, they also sometimes admit that the dissenter adheres to a code which justifies to an extent his irritating superiority.[5] Ordinarily the zealot is verbose and noisy, condescendingly holy, and eternally in a pious fury. Fletcher's Hope-on-High Bomby, whose name reflects his religious zeal, rages at the evils of a hobbyhorse.[6] What he says has no very clear bearing on sin, or the Christian church, or rites and practices; it is rather a wrathful denunciation of something which gives pleasure to others; in addition, he argues, the hobbyhorse came from Rome. Bomby's offensive manner is typical of most of his kind. There is the same florid manner which marked the sermonizers in John Taylor, there is the hint of a biblical vocabulary, and there is the apocalyptic tone. Here the Puritan is not declaiming from a tub, nor talking about rite and worship. He is expressing the quality of preciseness by his overconcern with innocent things, his eagerness to find sin everywhere, and his deep suspicion of pleasure. The failing was certainly to be found in some of the reformers to a degree; upon a valid basis, slight or considerable, the stage writers are able to construct a clownish zealot with a most irritating manner. Sometimes hypocrisy is not a part of the manner: ". . . yet she's so precise, and over-honest," means just that.[7] She should be less meticulous; she is

5. As, for example, in *The First Part of Sir John Old-castle* (1599), IV, iii, 153:

> . . . I am neither heretike nor puritane, but of the old church: ile sweare, drinke ale, kisse a wench, go to masse, eate fish all Lent, and fast fridaies with cakes and wine, fruite and spicerie, shrive me of my old sinnes afore Easter, and beginne new afore whitsontide.

6. Fletcher, *Women Pleas'd* (1620), IV, ii, 283–4:

> The Beast is an unseemly, and a lewd Beast,
> And got at Rome by the popes Coach-Horses . . .
> I do defie thee, and thy foot-cloth too;
> And tell thee to thy face, this profane riding,
> I feel it in my conscience, and I dare speak it,
> This unedified ambling, hath brought a scourge upon us,
> This Hobby-horse sincerity we liv'd in
> War and the sword of slaughter: I renounce it,
> And put the beast off; thus, the beast polluted,
> And now no more shall hop on high Bomby
> Follow the painted pipes of high pleasures,
> And with the wicked, dance the devils measures;
> Away thou pamper'd jade of vanity,
> Stand at the Livery of lewd delights now,
> And eat the provinder of prick-ear'd folly,
> My dance shall be to the pipe of persecution.

7. Shirley, *The Gamester* (1633), III, i, 226.

inhuman. In the preciseness, piety is an important element; the Puritans
have an exclusive way to salvation and ordinary mortals are excluded.
But the feeling is an understandable protest against the doctrine of
election, particularly since the election seemed to exclude all Anglicans.
In the question: "How now, Will? become a precissian?"[8] the speaker
is not chiding Will for hypocrisy but for niceness in his scruples.

Various habits of dress and conversation enforce the pious superiority
and inhuman asceticism. If the term *roundhead*[9] came under Charles I
to be the name of a dissenter, short hair was a satiric item for the dramatists of Elizabeth's time. A serving man compelled to have his hair cut
short complains because he looks like a Brownist; a ruff might be a
symbol of the stiffness of the precisian; the eyes rolled heavenward and
the nasal whine were a part of the traditional manner.[1] In the anonymous *How a Man May Chuse a Good Wife from a Bad* (1602), Master
Fuller tells a long and funny story of how he could not seduce a Puritan
girl until he convinced her that he was just as devout as she. At the
opening of the campaign, Fuller operated under the handicap of conventional clothing; he met with no success. But then he dressed as a
Puritan. When he approached her, he "turn'd up the white of eye." His
success was immediate and complete. The incident is told in much the
manner of the obscene ballads about the Puritans.[2]

In addition to the lenient morals of the female Puritan, there is the

---

8. *The Lamentable and True Tragedy of M. Arden of Fevershame* (1591), III, ii, 16.
D'Avenant's *Temple of Love* (1635) 295, complains of the Puritan's monopoly of virtue:

> To these I'll add a sect of modern devils;
> Fine precise fiends, that hear the devout close
> At ev'ry virtue but their own, that claim
> Chambers and tenements in heaven, as they
> Had purchas'd there, and all the angels were
> Their harbingers . . .

9. The *OED* dates *roundhead* 1641.

1. *Sir Thomas More* (1595), III, ii, 402: "Heers a lowsie jest! but, if I notch not that
Rogue Tom barbar, that makes me looke thus like a Brownist, hange me!" In Shirley's
The Cardinal (1641), II, iii, 302, the duchess says:

> . . . the short-hair'd men
> Do crowd and call for justice . . .

Fletcher's *The Night-Walker* (1614), III, 348, has the lines:

> So many a Puritans ruff, though starch'd in print,
> Be turn'd to Paper, and a Play writ in 't.

Brome's *The English Moor* (1637), v, iii, 85, describes the whining manner:

> Forgiv' me for swearing, and turn Precisian, and pray
> I' the nose that all my brethren whoremasters spend no worse.

2. *How a Man May Chuse a Good Wife from a Bad* (1602), 52–3:

> . . . But ever somewhat did offend her sight,
> Either my double ruff, or my long haire:

tradition that she is frequently a shrew. When a scene of lechery fails the writer, he can present the wife sitting with her Bible, rolling her eyes, swinging a cudgel in one hand, and terrifying her husband and the servants with Old Testament wrath; while the husband, in his total depravity, may even feel that he deserves the treatment he gets.[3] The Puritan woman likewise reduces music to hymns, and she can denounce bear-baiting as eloquently as any man.[4]

An extended account of the Puritan manner at its pettiest comes from Chapman's D'Olive when he tells how a precisian talked of tobacco as though it burned with the smoke of hell. The account is at second hand; the speaker tells how a Puritan has made a fool of himself with a dreary disquisition on the evils of the habit; the speech is a comment on the fanatic's appearance and manner:

> Upstart a weaver, blown up b'inspiration,
> That had borne office in the congregation,
> A little fellow, and yet great in spirit;
> I shall never forget him, for he was
> A most hot-liver'd enemy to tobacco,
> His face was like the ten of diamonds

> My skarfe was vain, my garments hung too low,
> My spanish shooe was cut too broad at toe.

He describes his Puritan costume:

> My shooes were sharpe-toed, and my band was plaine,
> Close to my thigh my metamorphos'd breech:
> My cloake was narrow Capte, my hair cut shorter . . .

3. *Two Wise Men and All the Rest Fools* (1619), III, ii, 46, gives an elaborate picture of the Puritan shrew:

> *Rust:* (She openeth her Bible, and makes shew to reade, and many times turnes her eyes with the white upward.) That is her rod of discipline, and a strange thing it is which now I tell you. She is never so rapt up in her devotions, but if I commit the least fault (as wretched man that I am many times I doe, and my best actions are abhominable) she perceives it presently (and yet is deafe to all other noise) and she comes to me fiercely in the heate of her charitie, and corrects mee verie handsomely with that wand.

4. Massinger, *The Emperor of the East* (1631), III, ii, 293:

> *Arcadia:* . . . I have not learned to dance yet,
> Nor sing, but holy hymns, and those to vile tunes too;
> Nor to discourse but of schoolmen's opinions.

Brome, *The Antipodes* (1638), IV, i, 295–6:

> *Maid:* Fie Granny fie, can no perswasions,
> Threatnings, nor blowes prevaile, but you'll persist
> In these prophane and Diabolicall courses,
> To follow Bear baitings . . .
> Let me entreat you
> Forbeare such beastly pastimes, th'are Sathanicall.

Pointed each where with pushes, and his nose
Was like the ace of clubs
. . . the colour of his beard
I scarce remember; but purblind he was
With the Geneva print, and wore one ear
Shorter than t'other for a difference . . .
Said 'twas a pagan plant, a profane weed,
And a most sinful smoke, that had no warrant
Out of the Word; invented, sure by Sathan
In these our latter days to cast a mist
Before men's eyes that they might not behold
The grossness of old superstition,
Which is, as 'twere, deriv'd into the Church
From the foul sink of Romish popery,
And that it was a judgment on our land
. . . the smoke of vanity
. . . a rag of popery . . .
And speaking of your Grace behind your back,
He charg'd and conjur'd you to see the use
Of vain tobacco banish'd from the land. . . .[5]

The account of the traditional Puritan manner is fairly complete: he is of humble occupation, of small size, but great in noise. He is sour-visaged, squint-eyed, contrary, and stubborn, able to see Rome everywhere; he is eager to impose his moral judgment on the whole community.

The general threat of the closing of the theaters and the particular rantings of William Prynne furnished material for the dramatists; and in the lines which they produced satire blends into denunciation. The attacks are of no significance to the development of the stage Puritan; they do, however, indicate the vigor of the drama, its ability to speak in its own behalf, and its close connection with contemporary life. Thomas Heywood says that one of his own plays is safe from the *Histrio-Mastix;* the ironic dedication of Shirley's *The Bird in a Cage* (1633) is to Prynne in jail; and an amusing bit of dialogue from D'Avenant refers to Wither, Prynne, and to Shirley's play.[6] In addition, the writers list the threats to

5. Chapman, *Monsieur D'Olive* (1604), II, ii, 330. Opinion was divided on tobacco. The Wife in Beaumont's *The Knight of the Burning Pestle* (1607), in I, i, 172, delivers an amusing denunciation. The authors are obviously making fun of her. She is not a Puritan.
6. Thomas Heywood, *A Maiden-Head Well Lost* (1633), "To the Reader," 99. The mock dedication to William Prynne of Shirley's *The Bird in a Cage* (1633) reads in part: "Sir, the fame of your candour and innocent love to learning, especially to that musical part of humane knowledge, Poetry, and in particular to that which concerns the stage and scene (yourself, as I hear, having lately written a Tragedy) doth justly challenge from me this Dedication. I had an early desire to congratulate your happy re-

the drama: the plague, the critics, and the Puritans; while Jonson
defends the actors through his puppets at Bartholomew Fair as a
decently conducted company of workmen.[7] Perhaps the most eloquent
of all the defenses of acting and the drama is Massinger's *The Roman
Actor* (1626). The play is not anti-Puritan and it is not satire; it instead
offers the serious justifications that the drama can be an accurate reflection of human experience, that it can evaluate men's deeds, and that
it can be an active force for good.[8] But the personal attacks from the
dramatists on their detractors and the larger defense of the theater
against the Puritans are, after all, only repetitions of the old objections
to the sour precisian: "O mother, cold sobriety and modest melancholy
becomes the face . . . un-edifying gawdes are Prophane vanities.
Mirth is the fat of fools, onely vertue is the nourishment of purity and
unsinning sincerity." [9]

---

tirement . . . how aptly I may present you at this time, with the *Bird in a Cage* . . ."
D'Avenant's *The Cruel Brother* (1627), II, i, 141–2:

> *Dorido:* Good morrow to the court satirist!
> *Castruchio:* . . . We cannot meet
> In duel: the heralds stand between.
> But my fine thrush can sing you a new libel.
> *Dorido:* We shall have your thrush in a cage shortly.
> Remember whom you deal withal . . .
> Prithee, sweet Castruchio! Leave thy barking.
> 'Twill be treason shortly for any man
> To carry ears within three miles of thy tongue.
> *Castruchio:* Why signior, what faction are you of?
> *Dorido:* Not of your faction, sir, if none return
> Unto the prison for your libelling.
> You remember your vices strip'd and whip'd . . .

7. Middleton, *A Mad World My Masters* (1606), v, i, 339:

> *Sir Bounteous:* Players? by the mass, they are welcome; they'll grace my entertain-
> ment well. But for certain players, there thou liest, boy; they were never more
> uncertain in their lives; now up, and now down; they know not when to play,
> where to play, nor what to play: not when to play, for fearful fools; where to
> play, for puritan fools, nor what to play, for critical fools.

Jonson, *Bartholomew Fair* (1614), v, iii, 120:

> *Cokes:* Well, they are a civill company, I like 'hem for that; they offer not to
> fleere, nor geere, nor breake jests, as the great Players doe: And then, there
> goes not so much charge to the feating of 'hem, or making 'hem drunke, as to
> the other, by reason of their littlenesse. Doe they use to play perfect? Are they
> never fluster'd?
> *Lanterne:* No, Sir. I thanke my industry, and policy for it; they are as well govern'd
> a company, though I say it . . .

8. See particularly the speech of Paris on the moral worth of the drama, II, i, 355–6.
Massinger's *The Emperor of the East* (1631), III, ii, 292–3, has the following lines:

> . . . I am so tired
> With your tedius exhortations, doctrines, uses,
> Of your religious morality . . .

9. Brome, *The City Wit* (1628), v, 363.

THE
DEVIL TURN'D
ROUND-HEAD:

OR,
PLVTO become a BROWNIST.

Being a juft comparifon, how the Devil is become a *Round-Head?* In what manner, and how zealoufly (like them) he is affected with the moving of the Spirit.

With the holy Sifters defire of Copulation (if he would feem Holy, Sincere, and Pure) were it with the Devill himfelf.

As alfo, the Amfterdammian definition of a Familift.

The Climax of the Tradition: Shakespeare, Middleton and Jonson.

B ETWEEN 1600 and 1615 there appeared several plays which mark a
climax in respect to anti-Puritan satire on the stage. The plays deal
either with the Puritan in detail or they treat particularly the characteristic of preciseness as a source for humor; in all of the plays major figures
are Puritans or are tarred with the Puritan brush, and in some of the
plays Puritanism is the moving force for a large part of the action. At
the hands of the authors the precisians receive varying treatment, but
they are all highly developed personalities.

Malvolio in Shakespeare's *Twelfth Night* (1600) is of such complexity that it is impossible to speak with certainty about him. His fellows
in the play say that he is somewhat like a Puritan, and then they say that
he is not one; and scholars and critics who have examined him are not
in agreement.[1] One of the difficulties behind any estimate of Malvolio is

1. *Twelfth Night* (1600), II, iii, 129-30:

    Maria: Marrie sir, sometimes he is a kinde of Puritane . . .
    The div'll a Puritane that hee is, or any thing constantly but a time-pleaser . . .

Twelfth Night, A New Variorum Edition of Shakespeare, ed. Horace H. Furness
(Philadelphia, Lippincott, 1901), 130, and 396-402, gives samples of the differences of
opinion: ". . . Rolfe (*Poet-Lore,* July 1898, p. 420): Malvolio at no time talks like
a Puritan, as he would naturally have done if he had been one, when he came in to re-
prove the midnight roysterers. . . . Charles Lamb ([*Works,* 1870], ii, 369): . . . he
might have worn his gold chain with honour in one of our old round-head families, in the
service of a Lambert or a Lady Fairfax . . . Hunter ([*New Illustrations of Shakespeare*], 1845, i, 381): . . . in this play . . . there is a systematic design of holding them
up to ridicule, and of exposing to public odium what appeared to him the dark features
of the Puritan character . . . In Malvolio's general character the intention was to make
the Puritan odious . . . William Archer (*Macmillan's Magazine,* August 1884, p. 275):
. . . The theory, so popular with German, and with some English, commentators, which
makes of him a satirical type of the Puritan as Shakespeare conceived him, will not hold
ground for a moment. It is founded on one or two detached speeches wrested from their
context . . . J. W. Hales (*Contemporary Review,* Jan. 1895, p. 65): "Thus Shakespeare
took no part in the Puritan-baiting that became a favourite dramatic pastime. And this
forbearance is to be accounted for not only by the general fairness and comprehensive
sympathy of his nature . . . but also by the fact, that at Stratford he was brought into
such close and intimate contact and acquaintance with so many specimens, public and
private, of the Puritan breed . . ." Recent opinion does not make him a Puritan.
Twelfth Night, ed. Sir Arthur Quiller-Couch and John Dover Wilson (Cambridge,
University Press, England, 1930), "Introduction," xxiv: "Malvolio, of course, is not a
'Puritan' in any historical sense, but a Puritan only as an incarnation of the abstract
Puritan's besetting foible—that of self-righteousness, of making himself a judge of
others. Through this, and through the complacent arrogance bred by that habit of mind,
he comes to grief." Alwin Thaler, "The Original Malvolio?" *Shakespeare Association
Bulletin,* 7 (1932), 57-71, identifies Malvolio with "William Ffarington (1537-1610) of
Worden, Lancashire, steward (until 1594) to Lord Ferdinando Strange, Earl of Derby
and patron of Shakespeare's company." Thaler sees no element of Puritanism in the
character. Paul Mueschke and Jeanette Fleischer, "Jonsonian Elements in the Comic
Underplot of 'Twelfth Night,'" *PMLA, 48* (1933) 722-40, argue that Malvolio is pat-
terned on Jonson's comic method developed in *Every Man in his Humour* and *Every
Man out of his Humour,* produced by the Lord Chamberlain's Company in 1598 and 1599,

that Shakespeare's religious views are not certainly known, although the presumption is that they were Anglican. Were it, for instance, possible to demonstrate that he was a Roman Catholic or a Presbyterian, a good deal of Malvolio's ambiguity would disappear. But no such demonstration is possible—the attempts of those who have tried reveal diligence rather than fact [2]—and it is also true that Shakespeare gave no clear indication of his opinion of Puritanism. His few references to the reformers are colorless, or, at worst, gentle quips.[3] If it is fruitless to speculate on Shakespeare's attitude toward Puritanism, it is also unnecessary as far as a satisfactory understanding of Malvolio's character is concerned.

In certain respects Shakespeare follows the tradition of the stage precisian, but at the same time he makes his satire more complicated than a mere picture of excessive religious zeal. Indeed, Malvolio shows no sign of religious eccentricity in the course of the play; it is, rather, in other respects that he gives the impression of being Puritanical. In his first speech he sets his character for the course of the action, and particularly for the comic humiliation which he is to suffer : he is too solemn

---

respectively. They date *Twelfth Night* 1600–1. In addition, Shakespeare led the list of actors for *Every Man in his Humour* in the Jonson folio of 1616. Their conclusion is that ". . . Shakespeare's adaptation of the Jonsonian 'humour' character in Malvolio [is] no longer to be conceived as a satiric portrait of the Puritan but rather as a felicitous combination of psychological humorist and social attitudinizer, through whom Shakespeare attains comic effects superior to those of his model, Jonson." They differ from Thompson, *Controversy*, 250, who would make Malvolio a Puritan: "Undoubtedly, Malvolio is in conception a humour study in Puritan character with the Puritan abhorrence of bear-baiting and the like, for which inclination Sir Andrew threatens to beat him."

2. Shakespeare's echoes of the Bible are from the Bishops' and the Geneva, but his religion is usually that of the critic who is writing about him. The accounts are very numerous, and the variety of conclusions is indicated by the following. Thomas Carter's *Shakespeare Puritan and Recusant* (1897) proves that both John and William Shakespeare were Puritans. Henry Sebastian Bowden's *The Religion of Shakespeare* (1899) demonstrates on the basis of the facts of Shakespeare's life and the contents of his plays that he was a Roman Catholic. Henry C. Beeching's *The Religion of Shakespeare* (Stratford-on-Avon, 1907) assumes that Shakespeare was an Anglican; Sister Maura in *Shakespeare's Catholicism* (Cambridge, Riverside Press, 1924), comes to a different conclusion. George Seibel, *The Religion of Shakespeare* (Watts, 1924), surveys critical opinion and concludes that Shakespeare was a skeptic.

3. F. G. Fleay, "Shakespeare and Puritanism," *Anglia, 7* (1884), 223–31. Fleay lists references to Puritans: "In Twelfth Night II.3 Maria says that Malvolio is 'sometimes a kind of puritan' but when Sir Andrew says that in that case 'he would beat him like a dog' she goes on 'the devil a puritan that he is, or anything constantly but a timepleaser, an affectioned ass &c.' In Alls well that Ends well I.3 the Clown says 'Young Charbon the Puritan, and old Poysam the Papist, howsome'er their hearts are severed in religion, their heads are both one' and further on in the same scene he says 'Though honesty be no Puritan, yet it will do no hurt: it will wear the surplice of humility over the black gown of a big heart.' Finally in Winter's Tale IV.3 the Clown says there is but one Puritan among the shearers 'and he sings psalms to hornpipes.'" Fleay observes properly that "Shakespeare is singularly unlike his contemporaries in [his] abstinence from satirizing the Puritans. . . ."

and sad: he talks unnecessarily of decay and death.[4] If his conversation proves nothing about his religion, it does establish him as being over-serious and in considerable contrast to the group of people around him. In addition, he shows a pompous sententiousness which makes him vulnerable to those of a less serious turn of mind. However, in his speeches in later scenes, Malvolio has no trace of the traditional idiom or phrase of the precisian: he talks as a well-trained steward in an important household should. When he addresses his mistress, he speaks with respect and he sticks to the subject, although it is also true that he is somewhat wordy.[5] When Sir Toby gets drunk and his party makes a great deal of noise in the night, Malvolio enters and protests. Were he a stage Puritan, he probably would talk of vain revelry and fleshpots; instead, he is angry at the disturbance of the peace, the disrespect shown to his mistress, and, indeed, compares the revelers to low tinkers, a simile which no good sectary would use.[6] Nowhere in the scene does he call the offenders ungodly.

In several other respects Malvolio departs from what the stage Puritan should, conventionally, be. As he meditates with conceited delight over his conquest of Olivia, he gives credit to Jove, and thanks him.[7] A stage Puritan would not lightly traffic with the heathen Jove, nor with the Christian God. Finally, when he writes his sad letter to Olivia in which he pleads his sanity, he begins with an oath which would have been an abomination on the lips of one of the saints.[8] Thus, in a number of situations, Malvolio has violated established conventions for the satiric portrayal of the precisian.

But it is not without reason that Malvolio has been called a Puritan, and that to generations of readers and playgoers he is remembered as a stage Puritan, for in his character there is just enough of the precisian so that the audience thinks of him as something more complicated than merely melancholic. There is, for instance, the specific discussion of his Puritanism after he has objected to the noise at Sir Toby's party.[9]

4. *Twelfth Night*, I, v, 69: "Yes, and shall do, till the pangs of death shake him: Infirmity that decaies the wise, doth ever make the better foole."

5. *Ibid.*, I, v, 76–7: "Madam, yond young fellow sweares hee will speake with you. I told him you were sicke, he takes on him to understand so much, and therefore comes to speake with you. I told him you were asleepe, he seems to have a fore knowledge of that too, and therefore comes to speake with you. What is to be said to him Ladie, hee's fortified against any deniall."

6. *Ibid.*, II, iii, 122: "My masters are you mad? Or what are you? Have you no wit, manners, nor honestie, but to gabble like Tinkers at this time of night? Do yee make an Alehouse of my Ladies house, that ye squeak out your Coziers Catches without any mitigation or remorse of voice? Is there no respect of place, persons, nor time in you?"

7. *Ibid.*, III, iv, 222: ". . . it is Jove's doing . . ." It has been suggested by various editors that *Jove* originally read *God*, or that *Jove* should be emended to *Love*. Either emendation is unappropriate to a stage Puritan.

8. *Ibid.*, V, i, 307.

9. The passage, II, iii, 129–30, has been quoted in part above. G. L. Kittredge in his edition of *Twelfth Night* (Boston, Ginn, 1941), 118, says: "Maria uses *Puritan* in the

Although the decision is that he is not really a Puritan, it is clear that he does have the failing of an overhigh regard for his own worth, and from that fault arises the plot against him with his final humiliation. Conceit and self-righteousness were two of the sins central to preciseness in the stage Puritan, and in the discussion of Malvolio, his Puritanism and his conceit follow one after the other. As Maria talks about the steward, she does not quite say that he is a Puritan; in the failure to note that, discussions of his character have gone wrong. She does say that "sometimes he is a kind of Puritan." In other words, in some ways, he on occasion acts like a Puritan. A few lines later she says that he is not a Puritan; she is not contradicting herself because she never said that he was one. But in the course of the scene Maria, with the assistance of Sir Toby and Sir Andrew, has attached at least the shadow of Puritanism to Malvolio. A little later, Fabian makes a reference as traditional to the stage Puritan as a whining voice: Malvolio got Fabian into trouble over a bear-baiting. Then Sir Toby says that they will have the bear in once more to make Malvolio furious.[1]

Malvolio has, then, been portrayed as an overserious, even melancholic, man; in addition, he has the preciseness and the self-righteousness of the Puritan. In his subsequent humiliation it is this somber self-love which is turned against him. His pride betrays him into believing that he is preeminently worthy of Olivia, and he struts about, a parody of what the lover should be. His last line leaves him uncured: he is still better than the others, more virtuous, more wise, more worthy, the victim of persecution.[2]

Shakespeare's creation has been raised to a level of complexity where he is largely removed from the traditional Puritan: there is left haughty conceit and suspicion of the pleasures of the flesh. He can be called a Puritan, or he can be simply the fool who is perfect and the meddler who would recast the world in one perfect mold. But the same figure had walked the stage before, for Sir Toby's question sums up the old charge: "Dost thou thinke because thou art vertuous, there shall be no more Cakes and Ale?"[3]

Within the same period as that of *Twelfth Night,* Shakespeare presented in the figure of Angelo of *Measure for Measure* (*c.* 1603–04) a serious complement to the comic creation of Malvolio. In a number of

---

loose sense: 'a Puritanical or strait-laced person.' Sir Andrew takes the word in its strict sense as denoting a member of the Puritan party in the Church. Sir Toby's question ('Thy exquisite reason?') is prompted by a desire to hear Sir Andrew dilate on ecclesiastical questions; but Sir Andrew refuses to be drawn . . ."

1. *Twelfth Night* (Variorum ed.), II, v, 153.
2. *Ibid.,* II, v, 156; V, i, 313.
3. *Ibid.,* II, iii, 126.

important respects, Angelo reflects elements in the character of Malvolio, even though the effect of Angelo is entirely different. Commentators on the play have generally been concerned with an explanation of its puzzling tone and the interpretation of its meaning as a complex allegory based in some way on the biblical text which suggests the title. Concern with the over-all meaning of *Measure for Measure* and, on a more particular level, the explanation of the ambiguous figure of Isabella, have obscured generally the fact that in the portrayal of the villainous Angelo Shakespeare has drawn to an extent on the stage tradition of the Puritan.[4]

For the chief sin of Angelo is one which accords with the long tradition of the evil Puritan. Angelo, who is supremely virtuous, and to whom the term *precise* is explicitly attached,[5] is put in charge of Vienna by the Duke, who disappears. Angelo promptly charges Claudio with a sexual irregularity under a law which has fallen into disuse, and he is sentenced to die. Claudio's sister Isabella pleads before Angelo for her brother's life, and Angelo grants it on condition that Isabella will give herself to him. Angelo believes that she has consented and has fulfilled her part of the bargain—actually, another woman has been substituted for Isabella—but he still orders the execution of Claudio. In the comic ending of the play Isabella is shown to be perfectly virtuous; the brother is alive; and the villainy of Angelo is exposed.

In the course of the play, Angelo is never called a Puritan, and in no particular sense is he a Puritan: he belongs to no sect, he makes no pretense of a particular religious doctrine, and he has few of the conversational tags which labeled the stage Puritan for the audience. But at the same time, he has about him a good deal of the evil which was peculiarly Puritanical: the most notable trait of his character is his hypocrisy. He begins with the endeavor of perfect virtue, and perfect virtue is the repu-

---

4. The widely differing estimates and interpretations of the play are summarized in the first section of Roy W. Battenhouse's *"Measure for Measure* and Christian Doctrine of the Atonement," *PMLA, 61* (December, 1946), 1029–59. Some recent discussions of importance are in W. W. Lawrence's *Shakespeare's Problem Comedies* (New York, Macmillan, 1931), 78–121; R. W. Chambers' *The Jacobean Shakespeare and Measure for Measure, Proceedings of the British Academy, 23* (1937); G. Wilson Knight's *The Wheel of Fire* (Oxford University, Press, 1949), 73–96; and E. M. W. Tillyard's *Shakespeare's Problem Plays* (Chatto & Windus, 1950), 118–38. S. J. Mary Suddard in *Studies and Essays* (Cambridge, University Press, 1912) 136–52, treats the entire play as a study of Puritanism.

5. *Measure for Measure,* I, iii, 13–14:

> . . . Lord Angelo is precise;
> Stands at a guard with envy; scarce confesses
> That his blood flows; or that his appetite
> Is more to bread than stone; hence shall we see,
> If power change purpose . . .

The Duke is speaking.

tation which he enjoys in Vienna.[6] But as soon as he is in power, he betrays his position and bargains a life for the chastity of an unwilling woman. Angelo's conduct in the past had been at least questionable: he had deserted his fiancée to whom he had been pledged in a solemn rite of the church. But his worst crime of hypocrisy and betrayal is that he orders the execution of the convicted man after the sister has supposedly given herself to Angelo: he would take a life which has been paid for.

Now, throughout the scenes in which Angelo appears, he preserves the icy external of the precisian—which he is called—and at the same time has the covert passion of the religious hypocrite. Like so many of the comic figures of the Puritan, Angelo is the prey of sexual lust, and that Shakespeare has made the lust unattractive by attaching to it both rape and something akin to murder, does not alter the fact that the deeds are a part of Angelo's preciseness; they correspond to the stiff, presumptuous, and false virtue of the stage Puritan. The exact nature of Angelo as a symbol is indeterminate, as it should be; but in the fault of preciseness he might be regarded as the evil obverse of Malvolio, who is another generalized but comic version of the stage Puritan.

Angelo and Malvolio meet in certain areas: both, for instance, take their virtue too seriously, both have pretensions to propriety which are so noticeable as to be annoying. Both men are addicted to an inordinate solemnity: for Malvolio it is out of proportion because a steward is not that important; for Angelo it is unsuitable in view of his sexual habits both before and during the action. And again, both men to an extent derive their force of personality from the fact that they are in a Jonsonian humor. Malvolio is in a humor when he pretends to the position of the suitor of his mistress, and Angelo is put in a humor when the true Duke of Vienna places him in charge of the state, a position for which he has neither the experience, the understanding, nor the virtue. The destruction of the two figures follows the classic pattern for the stage Puritan. If Malvolio's downfall comes by his conceit, Angelo's comes by his hypocrisy; and conceit and hypocrisy were two of the dominant elements in preciseness. The differences between the two figures serve to reinforce Shakespeare's generalized intention in both: neither character is connected with a particular religious sect, but in the two are two aspects of moral zeal and its downfall.

Thomas Middleton's *The Family of Love* (1602) is a long distance from Shakespeare's comedies; but Middleton's play was produced at

6. In I, iv, 16, Lucio reinforces the Duke's account of Angelo:

> . . . a man whose blood
> Is very snow-broth; one who never feels
> The wonton stings and motions of the sense;
> But doth rebate and blunt his natural edge
> With profits of the mind, study and fast.

about the same time as *Twelfth Night,* both are comedies, and both lean heavily on the characteristic of preciseness for comic effect. Instead of Shakespeare's single character, Malvolio, compounded of a selection of Puritanical characteristics, Middleton offers a crowd of hypocrites who talk devoutly and act profanely. Malvolio's story is incidental to the main plot, whereas the central narrative of *The Family of Love* concerns the sectaries. The subtlety and complexity of Shakespeare's portrayal is entirely absent from Middleton: his picture of Puritanism is not subtle or complex, but it is not intended to be.

The Family of Love is a laboratory specimen, with appendages complete, of the anti-Puritan comedy. It is a well-constructed farce with a plot which falls neatly into two divisions. The conventional demands of a romantic problem are satisfied with the love of Maria and Gerardine: their affair opens the play and with the last act they are finally successful in their efforts to be married. The second plot concerns the efforts of Lipsalve and Gudgeon, two frankly corrupt gallants of the city, to seduce Mistress Purge, lascivious practitioner in the Family of Love. The story is, however, actually about Puritans and their hypocrisies; Middleton has used the name of the sect only because it had to his audience an aura of Paphian rites and secret sins. The picture of corruption differs in no way from that presented in the casual references in plays not on the precisians; but Middleton does gain by detail and the sustained development of character and situation. His names, for instance, fit his characters, and each one is dominated by a single humor of the sort which makes him a suitable person for the farcical action.[7] Only the lovers lack ridiculous overtones. In the course of the scenes involving the sect and the discussions of religious practices, Middleton manages to cover most of the topics which were commonly a part of anti-Puritan satire: his ear is good for the rhythm of conversation; he can exaggerate and still leave the original recognizable; and he is able to exploit situation and action for the grotesque to the humiliation of his victims. Mistress Purge, "an elder in the Family," does not like plays, and she denounces them in an extended speech which covers both the serious objections of the Puritan writers and some irrelevant ramblings about there having been no theater in the primitive church.[8] Again, there is the description of a sermon from the wife of a bellows-

7. Middleton, *The Family of Love* (1602), 10, "Dramatis Personae":
   Glister, a doctor of physic.
   Purge, a jealous apothecary.
   Dryfat, a merchant, a brother of the Family . . .
   Lipsalve,
   Gudgeon, two gallants that only pursue city lechery . . .

8. *Ibid.,* I, iii, 26–7: "Fie, fie, 'tis pity young gentlemen can bestow their time no better: this playing is not lawful, for I cannot find that either plays or players were allowed in the prime church of Ephesus by the elders."

mender: the bawdy piety of the woman parodies the pronouncements of the sectaries on the equality of all men before God.[9] Throughout the scenes, the details of strange and strained religious practices, such as terror at eating fish on Friday, accumulate. Gerardine sums up the preciseness and the hypocritical piety which he has learned from his Familist friends: ". . . I never rail nor calumniate any man but in love and charity; I never cozen any man for any ill will I bear him, but in love and charity to myself; I never make my neighbour a cuckold for any hate or malice I bear him, but in love and charity to his wife." [1] The final list of virtues which he numbers over includes bastardy, adultery, bribery, fornication, and seduction.

The events in the meetinghouse are retailed necessarily at second hand, but when the brothers and sisters have gathered, the lights are put out and the congregation, in the traditional phrase of the Family, love one another.[2] Dialogues on religious rites parody the arguments of the serious reformers for a simpler service: Mistress Purge protests her hatred of all organs, church or corporeal.[3] The climax of the action involves a visit by the two gallants to the church during a service and Mistress Purge's loss of her wedding ring. She thinks that in the dark she has given it to an unknown lover; actually, she has given it to her husband. The last speeches are centered on the impenetrable hypocrisy of the Familists, for despite the evidence of the gallants and the wronged husband, the lady explains that she turned the ring over to help "dis-

---

9. *Ibid.*, IV, i, 69–70:

   Lipsalve: . . . Hadst thou heard the protestations the wife of a bellows-mender made but yesternight against gallants, thou hadst for ever abjured crimson breeches. She swore that all gallants were persons inferior to bellows-menders, for the trade of bellows-making was very aerial and high; and what were men and women but bellows, for they take wind in at one place and do evaporate at another;—evaporate was her very phrase.

1. *Ibid.*, IV, ii, 77.

2. According to the apprentice, Club (II, iv, 39), they improve on the principle, for they ". . . love their neighbours better than themselves . . . for they love them better than their husbands, and husband and wife are all one; therefore, better than themselves." The speech is a typical piece of burlesqued logic of the sort the Puritans supposedly use to get themselves out of difficulties. Dryfat and Mistress Purge give an account of the "service," III, iii, 57:

   Mistress Purge: To the Family, master Dryfat, to our exercise.
   Dryfat: What, by night?
   Mistress Purge: O Lord, ay, sir, with the candles out too: we fructify best i' th'
        dark: the glance of the eye is a great matter; it leads us to other objects be-
        sides the right.
   Dryfat: Indeed I think we perform those functions best when we are not thrall to
        the fetters of the body.

3. *Ibid.*, III, iii, 57:

   Mistress Purge: Organs? fie, fie, they have a most abominable squeaking sound in
        mine ears; they edify not a whit; I detest 'em: I hope my body has no organs.

tressed Geneva." Throughout the scene she has been the innocent lamb:

> Here I am,—O time's impiety!—
> Hither I come from out the harmless fold
> To have my good name eaten up by wolves:
> See, how they grin! Well, the weak must to the wall;
> I must bear wrong, but shame shall them befall.[4]

Mistress Purge slips with the greatest ease into doggerel verse on the order of a bad hymn. Her lines are full of trite rhythms, trite thoughts, and trite figures of sheep and wolves. The validity of the parody is apparent: the wolves, sheep, and shepherds of the *Shepheardes Calender,* a generation earlier, and *Lycidas,* a generation later, bear witness to that fact.

The Family of Love succeeds admirably as a farcical account of the Puritans. There are dull stretches of dialogue, but they are not in the scenes when religion and religious practice are under discussion. The satire is centered on a group of people who go through the rites of an outlandish practice: both situation and character make Puritanism funny. But throughout the play Middleton has preserved a feeling of good humor; there is no wrath over the sectaries, and the criticism of their morality is plainly directed against their hypocrisy rather than the sins in themselves. Middleton makes his most telling point by the ironic contrast which he uses time after time, the difference between what might be called the honest corruption of the city gallants and the hypocritical corruption of the Puritans. As the action is resolved, it is for the gallants to offer, by contrast with Mistress Purge, an ideal of conduct which, although it is base, is still higher than the dark depravities of the Familists. Basing his narrative on traditional immoralities, Middleton has made the satire hinge largely on the comparison of sexual mores. The tone of the play is, as a result, low; but it is also funny.

The material of Jonson's comedy of humors was the man who was ruled by a single passion and whose character could be developed in terms of this one dominant trait. Shakespeare improves on the formula in Malvolio, the victim of self-love and a melancholic humor, for Malvolio is as far above Jonson's humors as Falstaff is above Bobadill. The physiology of Middleton's Puritans is in accord with Jonson's pattern of character, and although Middleton's Puritans are inferior, they are not essentially different. If the humor is at the basis of Jonson's Puritans, there is also his metaphor that the conflict in humors is the cause of all disagreement in church and state. In addition, Jonson had stated

---

4. *Ibid.,* v, iii, 109. In v, iii, 112, she explains the loss of the ring: ". . . E'en the sanctuary of a safe conscience: now, truly, however he came by that ring, by my sisterhood, I gave it to the relief of the distressed Geneva."

RELIGIONS
ENEMIES.

WITH A BRIEF AND INGENIOUS
Relation, as by *Anabaptiſts, Browniſts, Papiſts,*
Familiſts, Atheiſts, and *Fooliſts,* ſawcily
preſuming to toſſe Religion in
a Blanquet.

The Anabaptiſt.   **The Browniſt.**

By JOHN TAYLOR

The Familiſt.   **The Papiſt.**

Printed at *London* for *Thomas Bates* in the Old-baily. 1641.

his intention of dealing with folly and not with the shocking or violent; in *The Alchemist* (1610) and *Bartholomew Fair* (1614) the folly and contentiousness of the Puritans furnish a good part of the food for the satiric feast.[5]

In *The Alchemist,* gullibility, hypocrisy, and the desire to get something for nothing dominate the action and the persons; the chief mediums for the exposition of these themes are alchemy and Puritanism. If Jonson had no faith in alchemy, he also believed that the sects would produce spirituality and virtue as soon as lead would produce gold, and in the two characters of Tribulation Wholesome, a dissenting pastor from Amsterdam, and his deacon Ananias, he presented his satiric picture of Puritans. Later, in *Bartholomew Fair,* he enriched his canvas with new details. For complexity and sharpness of delineation, he surpassed the attempts which had been made before him; after he had done, there was little to be added from the theater; and indeed, in the years which followed, anti-Puritan drama consisted largely of a repetition of his characters but with less than his wit and invention.[6]

The force of the anti-Puritan satire in *The Alchemist* arises from the careful manipulation of character in situation: the two elements are adjusted so appropriately that each illuminates the other. The troubles which befall the saints from Amsterdam are of the sort which should come to men of their ambitions and intentions; the incidents serve to

5. Charles R. Baskervill, *English Elements in Jonson's Early Comedy* (Austin, Texas, University of Texas Press, 1911), discusses the theory of humors. Baskervill, 34, says: "Jonson's celebrated definition of humour has fixed the meaning of the word for us in connection with the comedy of manners. As Jonson defines the term, it is fairly inclusive and may represent almost any decided moral inclination or mental attitude. Beginning with the broadest definition of the term in the physical sense, he proceeds to the figurative meaning of the word (*Every Man out, Induction*) :

> . . . As when some one peculiar quality
> Doth so possess a man, that it doth draw
> All his effects, his spirits, and his powers,
> In their confluctions, all to run one way,
> This may be truly said to be a humour."

The quotation is in the Herford edition of *Every Man out of his Humour* (1599), "After the Second Sounding," 432. John L. Palmer's *Ben Jonson* (Viking, 1934), 22–39, stresses the realistic element in Jonson's comedy of humors, and makes the point that Jonson's method keeps him close to contemporary life. Oscar J. Campbell's *Comicall Satyre* (San Marino, Calif., Adcraft, 1938), 54–134, offers an illuminating discussion of Jonson's development of humor comedy from *Every Man out of his Humour* (1599) through *Cynthias Revels* (1601) and *Poetaster* (1601). In *Every Man in his Humour* (1598), "Prologue" (ed. Herford, 303), Jonson states his intention of making sport of human follies. *The Magnetick Lady* (1632), "The Induction" (ed. Herford, 511), has the passage on humors and religious schism: "A bold undertaking! and farre greater, then the reconciliation of both Churches, the quarrell betweene humours having beene much the ancienter, and, in my poore opinion, the root of all Schisme, and Faction, both in Church and Common-wealth."

6. Thompson, *Controversy,* 255: "Though other dramatists showed just the same feelings, we find in no other place such a complete exposition of Puritanism as in Jonson."

display their hypocrisy and greed. Subtle, the heroic scoundrel of the piece, sets himself up as an alchemist with the aid of a number of unscrupulous assistants in an empty house; he is visited by customers who would be rich or young, and he does a thriving trade on his promises until Lovewit, the master of the house, returns and puts him out of business. The events are united around the themes of human vanity and greed, and the dramatic action takes no more time than the events which it represents. The two Puritans thus enter to ring their particular variations on the leit motif, the variations peculiar to religious hypocrisy.

Ananias and Tribulation Wholesome function in the plot as two of the dupes of Subtle. The sectaries have come to make money for their congregation through the alchemist: by the transmutation of metals, they will all become rich; for his labor, the alchemist must be paid.[7] Their first venture is the frame on which Jonson hangs the label of Puritan gullibility. Ananias and Tribulation never ask the obvious question: if Subtle can make gold, why should he want gold from others? Their second venture compounds the satire, for hypocrisy and dishonesty are added to stupidity. Subtle assures them that he can coin money for them. Although they will have to pay him for this too, the profits will be enormous. Again the saints do not ask the obvious question; their only objection is that counterfeiting is illegal. But *hen, with a labyrinthine explanation in the tradition of the theo.ogy of the stage Puritan, they decide on Subtle's suggestion, that "casting" is not counterfeiting, not illegal, and not a sin.[8] Consequently, at the end of the play they get no gold, they get no coin, and they are gulled of the money which they have paid Subtle. In the course of the plot, the humiliation of the Puritans is linked to that of the other victims; at the climax, Lovewit simply arrives and resolves the situation. The greed of the two Puritans has met another greed which is as great, and which is combined with intelligence; in their stupid efforts to cheat, they are cheated.

However, it is through details of character that Jonson chiefly develops his satire and makes the slight narrative adequate to the demands of five acts. The first scene in which one of the Puritans appears is devoted to exposition [9]—although Ananias does denounce all foreign lan-

---

7. *The Alchemist*, II, v, 336. *Ben Jonson*, ed. Herford, *1* and *2, The Man and His Work* (Oxford, 1925), *2*, 104: "The Puritan dupes, Ananias and Wholesome, on the other hand, make a new departure. Jonson, as a professed Catholic during the previous ten or eleven years, can never have felt any attraction to the 'saints' of the Reformation: but this was his first undisguised exposure of Puritan foibles on the pillory of the stage. In this sense *The Alchemist* foreshadowed *Bartholomew Fair*. His attitude to Puritanism was indeed not unlike his attitude to alchemy. Both were, for him, social pests, offensive by their hypocritical pretensions and their masquerade of hollow questionable learning. He treats the two Puritans indeed with a palpably deeper contempt than any of the other dupes . . ."

8. *Ibid.*, III, ii, 347. Ananias leads the argument; Tribulation hesitates slightly.

9. *Ibid.*, II, v, 334, ff.

guages except Hebrew—, but presently Ananias, Tribulation, and
Subtle appear together and talk on a variety of subjects. Through the
development of the characters of the two Puritans and the contrast
of their dishonesty with Subtle's, Jonson makes them absurd in their
petty guile. The three are discussing the project of transmuting metal
for the profit of the congregation at Amsterdam, and at the beginning
of the conversation the precisians carp at the terms which always filled
the stage Puritan with horror: Christmas is unmentionable.[1] Their
talk becomes increasingly pious until Subtle loses patience with them and
tells them off for their hypocrisy and immoderation. His speech is so
indignant that it violates the suavely comic tone of the scene; but it can
be taken in all its bitterness for Jonson's opinion of Puritans.[2] The answer of the two precisians is that the end justifies the means; Subtle
recovers the solemn manner which complements that of his opposites and
the three go on with their talk about alchemy. The scene ends with the
discussion of counterfeiting. In the argument over whether the holy
can in conscience approve of the project, there is a nice difference of
character made between the timorous Tribulation and the more aggres-
sive Ananias: both reveal themselves as crooks, but Tribulation prefers
petty thievery to grand larceny on the ground of safety.[3] As the con-

1. *Ibid.*, III, ii, 343–344:

> *Subtle:* And, then, the turning of this Lawyers pewter
>   To plate, at Christ-masse—
> *Ananias:* Christ-tide, I pray you . . .

2. *Ibid.*, III, ii, 344:

> *Subtle:* No, nor your holy vizard, to winne widdowes
>   To give you legacies; or make zealous wives
>   To rob their husbands, for the common cause:
>   Nor take the start of bonds, broke but one day,
>   And say, they were forfeited, by providence.
>   Nor shall you need, ore-night to eate huge meales,
>   To celebrate your next daies fast the better:
>   The whilst the Brethren, and the Sisters, humbled,
>   Abate the stiffenesse of the flesh. Nor cast
>   Before your hungrie hearers, scrupulous bones,
>   As whether a Christian may hawke, or hunt;
>   Or whether, Matrons, of the holy assembly,
>   May lay their haire out, or weare doublets:
>   Or have that idoll Starch, about their linnen . . .
>   Nor shall you need to libell 'gainst the Prelates,
>   And shorten so your eares, against the hearing
>   Of the next wire-drawne grace. Nor, of necessitie,
>   Raile against playes . . .

3. *Ibid.*, III, ii, 347:

> *Subtle:* . . . I have [a] trick
>   To melt the pewter, you shall buy now, instantly,
>   And, with a tincture, make you as good Dutch dollers,
>   As any are in Holland.

versation goes on, the themes of hypocritical corruption and excessive religious zeal alternate: Ananias decides that the "casting of dollars" is lawful and makes the solemn announcement, hedged about with pious pronouncements and denunciations of the world and the flesh, and then he gets himself into an irrelevant quarrel over idolatrous clothing.[4] In the last act Ananias delivers a parody of Puritan pulpit oratory; when the two sectaries realize that they have been cheated, they beat at the locked door of Subtle's place of business and curse the alchemist. In the turmoil of disappointed clients, Ananias must share attention with the other victims, but he makes a beginning of a memorable biblical curse.[5] Finally, he delivers an imprecation worthy in vocabulary, syntax, and imagery of Job and the Book of Revelation;[6] but there is the intrusion

---

> *Tribulation:* Can you so?
> *Subtle:* I, and shall bide the third examination.
> *Ananias:* It will be joyfull tidings to the Brethren.
> *Subtle:* But you must carry it, secret.
> *Tribulation:* I, but stay,
>   This act of coining, is it lawfull?
> *Ananias:* Lawfull?
>   We know no Magistrate. Or, if we did,
>   This's forraine coine.
> *Subtle:* It is no coining, sir.
>   It is but casting.
> *Tribulation:* Ha? you distinguish well.
> Casting of money may be lawfull.
> *Ananias:* 'Tis, sir.

4. *Ibid.,* IV, vii, 383–4:

> *Ananias:* Peace to the household . . .
>   Casting of dollers is concluded lawfull
>   . . . They are profane,
>   Leud, superstitious, and idolatrous breeches.
>   Avoid Sathan,
>   Thou art not of the light. That ruffe of pride,
>   About thy neck, betrayes thee: and is the same
>   With that, which the uncleane birds, in seventy-seven,
>   Were seene to pranke it with, on divers coasts,
>   Thou look's like Antichrist, in that leud hat.

5. *Ibid.,* v, iii, 393:

> *Ananias:* Come forth, you seed of sulphure, sonnes of fire,
>   Your stench, it is broke forth: abomination
>   Is in the house . . .
>   Sathan, avoid, and hinder not our zeal.

6. *Ibid.,* v, v, 405:

> *Ananias:* I doe defie
>   The wicked Mammon, so doe all the Brethren,
>   Thou profane man. I aske thee, with what conscience
>   Thou canst advance that Idol, against us,
>   That have the seale? Were not the shillings numbred,
>   That made the pounds? Were not the pounds told out,

of the nature of the man who is delivering the curse and the occasion for its delivery. In the course of the scene, Tribulation accompanies Ananias with trite murmurings on patience.

Throughout the play, Jonson has skillfully balanced the elements of his satire. Ananias and Tribulation are not simple sectaries with a few silly lines; they are differentiated sufficiently so that each manages to be offensive in his own way; the action encourages them and reveals them; and their lines review most of the charges which had been made in the past against the Puritan. The two saints, hypocritical enough so that they should have been protected against any deceit, still unknowingly encounter a swindler far more accomplished than they; and the audience watches the approach of the catastrophe which the zealots deserve.

Bartholomew Fair (1614) repeats and enlarges upon the observations of *The Alchemist*. The plot of the new play is even slighter than that of the earlier; but there is richer detail in the character of the religious zealot; and the action is more singly directed to the exposure of hypocrisy and religious excess. There is now no plot of gulls and scoundrels to be defeated by other scoundrels who are more clever. The narrative is simple enough: a number of people pay a visit to Bartholomew fair, a popular center of amusement.[7] There are, among others in the Jonsonian array, a foul-mouthed harridan, a justice, a seller of gingerbread, and a lady. By the end of the play they have gone through small adventures of no importance and are happy. One of the leaders in Jonson's parade is a Puritan, Zeal-of-the-Land Busy; there are several other precisians around him, but he dominates them by the amount of his talk and by the difficulties into which he gets himself. He is the brother of Ananias or Tribulation, but he is larger and noisier than they; he is the ultimate exaggeration of the Puritan manner.[8]

> Upon the second day of the fourth weeke,
> In the eight month, upon the table dormant,
> The yeere, of the last patience of the Saints,
> Sixe hundred and ten? . . .
> I will pray . . .
> Against thy house: may dogs defile thy walls,
> And waspes, and hornets breed beneath thy roofe,
> This seat of false-hood, and this cave of cos'nage.

7. *Bartholomew Fair*, ed. C. S. Alden (New York, Holt, 1904), x–xii, contains a summary of the history of the fair.

8. *Ben Jonson*, ed. Herford, 2, 144: ". . . he (Busy) cannot sustain the comparison he invites with Tartuffe. Jonson commands the Puritan jargon . . . but his satire does not touch the deeper strata of Puritan thought . . . Like Jonson's hypocrites in general he is not profoundly plausible, and it is significant that he makes no dupes." Palmer, *Ben Jonson*, 205, says: "Zeal-of-the-Land Busy is a true picture. His style of speech, with its meaningless repetitions, and tiresome playing with worn tags and phrases, was as characteristic of the nonconformist orators of the sixteenth century as of their present heirs."

The spirit of the satire is set in the first act by the device which Jonson employs to move his Puritans to a place as improbable as Bartholomew fair : the pregnant Win-the-Fight Littlewit lusts for pork. Although her desire is plainly ungodly, the dangers of denying her strike her husband, so Busy is asked for advice. The weight of his answer is paralyzing : it is a speech of epic scope; it surveys pigs, fairs, the carnal lusts of women, heaven, and human vanity; it concludes that a trip to the fair, if taken with devout humility, is permissible.[9] In the speech, Busy is delivering a sectarian "lecture" of the sort which John Taylor parodied in his pamphlets and which the Anglican apologists objected to as wild and private judgments. But Busy surpasses Taylor's sectaries on a number of points : for one thing, Busy's lecture is spoken and is thus closer to a sermon; for another, it is even more concentrated, for Taylor's pages have been reduced to lines, and the impression of interminable length and dullness has been preserved. After Busy gets to the fair, his talk on the most trivial subjects matches his pronouncement on pig. Idolatry and the snares of Satan are in everything, and everything produces a lecture of redundancies. One of the Puritan's chief themes is necessarily Rome and the whore of Babylon : his denunciations come to a climax when he finds that the gingerbread dolls are popish images and he overturns the basket. Presently, he makes so much trouble that he is thrown into the stocks, but he does not complain. The punishment is an opportunity for him to be persecuted and to display fresh aspects of religious fervor. Martyred, he rejoices in his suffering at the hands of the unrighteous, or at least he does until he has a chance to escape. Then he skips off, delivered by a miracle from heaven.[1]

9. *Bartholomew Fair,* i, vi, 37 :

> *Busy:* Verily, for the disease of longing, it is a disease, a carnall disease, or appetite, incident to women: and as it is carnall, and incident, it is naturall, very naturall : Now Pigge, it is a meat, and a meat that is nourishing, and may be long'd for, and so consequently eaten; it may be eaten; very exceeding well eaten: but in the Faire, and as a Bartholmew-pig, it cannot be eaten, for the very calling it a Bartholmew-pigge, and to eat it so, is a spice of Idolatry, and you make the Faire, no better then one of the high Places. This I take it, is the state of the question. A high place . . . Surely, it may be otherwise, but it is subject, to construction, subject, and hath a face of offence, with the weake, a great face, a foule face, but that face may have a vaile put over it, and be shaddowed, as it were, it may be eaten, and in the Faire, I take it, in a Booth, the tents of the wicked: the place is not much, not very much, we may be religious in midst of the prophane, so it be eaten with a reformed mouth, with sobriety, and humblenesse . . .

1. The following are samples of Busy's Puritan eloquence.
Busy says of Smithfield and the fair (*ibid.,* iii, ii, 63) :

> Look not toward them, harken not: the place is Smithfield, or the field of Smiths, the Grove of Hobby-horses and trinkets, the wares are the wares of divels. And the whole Faire is the shop of Satan! They are hooks, and baites, very baites, that are hung out on every side, to catch you, and to hold you as it were, by the gills; and by

The final display of Busy's zeal is in an argument with a puppet and a puppeteer. The Puritan damns the stage and all who are connected with it; the puppet and his master defend. The scene is obviously a review of the old conflict of the Puritans and the drama, for point after point is covered. Ostensibly, it is a defense of the puppets, but Jonson is defending the actors and the whole stage. At the end of the play, Busy marshals most of the points from the antistage literature: the actors are licentious, unlawful, profane, and, in violation of biblical instruction, they wear women's clothes.[2] The puppeteer refutes Busy too easily, and in an unconvincing conclusion he is brought over to become a willing part of the audience.

At the head of the list of stage Puritans, Zeal-of-the-Land Busy maintains his position not by his departures from'the tradition but by the conventional details which make him the enduring symbol of religious hypocrisy, greed, and meddlesomeness. Malvolio is a far more complex man than Busy, but Busy is a greater Puritan; and in his messianic romp through Bartholomew fair he achieves by sheer verbosity a variety which the rather simple figures of the *Family of Love* cannot have. It has been objected that Busy fails as a supreme example of religious hypocrisy, that he does not, like Molière's Tartuffe, ensnare any dupes. The objection is scarcely valid if one understands the conventional picture which Jonson is presenting. Busy does reflect accurately the preciseness and the hypocrisy which the seventeenth-century playwright associated with the Puritan, and it is not accurate to say that he made no dupes. He deceives himself: the self-deception is demonstrated

---

the nostrills, as the Fisher doth: therefore, you must not looke, nor turne toward them— The Heathen man could stop his eares with wax, against the harlot o' the sea: Doe you the like, with your fingers, against the bells of the Beast.

Busy sees the gingerbread woman (III, vi, 83–4):

The provander that pricks him up. Hence with thy basket of Popery, thy nest of Images: and whole legend of ginger-worke . . . the merchandize of Babylon againe, & the peeping of Popery upon the stals here, here, in the high places . . .

Busy rejoices at being in the stocks (IV, vi, 109):

I doe obey thee, the Lion may roare, but he cannot bite. I am glad to be thus separated from the heathen of the land, and put apart in the stocks, for the holy cause.
Waspe: What are you, Sir?
Busy: One that rejoyceth in his affliction, and sitteth here to prophesie the destruction of Faires and May-games, Wakes, and Whitson-ales, and doth sigh and groane for the reformation, of these abuses.

Busy escapes from the stocks (IV, vi, 112):

Wee are delivered by miracle; fellow in fetters, let us not refuse the meanes, this madnesse was of the spirit: The malice of the enemy hath mock'd it selfe.
2. *Ibid.*, v, v, 133 ff.

by the fact that he can be converted from his hatred of the stage. The pure hypocrite may be discovered, but he can scarcely be converted from a belief which he never held. To dismiss Busy as the pure hypocrite is to miss the complex nature of the Puritanism of Jonson's comedy, a Puritanism which is partly assumed but largely genuine, like the protestations of loyalty to the crown from earnest writers of the polemics of reform. Again, if it is still argued that dupes are lacking around Busy, the attendant precisians, like sycophants to a king, are forgotten. They ask eagerly for his opinion, they listen religiously to what he says, they follow assiduously his advice. They are also self-deceived, and at the bottom of their trouble is a narrow Puritanism of which Busy is the speaking symbol. Busy's conversion at the end of the play is certainly a weak resolution, sudden, unmotivated, and ambiguous to the extent that it does not make clear whether the precisian has been converted, or has merely been cured of his narrow dislike of the theater. But the difficulty is not serious, and the change of heart is consistent with comic resolutions which Jonson had used before.[3] The change, partial or complete, makes Busy a better exemplar of the Jonsonian formula than the two sectaries of *The Alchemist;* consequently, he is a more optimistic statement of the capacity of man to be converted from folly to reason. At any rate, it cannot be disputed that *Bartholomew Fair* is unmixed gaiety from beginning to end and that Jonson's satire of the Puritan is far less brutal than it might have been or, indeed, than it had been, even from Jonson's own hand.

For from his picture of the Puritans he omits the harshness and sexuality which are commonly a part of the satire from other writers. His zealots are, for instance, not cruel, as they often are in the casual references in the drama; and they would not betray the government and the nation, as they so often do in the pamphlets and the poetry. In eliminating the traditional sexuality of the stage Puritan Jonson deprived himself of obvious material for comedy: even his Puritan wives, old symbols of adultery on the stage, are no worse than hypocritical frauds with an eye on the moneybags when a marriage is to be arranged.[4] It is consequently true that Jonson discarded one of the least credible, if most amusing, of the charges. His attack was centered on the immodera-

---

3. In the last act of *Every Man out of his Humour,* the victims of humors are cured and are thus no longer comic.

4. Dame Purecraft does not have the adulterous habits of Middleton's Puritan wives. Purecraft tells of her adventures, *Bartholomew Fair,* v, ii, 114–15:

> . . . These seven yeeres, I have beene a wilfull holy widdow, onely to draw feasts, and gifts from my intangled suitors: I am also by office, an assisting sister of the Deacons, and a devourer, in stead of a distributer of the alms. I am a speciall maker of marriages for our decayed Brethren, with our rich widdowes; for a third part of their wealth, when they are married, for the reliefe of the poore elect: as also our poore handsome yong Virgins, with our wealthy Batchelors, or Widdowers; to make them steale from their husbands, when I have confirmed them in the faith . . .

tion of the Puritan and the old charge of preciseness. Their meddling, their self-righteousness, and their hypocrisy furnished the material for the comedy and, in his greatest Puritan, there was at least a partial cure.

The folly which Jonson treats and the folly which appears in the stock portrayal of the stage Puritan are in effect fairly precise indictments of the victims rather than general or vague protests against immorality and hypocrisy. In a stratified society where differences of manner, speech, dress, and even morals, are more marked than in a time of greater congruity of conduct among classes, it is inevitable that there should be an awareness of what is morally and socially fitting to a particular place in the hierarchy. This awareness includes much more than the superficial aspects of manners; it involves a total pattern, all details of which would be appropriate to the position; and if man in society conducts himself in accord with the demands of his position, he will not be guilty of folly and he will not be the proper subject of satire.

But a violation of the code by conduct inappropriate to a situation and a social position produces that kind of humor which particularly concerns the Puritan on the stage. If Ursula the pig woman at Bartholomew fair uses language which is coarse and low, she produces amusement in the audience; the amusement is that of surprise at the glimpse of low manners, or superiority at the contrast between the pig woman and the observer, or admiration of the rich vulgarity of her talk. If, however, the pig woman pretends to be a duchess, a new sort of humor arises: there are the incongruities of speech and manner between a pig woman and a duchess, and the folly of the attempt of the pig woman to be a duchess. Jonson's pig woman does not attempt to be a duchess; but his Zeal-of-the-Land Busy does pretend to be virtuous, honest, and pious, and a large part of the humor of Puritan conduct arises from these incongruities.

From the developed pictures, all done after 1600 by writers like Shakespeare, Middleton, and Jonson, come the enduring pictures of the Puritan on the stage. Before 1600, the allusions are fairly common, but they are generally slight. Around 1580 they begin, and although in the early years the writer will make a fairly elaborate reference to the Puritans, there is no great Puritan on the stage and there is no detailed account of the sectaries.[5] As the years go by, the parody of the traditional manner of the precisian continues. The author of the comic parts of Marlowe's *Doctor Faustus* (1592), for instance, satirizes their bibli-

---

5. *Mucedorus* (1590), 208: ". . . Well, I'll carry home my bottle of hay, and for once make my father's horse turne Puritan and observe Fasting-days, for he gets not a bit." The casual reference is typical of the early period. Myers, *Representation*, 27, says: "The reading of over two score plays extant from 1570–1580 discloses no mention of the Puritans . . . During the late eighties and early nineties mere allusions are occasionally found."

cal language as overheavy.[6] His attention is chiefly on the manner of
the Puritan in general; he makes no attempt to present one in person.
With the turn of the century, the Puritan moves, so to speak, out of
the church and into the street: the account of him swells and he engages
in an unlimited number of human activities. Although he is built up
for the most part in the same fragmentary way as before, he is at least
now an individual, and he is of some complexity. The tradition has
produced at least a stock figure: the sectary of Chapman's *Monsieur
D'Olive* is convincing and is a worthy comic creation.

But Malvolio and the precisians of Middleton and Jonson are far more
memorable. In them there is less of a difference in kind—except for
Malvolio—than richer detail and a larger participation in situation.
They are very important to the action or they dominate the plays in
which they appear. As a result, Jonson's redaction of the material which
he had inherited out of the past marks a high-water mark: later Jacobean
and Caroline drama add nothing of note.[7] Chapman and Dekker both
have many allusions to the Puritans; they present fairly developed satire
in short passages, but neither turns his attention seriously to an account
of a precision as a major character. The references in Marston are
sneering but slight. Beaumont and Fletcher frequently make fun of the
Puritan. Massinger's *The Roman Actor* (1626) is an answer to the
Puritan attack on the theater, but Massinger speaks outside the comic
tradition and in a serious manner similar to Jonson in *The Sad Shepherd*
(1637). In Randolph's *The Muse's Looking Glass* (1630) there is the
conventional story of the Puritans who watch a play at first with horror
and then with delight; the action and the dialogue are sufficiently amusing, but they are no advance over what had been done before. Jonson's

6. Marlowe, *Doctor Faustus*, I, ii, 67: ". . . I will set my countenance like a precisian,
and begin to speak thus:—Truly, my dear brethren, my master is within at dinner, with
Valdes and Cornelius, as this wine, if it could speak, would inform your worships; and
so the Lord bless you, preserve you, and keep you, my dear brethren."

7. The more important dramatic portrayals of the Puritans are summarized in the
following, with Harbage's estimated dates of first performances:

    1600: Shakespeare, *Twelfth Night*.
    1602: Middleton, *The Family of Love*.
    1610: Jonson, *The Alchemist*.
    1614: Jonson, *Bartholomew Fair*.

Several plays of Middleton have anti-Puritan lines or scenes, but he nowhere equals his
effort in *The Family of Love*. His *A Chaste Maid in Cheapside* (1611) has a Puritan
christening party (III, ii, 52–64). The ladies drink too much; the lines are conventional.
In *The Mayor of Queenborough* (1618), the anachronistic figure of "Oliver the Puritan"
is compelled to watch a play. He is inevitably converted from his hatred of the drama
(v, i, 96–103). *The Puritan, or the Widow of Watling Street* (1606), possibly by
Marston, has a deceptive title: there is no extended or striking satire of the Puritans.
Master Ful-bellie, the preacher who eats pig, sounds like Jonson's Zeal-of-the-Land
Busy; but Ful-bellie is only described at second hand (I, iii, 225). The attendants on
the Widow are stock Puritans with the clichés of the breed: they will lie, but will not
swear (I, iii, 224–5).

servant Richard Brome continues his master's attacks on the Puritans, but Brome lacks the eloquence and the wit to create a new Busy or Ananias. Shirley and D'Avenant both contain allusions to the Puritans, but no great Puritan characters.

The deterioration of the tradition just before the closing of the theaters is exemplified in Killigrew's *The Parson's Wedding* (1641). The play presents a developed but undistinguished account. The Parson —that is his only name—is fooled into marrying the captain's mistress. Supposedly, the Parson is a Puritan, but he has given his wife a wedding ring and at one point says: "I'll complain to the bishop of this insolence." [8] The character is less a precisian than a nondescript divine who is a stage fool. In Abraham Cowley's *The Guardian* (1642) there is a rather undifferentiated group of Puritans who repeat the classic sins. Two dramatists who write against the Puritans in the 30's are perhaps of particular interest: Jasper Mayne and William Cartwright were both Anglican clergymen. Cartwright is cruel in an unoriginal way when he portrays the Puritans. Mayne is rather more pleasant: in *The City Match* (1637) there is a detailed picture of the zealous Puritan free of hypocrisy and sexual promiscuity. The serving girl Dorcas drives her mistress almost insane with sermons and pious phrases in the course of the play; but finally the young precisian is lured away from her beliefs by Plotwell, who marries her. There is all the old manner and talk of the Puritan; but the girl Dorcas means it, or at least she thinks that she means it until a man cures her.[9] If the characterization is of the most conventional sort, it is at least free of the false though amusing charges of more accomplished writers like Middleton.

In most of the plays from 1600 to 1642 the treatment of the Puritan is in the nature of a cartoon: things are generally black or white; there are repetitious details which serve to identify the subject, and the details are of less importance than the bold strokes which accentuate the weaknesses. After Shakespeare and Jonson subtleties are lost and the account operates on the fairly elementary level of loud talk, lewd lines, and burlesque situations. However, if there was no advance in the dramatic satire of the Puritan after 1614 and *Bartholomew Fair,* it might also be pointed out that English comedy did not advance notably after Shakespeare and Jonson. The possibilities of religious satire had for the time been exhausted, and after the Restoration new treatments of the old material came from other literary forms.

Before the closing of the theaters, Jonson and Massinger, as they speak seriously of the Puritan, suggest, as have other dramatists and poets, their closeness to the central points of the polemical and philosophi-

8. Killigrew, *The Parson's Wedding*, IV, i, 537.
9. There is a description of Dorcas' Puritan manner—it is entirely conventional—in *The City Match*, II, i, 248.

cal defenders of Anglicanism. Massinger defends the theater not as perfect but as something which is good as well as bad; in short, he rejects the oversimplification of the extremist like William Prynne. Jonson likewise centers his serious complaint on the extremism of Puritanism. And both Jonson and Massinger echo in literary terms a Baconian skepticism about dogmatic and simple answers to moral and religious questions.

A Cluster of
COXCOMBES:
OR,
A Cinquepace of five forts of Knaves and Fooles : Namely ;
The *Donatifts, Publicans, Difciplinarians, Anabaptifts,* and *Brownifts;*
Their Origina!s, Opinions, Confutations, and (in a word) their
Heads Roundly jolted together.

Alfo fhewing how in the Raignes of fundry Kings, and in
the late Q *Elizabeths* Raign the Anabaptifts have bin burnt
as Hereticks, and otherwayes punifhed.

And that the Sect of the Brownifts is fo new, that many are alive
who knew the beginning of it.

With other Sects difplayed. By John Taylor.

July 12. *Printed for Richard webb,* 1642.

4. The Formula of Moderation

As two genres, dramatic and nondramatic satire against the Puritans have certain qualities peculiar to each; together they exploit in a fairly inclusive manner most of the major questions at issue in the serious dispute over religion. Both groups range from the trivial, the casual, and the highly ephemeral to the intricate, the developed, and, occasionally, the enduring. It is impossible to dismiss one group as markedly inferior to the other: if Spenser wrote memorably on Puritanism, so did Jonson, while the character writers established a fertile tradition which survived the interregnum.

Of the nondramatic satire there can be no question but that its strength lay in the variety of forms: by a multiplicity of approach it was able to display aspects of Puritanism denied to the stage. The varied prose and poetry suggest almost automatically the appropriate materials: the range of expression is as great as from folk poetry to *The Faerie Queene*. The scatological ballad, for example, denounced the Puritans with a roughness matched by the quality of the verse. The pamphlet was an ideal medium for the parodying of Puritan prose, and if the mock petitions and sermons are not subtle, they still catch the dull sententiousness of the uneducated zealot or the frenzy of the reformer with personal instructions from God. In addition, the prose, pro- and anti-Puritan, is rich in detailed reflections of the controversy: Martin Marprelate deals not only with the failings of the bishops but also offers a burlesque of serious theological dispute in the period. The reader who knows the Marprelate tracts will have a knowledge both of early satire and of the program of the religious left at the moment when Rome and the armada were attacking. The small form of the character produced pointed essays on eccentricities of rites and beliefs; but if the writer wished to be more particular, he could describe a single Puritan with the caustic disgust of a conforming Anglican sick of religious dispute. From the hand of the expert, the epigram could be a monument of wit over the grave of pious zeal.

The dramatic satire had its limitations, chiefly those of the simplicity and the directness of the passing references in the plays. In addition, the playwright was compelled to warp his material on religion, like everything which he used, to the dimensions of the stage: his Puritans could speak of sermons, but they could give little more than the dull beginning of one, for the audience would soon stop listening. The dramatist could set his scene outside the meetinghouse of the Family of Love, but he could not follow the pamphleteer inside to record the orgy which took place. Most compelling of all, however, was the fact that a large part of the controversy was unsuited for treatment on the stage. In the early years of the dispute, the rightness of one church over another was argued, but this direct treatment soon passed and there appeared instead the satirical representation of the group which the dramatist particularly opposed. The line about the Puritan became presently the direct portrayal of the Puritan, and the dramatist faced the necessity of restricting his type and actions to material which would be appropriate to the conventions and capacities of the medium. Theology and polity, however important they were, could receive little more than referential treatment in a play; they could serve for occasional, minor quips, but they were too static to produce either the movement or the interest in character necessary to keep plot moving.

The dramatist's solution was the necessary compromise of the stage and the necessary distortion of satire : his Puritan spoke against himself and said the things which the audience would listen to. He would say nothing, for example, of his belief in the worth of simple living and hard work, since the opinion would be both inappropriate for comedy and completely out of character for a satirical figure. Instead, the stage Puritan had to show vices which would make him ridiculous : he was the criminal without violent crimes, the villain who preserved the comic spirit. As the Puritan sloughed off his mortal skin of polity and doctrine, there remained the features by which he would be known in the future, the dour precisian opposed to all pleasures as evil. He has remained that to the present; and his survival is a tribute in large part to the success of the dramatists.

The question of the justice of the attack, both dramatic and non-dramatic, is interesting, but largely irrelevant. Not literal accuracy but perverse accuracy is the strength of satire. Satire must distort the truth so that it is at once less and more true than the reality; the faults and failings of the victim are overcolored and overstated, while his virtues are either banished or exaggerated to vices of excess. Within that technique anti-Puritan satire succeeded : it produced witty commentaries in prose and verse on the reformers, and on the stage a long parade of zealous fools who were near enough to the real thing to delight the spectators. At its best, the performance was a skillful juggling of politics, religion, morals, propaganda, and the creative imagination of the writer. A balanced judgment would necessarily record both delight in the spectacle and skepticism at its accuracy: ". . . it is an excellent play; the more I see it, the more I love the wit of it; only the business of abusing the Puritans begins to grow stale, and of no use, they being the people that, at last, will be found the wisest." [1] Samuel Pepys is speaking in 1668 and, reviewing the events, is occupying what might be called a middle position: he has just seen *Bartholomew Fair;* although he applauds the satire, he does not believe the picture of Puritanism. Further consideration of the propaganda and the events would compel an evaluation perhaps even more unsympathetic to both sides or, at least, devoid of the feeling that notable elements of right are to be discovered in one party to the discrediting of the other.

It is certainly true that the Anglicans wrote more, and that they sometimes wrote better, than the Puritans. But the Anglicans did not succeed in demonstrating that Puritanism was a wild notion in the heads of a few zealots, and the Anglicans did not win the open fighting which followed. The ultimate triumph of Anglicanism, if it can be called a triumph, came when the ideal of Laud had been displaced and uniformity, in any sense which he would have recognized, was unthinkable. The failure of the writing by quantity and quality to anticipate the outcome is easy enough to explain: orthodoxy commonly controlled the press, the pulpit, the theater; and orthodoxy had money for literary patronage. That the Anglicans spoke more eloquently and more often than the Puritans does not, then, alter the fact that the satirical writing is a generally valid measure of the controversy. Since there is a constant increase in the quantity of anti-Puritan writing through the years, together with some gain in quality, the conclusion, both obvious and obviously true, would be that Puritanism was of constantly increasing importance to the English people from the 1570's to the opening of the civil war in 1642. That the issue is of less importance at the beginning is supported by the fact that through 1590 there is no great amount of anti-Puritan satire. The serious debate has gone on in volume, but it has been restricted to the more special areas of church rite and church government; the points at issue have not come to be so commonly discussed that they are proper material for a popular form of art; and even in the serious dispute of the early years, nothing had appeared which could compare in importance with Hooker or, in the last years, with Milton. After 1590 there is a steady development in all the satirical forms. The amusing, merely libelous, pamphlet develops into the parody sermon; the miscellaneous verse, the characters, and the epigrams all improve in quality and increase in number; and the popular poetry, impossible to date exactly for composition, was most commonly printed after 1640. The drolleries and miscellanies, often uniquely concerned with the Puritans, flourished during and after the revolution. It can be said of no form that it reached a climax before 1600 and disappeared as the dispute became more bitter.

---

1. *The Diary of Samuel Pepys,* ed. Henry B. Wheatley (8 vols. Bell, 1923), *8,* 92 (4 September 1668).

But there are also, between the serious writers and the satirists, correspondences which involve both the immediate program of religious practice and the larger question of an ideal of conduct. The serious and the satirical writers are defending a point of view which embraces politics, economics, social behavior, and religion. Attitudes and ideals common to both groups reveal an identity of purpose larger than the recommendation of one particular set of ecclesiastical principles, and, consequently, a number of the polemicists meet on common ground with a number of the satirists. The serious Anglican apologists are often conscious of their espousal of an ideal, and at their most persuasive they are careful to avoid the offering of a narrow conformity as a necessary part of that ideal. The Anglican satirists are perhaps less aware, but they do make recommendations, and to a surprising extent what'they say corresponds to some of the central points of the Anglican apologists.

There was, for instance, the charge of hysterical extremism. It was one of the most rewarding sources for humor among the satirists; it appears in all the forms of writing from the unsophisticated ballads to the highly developed drama; and it made the Puritan ridiculous in the way that he had to be if he was to be satirized and not merely denounced. Behind the satire there is the implication that the ideal of conduct in religious matters is one of moderation. Among the more ardent pamphleteers, specifically Anglican recommendations do occur, but the satire on the more enduring level makes little or no mention of one church or one rite as better than another. The satirists, rather, recommend a code of conduct which implies the ideal of a moderate church, and the pattern of general advice to the sinner in respect to excess applies, almost without exception, from the lesser writers to the greater. John Taylor is a fierce royalist, and his pamphlets in support of Charles and the bishops are specific enough so that he can be described as devoted to the Anglican church. But Shakespeare is scarcely an ardent Anglican making fun of Puritans, and Jonson with his Roman Catholic background has nothing to say in his stage arguments on the specific worth of Catholicism, either Anglican or Roman, as a cure for excess. The avoidance of a narrow Anglicanism is notable in Hooker and in Bacon when they write of Puritan extremism: they warn of the dangers of the same hysterical enthusiasm against which the satirists speak. Bacon is, perhaps, an unfair example, since his transparent skepticism makes him incapable of anything more specific than impatience with a religious opinion that interferes with civil order. But it is also notable that in his attacks on the corruptions of the establishment, Bacon showed that he was not blind to Anglican failings. The fact remains that Bacon's recommendations center on moderation and order. He speaks in general for the English church because it works and because it offers the hope of social concord if it will adopt the recommendations of moderates like himself. At the extreme of the other side, he sees only chaos and the religious confusion which furnished the satirists with one of their best points of departure. Hooker is a fairer measure of the parallel ideal between satirist and apologist : in the preface to *Of Ecclesiastical Polity* he writes of Puritan extremism, but he does not speak for complete conformity and for the divinely right nature of Anglicanism. His defense is to a degree in accord with that of Bacon, and certainly in accord with Spenser : excess of change, self-righteousness, and zeal are destructive of order.

Again, when the satirist and the moderate polemicist treat the Puritans' hatred of elaborate ritual, there is an apparent union of intention which does not include the indispensable necessity of conformity to Anglican rite. The Puritan fear of bells, organs, crosses, vestments, and fish on Friday is silly not because it is un-Anglican, but because it is immoderate in relation to the dangers which attend these rites and practices : the Anglican church is not the Roman Catholic church and it will not become the Roman Catholic church if communicants eat fish on Friday. Whitgift, for instance, generally deals with his attacker in terms not of the unique perfection of the establishment, but of the importance of a number of the Puritan complaints. Indeed, Whitgift admits his Calvinistic sympathies and writes on occasion in such a manner that the reader might think that the words came from the pen of a Puritan ; they do, to the extent that numbers of Anglicans accepted the need for moderate change and rejected only the extreme proposals and pronouncements which furnished the satirists with material for the belittling of the whole Puritan position. And so Whitgift sides somewhat with the Puritans, but he objects in the reformers to the same things which make them play their role of fools in the satirical drama. The bibliolatry of the Puritans receives from the satirists and some of the moderate polemicists similar treatment. If biblical names and conversation are silly when the dramatist attaches them to the zealots, his observation is not so far removed from that of Hooker who, having paid his respects to the word of God, still insists that the law by which men live must include more than the Old and New Testaments.

The religious fragmentation, seemingly infinite, of the Puritans in the course of their examination of polity and worship met with similar treatment from the satirists and polemicists of moderate cast. What the stage or the prose pamphlets have to say on the Family of Love is not so far from what Hooker has to say on the Anabaptists or Bacon on the multitudes of worshipers, each whirling dervishwise in his own religious orbit. The complaint of the satirist is not that the Puritans are not Anglicans, but that they destroy in their immense eccentricity the cultural, moral, and religious uniformity which makes society a communicating whole : if the zealot in the play believes that the study of Greek is evil, there is one bit less of the common ground of reasonable agreement upon which Hooker founds his state. For Jonson as for Hooker, the solution is something larger than membership in the Anglican church. The confusion of the government of the church follows naturally upon the fragmentation of the sects. Poor material for satire by its abstract nature and its removal from human situations, ecclesiastical polity receives little attention. But significantly, the moderate Anglicans again offer no thundering defense of episcopacy divinely based on the word of God. Hall offers this defense, but here he is as immoderate as Milton on the opposite side, and although Hooker defends the government of his church as divine, his use of *divine* is totally different from that of Hall. Hooker's divinity in earthly affairs is the product of a reason not notably different from the "right Reason" which Milton was later to praise during what he regarded as the desperate unreason of the Anglican restoration.[2] Bacon's defense of Anglican polity is the defense of what works; and his defense echoes the prose gloss to Spenser in his satirical attacks on Anglican corruption: the government of the English church is what it should be; the performance is not. Spenser the satirist meets Bacon the polemicist. A divinely instituted polity is not what the satirists propose, and it is, in turn, out of harmony with the argumentative climate of the most persuasive of the Anglican apologists.

Church doctrine, like polity, does not lend itself readily to satire; and at any rate, the Anglicans were never very far from the Puritans doctrinally. Whitgift and Cartwright are in rough agreement on the most important points, and the continued agreement is perhaps an indication of the fact that both groups were headed by different roads toward the eventual destination of a moderate position. But even on doctrinal matters, when, for example, the Anglicans make fun of the Puritans for their belittling of works, the implication is not that the Puritans must become Anglicans, but rather that the Puritans should become less extreme, that they might admit the possibility of a connection between evil deeds in this world and damnation in the next. If later Puritan thought was to arrive at the perilously un-Calvinistic point at which good works could be the outward and visible manifestations of certain election, the saints were only moving closer to congruency with Hooker's general recommendations.

A specific consideration of the picture of Puritan vice as offered by several of the dramatists reinforces the generalization of a parallel pattern from Anglican polemic to Anglican satire. On the stage, the Puritan comes to be a symbol of self-love, conceit, and hypocrisy: the stage exploits the human situation and human vices as the propagandist cannot. But at the same time, removed as the dramatists are from polemical ma-

---

2. *Paradise Lost*, xii, ll.83–4:

> . . . true Liberty
> . . . which always with right Reason dwells . . .

terial and manner, they still make essentially the same moral recommendations as the serious writers. Shakespeare and Middleton, to pick two extremes of manner and material, are, in the implications attached to their precisians, not far from the observations of Hooker or Bacon. Malvolio has the central fault of immoderation in self-esteem and sobriety; but the cure for him will not be membership in the Anglican church, it will simply be moderation, a better understanding of his place in the world, a sense of humor, and a mixture of the elements which make a socially possible being. Angelo is not a satiric figure at all; he is rather something which has strayed out of tragedy into a play of moral problems, but he is also the victim of his immoderation, and he is undone by it. Angelo meets Middleton's Mistress Glister at least on the ground that they both are inordinately lustful. Mistress Glister is overloaded with an improbable sexuality, of use for the farcical effect which Middleton wants, but behind her lewd gambolings in the meetinghouse is the observation that excess is the besetting sin of the sects. In neither of these writers is there the suggestion that orthodoxy is the necessary means for salvation. Anglicans, it is true, do not conduct themselves as sectarians; but as far as the moral conditions imposed by the authors are concerned, the sectarians with the virtues of honesty and moderation could be as good as Anglicans.

Jonson, more seriously concerned with the Puritan than Middleton, and more specifically concerned with the Puritan than Shakespeare, also offers the ideal of moderation as the cure for the illness of hypocritical preciseness. Jonson discards the sexual immorality so commonly used by other dramatists, and the result is a satiric observation which conforms all the better to the principles urged by the polemicists. Ananias, Tribulation, and Zeal-of-the-Land Busy lie, cheat, and steal, while they talk unceasingly of morals: in short, they are, like other figures within Jonson's formula, the victims of an obsessive passion. To be cured they must be persuaded out of it, or driven out of it; then, perhaps like Busy at the end of the play, they will no longer be unbalanced. The cure is not Anglicanism; it is simply the balance which a religious zealot cannot have, a Christian should have, and a man of reason must have. Jonson's ideal state is not one which he can well portray on the stage; with him as with the other dramatic satirists, unless the natural order is askew, there is no material for satiric comedy. Jonson implies the ideal, and the satirist joins the serious reformer.

The satire on a more particular level, that which is merely pro-Anglican or pro-Puritan, fails by comparison. Martin Marprelate endures as a demonstration of the superiority of clownish chatter over sober polemic; but Martin is at his best when he is least Puritan, when he speaks of corruption, ignorant prelates, and the immoderate lives of the princes of the church. When he talks of the government of the church and describes the divine order of pastor, teacher, and deacon, he is less memorable. His argument is, certainly, of the greatest pertinence to his own time; to later times, it is of less interest. Behind his treatment of specific questions, there are also the larger questions of a nature not radically different from those with which his opponents dealt; for he offers at his best the unsectarian principle of virtue in learning and practice.

In the last years before the fighting, the satiric writing enforces the serious, and Puritan and Anglican become more hotly partisan: the pamphlets for and against the king, for and against episcopacy, for and against parliament, all confirm eloquently the civil and ecclesiastical perils which had already been suggested. A formula of connection between the literature and the events displays the intense concern of the time with religion and religious dispute and, more particularly, the passionate involvement of feelings on Puritanism. But the involvement does not end with the seventeenth century: historians, polemicists, and satirists alike in the eighteenth, nineteenth, and twentieth centuries have expended on Puritanism the most arduous study, and have produced the most colored pronouncements and fertile imaginings. Among scholars in the twentieth century, for all the accuracy of research and the painstaking examination of both sides, it is usually apparent that the writer is an Anglican, or a Presbyterian, or a Unitarian, or that the balance of right lay with the bishops, the reformers within the church, or the rising forces of the sects. Passionate appraisal did not stop with the closing of the theaters in 1642.

A general view of the mass of the controversy makes possible several attitudes: it may be felt that orthodoxy was right in its insistence on the preservation of old patterns in church and in state, and that, left to itself, it would have, in the course of time, remedied the undeniable evils against which the reformers spoke. Again, a strong case can be made out both for ecclesiastical and political Puritanism: the Restoration notwithstanding, the direction of the next centuries of English life was anticipated in more respects by the reformers than by the crown and the old church. It is also possible to adopt the pleasant but entirely naïve position that the Puritan revolution was an unnecessary mistake, that the bishops had no real differences with the Presbyterians, and that if both sides could have exercised intelligent restraint, apparent difference would, with time, have become agreement. Such an opinion disregards the fact that the nature of God and of His church was a question of major importance to the sixteenth and seventeenth centuries; that the question was scarcely one on which several right answers could be discovered; and that compromise with a different opinion was a compromise with the powers of evil.

A detached skepticism concerning both sides would revert in the direction of Bacon and, if it eliminated some of the joy of partisanship, might supply the compensating satisfaction of examining with a disinterested eye all claims to perfection, divine inspiration, and concord with the will of God. From such skepticism there might come a more calm appraisal of the cause and the development of the dispute. The Puritan movement, both with its strengths and its limitations, would emerge; and the nature of the opposition would be neither that of a beast having seven heads, nor a Red-Cross Knight. The violence of 1642 then becomes more understandable, and it is less possible to deplore what happened. The reader is less inclined to speculate pleasantly on how peace might have been preserved, for the bloody end of the discussion is consonant with the importance of the dispute and with the intellectual climate of the moment. The reader also hesitates to find an overbalance of fault or of virtue either in the Puritans or the Anglicans. He doubts that the Puritan movement was commonly concerned with intellectual freedom, with religious freedom, or with the consent of the governed, except as dire need for strength in the face of an old tyranny made a new tyranny amenable to modifications. Nor, on the other hand, will the Anglicans be the particular defenders of God's order on earth; they will rather be the defenders of a system which was sometimes adequate but often not, and which was heavy with the neglect and corruption of power generally safe from reform. The writing on both sides will appear, certainly, to be concerned with large questions of England's future, with such things as the evolution of religious freedom, the functions of the parliament, the place of the church in relation to society and the government, and the ultimate source for authority in the state; but more clearly, the writing will appear to be concerned with the moment at which it appears; and what it says will usually be a defense of a party or an order at a moment when it needs defense. As the polemicists and satirists go on their irremeable journey to revolution, they record with accuracy popular thoughts, feelings, tastes, and opinions; occasionally, at their best, they find answers to moral, religious, and social problems which reach back into their past and inform the future.

I. Editions used in references to the drama.

Arden of Feversham. *See* The Shakespeare Apocrypha.
Beaumont, Francis, and John Fletcher, The Works of Francis Beaumont and John Fletcher, ed. Arnold Glover, et al. (10 vols. Cambridge, University Press, 1905–12).
  The Chances, *4* (1906).
  The Elder Brother, *2* (1906).
  Fair Maid of the Inn, *9* (1910).
  The Knight of the Burning Pestle, *6* (1908).
  The Night-Walker, *7* (1909).
  The Spanish Curate, *1* (1905).
  Wit without Money, *2.*
  The Woman's Prize, *8* (1910).
  Women Pleas'd, *7.*
Brome, Richard, The Dramatic Works of Richard Brome (3 vols. 1873).
  The Antipodes, *3.*
  The City Wit, *1.*
  The English Moor, *2.*
  A Jovial Crew, *3.*
Cartwright, William, The Ordinary, Dodsley, *12* (1875).
Chapman, George, The Comedies of George Chapman, ed. Thomas M. Parrott (Dutton, 1914).
  Eastwood Ho
  Monsieur D'Olive
  Sir Giles Goosecap
Cowley, Abraham, The Complete Works in Verse and Prose of Abraham Cowley, ed. Alexander B. Grosart (2 vols. Edinburgh, 1881).
  The Guardian, *1.*
D'Avenant, Sir William, The Dramatic Works of William D'Avenant, ed. James Maidment and W. H. Logan (5 vols. 1872–74).
  The Cruel Brother, *1* (1872).
  News from Plymouth, *4* (1873).
  The Temple of Love, *1.*
  The Wits, *2* (1872).
Day, John, The Ile of Guls, ed. G. B. Harrison (Oxford, Oxford University Press, 1936).
Day, John, The Works of John Day, ed. A. H. Bullen (2 vols. 1881).
  Law Trickes, *2.*

Dekker, Thomas, The Dramatic Works of Thomas Dekker (4 vols. 1873).
    North-Ward Hoe, *3*.
    West-Ward Hoe, *2*.
    The Wonder of a Kingdom, *4*.
Dodsley, A Select Collection of Old Plays, ed. Robert Dodsley, John P. Collier, et al. (3d ed. 13 vols. 1825–33).
Dodsley, A Select Collection of Old English Plays, ed. Robert Dodsley, W. C. Hazlitt, et al. (4th ed. 15 vols. 1874–76).
Field, Nathaniel, Amends for Ladies, Dodsley, *11* (1875).
Fletcher, John. See Beaumont.
Glapthorne, Henry, Wit in a Constable (ed. 1640).
Heywood, Thomas, The Dramatic Works of Thomas Heywood (6 vols. 1874).
    The English Traveller, *4*.
    A Maiden-Head Well Lost, *4*.
How a Man May Chuse a Good Wife from a Bad, ed. A. E. H. Swaen (Louvain, Uystpruyst,1912).
Jonson, Ben, Ben Jonson, ed. C. H. Herford and Percy and Evelyn Simpson (11 vols. Oxford, Oxford University Press, 1925–52).
    The Alchemist, *5* (1937).
    Bartholomew Fair, *6* (1938).
    Every Man in his Humour, *3* (1927).
    Every Man out of his Humour, *3*.
    The Magnetick Lady, *6*.
    News from the New World, *7* (1941).
    The Sad Shepherd, *7*.
    The Staple of News, *6*.
    Volpone, *5*.
Jordan, Thomas, The Walks of Islington and Hogsdon (ed. 1657).
Killigrew, Thomas, The Parson's Wedding, Dodsley, *11* (1827).
The London Chaunticleers, Dodsley, *12* (1875).
Marlowe, Christopher, The Works and Life of Christopher Marlowe, ed. R. H. Case (6 vols. New York and London, 1930–33).
    The Tragical History of Doctor Faustus, ed. Frederick S. Boas, *5* (New York, 1932).
Marmion, Shackerley, The Dramatic Works of Shackerley Marmion, ed. James Maidment and W. H. Logan (1875).
    A Fine Companion.
Marston, John, The Works of John Marston, ed. A. H. Bullen (3 vols. 1887).
    The Malcontent, *1*.
    Parasitaster ; or The Fawne, *2*.
    What You Will, *2*.
Massinger, Philip, The Plays of Philip Massinger, ed. W. Gifford (4 vols. 1813).
    The Emperor of the East, *3*.
    A New Way to Pay Old Debts, *3*.

The Renegado, *2*.
The Roman Actor, *2*.
Mayne, Jasper, The City Match, Dodsley, *9* (1825).
The Merry Devil of Edmonton, Dodsley, *5* (1825).
A Merry Knack to Know a Knave, Dodsley, *6* (1875).
Middleton, Thomas, The Works of Thomas Middleton, ed. A. H. Bullen
    (8 vols. 1885).
    Anything for a Quiet Life, *5*.
    Blurt, Master-Constable, *1*.
    The Family of Love, *3*.
    The Inner-Temple Masque, *7*.
    A Mad World My Masters, *3*.
    The Mayor of Queenborough, *2*.
    The Roaring Girl, *4*.
    A Trick to Catch the Old One, *2*.
    The Widow, *5*.
    The Witch, *5*.
    Your Five Gallants, *3*.
Mucedorus, Dodsley, *7* (1874).
New Custom, Dodsley, *3* (1874).
The Pedlers Prophecy, ed. John S. Farmer (Tudor Facsimile Texts, 1911).
The Pilgrimage to Parnassus, ed. W. D. Macray (Oxford, 1886).
The Puritane or The Widdow of Watling-streete. *See* The Shakespeare
    Apocrypha.
Randolph, Thomas, The Muse's Looking Glass, Dodsley, *9* (1825).
Respublica, ed. John S. Farmer (Tudor Facsimile Texts, 1908).
Sampson, William, The Vow-Breaker, ed. Hans Wallrath, Materialen zur
    Kunde des älteren Englishen Dramas, *42* (Louvain, 1914).
The Shakespeare Apocrypha, ed. C. F. Tucker Brooke (Oxford, Oxford
    University Press, 1918).
Shakespeare, William, Measure for Measure, ed. Sir A. Quiller-Couch and
    J. Dover Wilson (Cambridge, University Press, 1921).
    Twelfth Night, A New Variorum Edition of Shakespeare, ed. Horace
    H. Furness (Philadelphia, Lippincott, 1901).
Shirley, James, The Dramatic Works and Poems of James Shirley, ed. Wil-
    liam Gifford and Alexander Dyce (6 vols. 1833).
    The Bird in a Cage, *2*.
    The Cardinal, *5*.
    The Gamester, *3*.
    The Gentleman of Venice, *5*.
    The Grateful Servant, *2*.
    The Lady of Pleasure, *4*.
    The Wedding, *1*.
Sir John Old-Castle. *See* The Shakespeare Apocrypha.
Strode, William, The Floating Island (ed. 1655).
Tourneur, Cyril, The Works of Cyril Tourneur, ed. Allardyce Nicoll (Fan-
    frolico, 1930).

The Atheist's Tragedie.

The Revenger's Tragedie.

Two Wise Men and All the Rest Fools, ed. John S. Farmer (Tudor Facsimile Texts, 1913).

Webster, John, The Complete Works of John Webster, ed. F. L. Lucas (4 vols. Chatto & Windus, 1927).

The Duchess of Malfi, *2.*

Wever, Richard, Lusty Juventus, ed. John S. Farmer (Tudor Facsimile Texts, 1907).

II. Selected Books and Articles on Anti-Puritan Satire.

Adkins, Mary G. M., "The Genesis of Dramatic Satire against the Puritan," *The Review of English Studies, 22* (1946), 81–95.

Fleay, F. G., "Shakespeare and Puritanism," *Anglia, 7* (1884), 223–31.

Mueschke, Paul, and Jeanette Fleischer, "Jonsonian Elements in the Comic Underplot of *Twelfth Night*," *PMLA, 48* (1933), 722–40.

Myers, Aaron M., Representation and Misrepresentation of the Puritan in Elizabethan Drama (Philadelphia, University of Pennsylvania Press, 1931).

Padelford, Frederick M., "Spenser and the Puritan Propaganda," *Modern Philology, 11* (1913), 85–106.

———— "Spenser's Arraignment of the Anabaptists," *Journal of English and Germanic Philology, 12* (1913), 434–48.

Thompson, E. N. S., The Controversy between the Puritans and the Stage (New York, Holt, 1903).

INDEX

Adamites, 58
Adkins, Mary G. M., 100 n. 5
Admonition to the Parliament, An, 14, 16–19, 21, 26, 31, 41 n. 7, 52, 72, 76, 91
à Lasco, 7
Alexander, John, 53
Amsterdam, 104, 104 n. 8, 104 n. 9, 105 n. 1, 106 n. 5, 108 n. 2, 133, 135
Anabaptists, 21 n. 8, 28, 39 n. 4, 42, 48, 52, 53 n. 2, 71 n. 7, 86 n. 1, 92, 108, 109 n. 4, 109 n. 5, 132, 145, 150
Andrewes, Launcelot, 94
Angelo, 126, 127 n. 5, 128, 128 n. 6, 152
Anglican: apologists, 33, 65, 71, 92, 138, 149, 151; arguments, 30, 35; Catholicism, 149; clergy, 45, 94; corruption, 43, 88; establishment, 16, 93, 150; extremists, 92; failings, 149; hierarchy, 16; honesty, 57; liturgy, 30; moderate, 30 n. 7, 86, 152; order, 28, 41; polemicists, 66, 151, 154; polity, 30, 44, 151; position, 21, 50, 72, 79; practices, 70, 77, n. 9; preachers, 72; reform, 102; restoration, 151; rites, 70, 150; satirists, 149, 151; services, 102; vestments, 150; virtues, 61, 152, 154; writers, 75
Anglican church, 2, 10, 15, 27, 31, 39, 56–7, 70–1, 88, 90, 149–51; differences from Puritanism, 6ff.
Anglicanism, 21–3, 26–7, 29, 35, 39, 43, 65, 72, 104, 144, 148–50, 152
Anglicans: conforming, 5, 27, 80, 124, 146, 150; extreme, 77 n. 6; moderate, 86, 149, 151–2; reforming, 2, 7, 87, 93, 102 n. 2; thoroughgoing, 88
Anne of Cleves, 8
Apostles, 18 n. 2
Aquinas, Thomas, 23 n. 4
Arber, Edward, 44 n. 1
Archer, William, 123 n. 1
Arians, 53 n. 2
Aristotle, 91
Articles of Religion, 17
Aston, Sir Thomas, 64 n. 6
Atheism, 2 n. 3, 109 n. 6
Atheists, 108, 132
Awdeley, John, 77 n. 6
à Wood, Anthony, 8, 9 n. 6
Aylmer, John, bishop, 50

Bacon, Francis, 26–9, 33, 65, 75, 75 n. 4, 81, 86, 93, 103, 149–52, 154
Bainton, Roland H., 5 n. 1
Bale, John, 14 n. 4
Bancroft, Richard, 21 n. 9, 40 n. 6, 46, 49 n. 7, 77
Baptism, 5, 17, 27, 106
Barclay, Alexander, 37
Barker, Arthur, 30 n. 7
Barlow, Jerome, 2 n. 2
Bartholomew Faire, 70 n. 6
Basel, 13
Baskervill, Charles R., 133 n. 5
Bastard, Thomas, 80
Bastwick, John, 84
Battenhouse, Roy W., 127 n. 4
Bayly, Lewis, 99 n. 9
Beard, Thomas, 99 n. 9
Beaumont, Francis, 103 n. 6, 104 n. 7, 104 n. 9, 120 n. 5, 142
Becon, Thomas, 103
Beeching, Henry C., 124 n. 2
Berdan, John M., 68 n. 3
Bible, 3–4, 6, 11, 13, 15–17, 20, 24–5, 30, 35–6, 40, 43, 50–1, 57, 59–60, 63, 77 n. 9, 78, 81 n. 1, 83, 99, 102, 106, 108, 110–11, 116–17, 119, 119 n. 3, 120, 124, 127, 136, 139, 150; Authorized Version of 1611, 7; Geneva, 8, 17–18, 29, 63, 107, 124 n. 2; interpretations of, 10, 106; translations of, 10, 40, 57 n. 3; Tyndale's, 7
Bolton, Robert, 99 n. 9
Bonnard, G., 44 n. 1
Boyce, Benjamin, 76 n. 5
Bowden, Henry Sebastian, 124 n. 2
Brant, Sebastian, 37
Brathwaite, Richard, 68, 82 n. 2, 83 n. 2
Brome, Richard, 105 n. 3, 108 n. 3, 118 n. 1, 119 n. 4, 121 n. 9, 143
Breton, Nicholas, 82 n. 2
Bridges, John, 22, 45–6, 50–1
Briefe and Plaine Declaration, A, 44
Brooke, C. F. Tucker, 94 n. 3
Brownists, 42, 47–8, 57–8, 61, 63, 65, 70, 71 n. 7, 73, 81 n. 1, 92, 104 n. 8, 108, 115, 118, 122, 132, 145
Bullinger, Heinrich, 7
Burton, Henry, 84